"A TRADE LIKE ANY OTHER"

"A TRADE LIKE ANY OTHER"

Female Singers and Dancers in Egypt

KARIN VAN NIEUWKERK

UNIVERSITY OF TEXAS PRESS
AUSTIN

Printed in the United States of America
Fifth paperback printing, 2006

♾ The paper used in this book meets the minimum requirements of American National Standard for Information Sciences—Permanence of Paper for Printed Library Materials, ANSI/NISO Z39.48-1984.

Library of Congress Cataloging-in-Publication Data

Nieuwkerk, Karin van, date
A trade like any other : female singers and dancers in Egypt / Karin van Nieuwkerk.—1st ed.
p. cm.
Revision of the author's thesis (doctoral)—Amsterdam, 1991.
Includes bibliographical references and index.
ISBN-13: 978-0-292-78720-9 (alk. paper)
ISBN-10: 0-292-78720-0
ISBN-13: 978-0-292-78723-0 (pbk.: alk. paper)
ISBN-10: 0-292-78723-5
1. Women entertainers—Egypt—Social conditions. 2. Belly dance.
3. Belly dance music—Egypt. I. Title.
PN2977.N54 1995 2006 94-26452
792.7′082—dc20

CONTENTS

FIGURES

ACKNOWLEDGMENTS

I wish to thank many people who advised, criticized, and stimulated me during the process of fieldwork and writing as well as rewriting my thesis. First of all I would like to thank Professor Jeremy Boissevain and Dr. Nico Kielstra, for their help, advice, and supportive comments. I am grateful to the University of Amsterdam, which financed the research and the fieldwork. I am indebted to the Amsterdam School for Social Science Research for providing seminars and research facilities. For valuable comments on parts of the text, I would like to thank Dr. Anna Aalten and Professor Willy Jansen. I am especially grateful for the long and stimulating discussions with my sister, Marja van Nieuwkerk, and for the critical comments and support of my partner, Hans Stukart.

There are many other persons who contributed directly or indirectly to this project. I would especially like to mention the friends whose support was invaluable during my stay in Egypt. First of all, my housemate, Gerdien Goede, whose good humor and patient ear provided an important safety valve. I would like to thank Muḥammed il-Ḥilmy and Ṣalâḥ for doing the boring job of checking newspapers and art magazines. I am grateful to Târiq Muṣṭafa Bahgat for his pleasant company and protection in "dangerous" nightclubs. Shamiyya's company and contacts with many Egyptians were also vital to my research. I am greatly indebted to my "assistant" and "big brother," Sayyid Ḥenkish. Without his guidance, knowledge, and contacts in the entertainment trade, this research would have been very difficult. I am grateful to the choreographer Muḥammad Ṭolba, first of all for introducing me to Egyptian music and dancing, but also for bringing me into contact with Sayyid. Most of all, I would like to express my gratitude to the many women in the trade who were willing to tell me about their lives. I am greatly indebted to

Ibtisâm, Bûḥa, Nagâḥ, Baṭṭa, Yasmîn, Magda, Karîma, Mona, Sayyida, ʿAida, Zeinab, Zûba, Umm Muḥammad (their names have been changed), and many others. Without their hospitality, friendship, and confidence, this book could not have come into existence. By creating more insight into and understanding about their way of living, I hope to repay partly my debt to them.

NOTE ON TRANSCRIPTION

The transcription system of *A Dictionary of Egyptian Arabic,* by Badawi and Hinds, has been used with minor changes. The long vowels ii, uu, aa, etc. have been replaced by î, û, â, etc., and the x has been replaced by kh. The more common transliteration is used for the Arabic consonants ɛ, ɣ, and ʃ—that is, ᶜ, gh, and sh, respectively. In quotations, the transcription system of the quoted author is followed. Some place names or words familiar to the reader, such as Cairo, Alexandria, and *sheikh,* have been written with their anglicized spellings; otherwise the strict transcription is used. In general, I have added an *s* to singular Arabic words to form an anglicized plural, with the exception of a few frequently employed terms. I mainly use the colloquial Egyptian Arabic, with the exception of official names—for instance, of newspapers—which are transcribed in standard Arabic.

"A TRADE LIKE ANY OTHER"

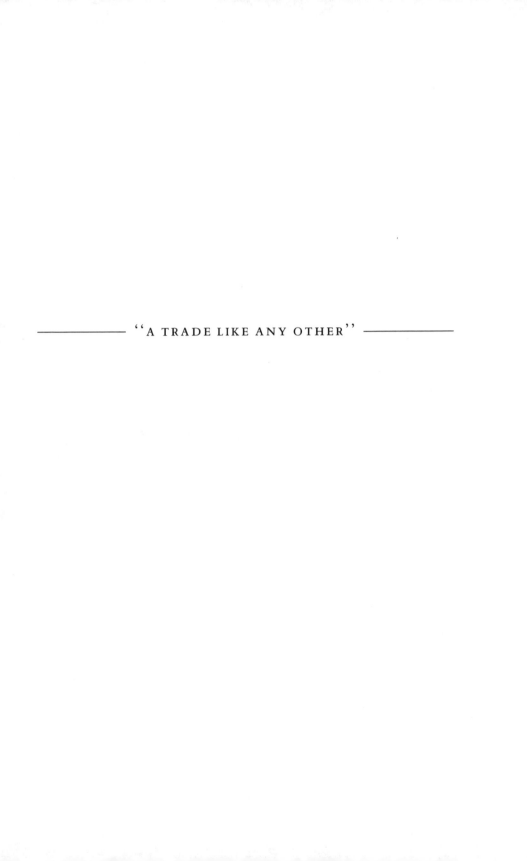

ONE

INTRODUCTION

Is entertainment a trade like any other? According to Egyptian performers it is. They usually shrug their shoulders and simply comment: "*mihna, zayy ayy mihna*," "a trade like any other." Like other jobs, entertainment fulfills a function in society and brings in money.

Yet many voices disagree with this opinion of performers. In the eyes of eighteenth- and nineteenth-century travelers, female singers and belly dancers were strange and exotic. The travelers were fascinated and shocked by the local dance. A member of the Napoleonic expedition wrote: "Their dance was at first voluptuous, but then it became lewd . . . it was no more than the most outrageous and indecent expression of bestial desires" (Denon 1803: 175). Today belly dancers still stand out as a symbol of the "sensual East." Nawâl al-Saʿadâwî, a leading Egyptian feminist and author, once remarked in an interview that the Western image of Arab women is either the oppressed and pitiable woman imprisoned in the harem or the voluptuous and exotic belly dancer.

The topic of this study could thus be taken as a preeminent example of "Orientalism." In this ethnography, though, I intend to "de-exoticize" the entertainment trade. By presenting the lives and views of female singers and dancers themselves, I hope to create more understanding of their livelihood. What bothers female performers most is not an "Orientalist misrepresentation," but the way they are regarded and treated by the middle and higher classes of their own society. By giving insight into their lives and backgrounds, I hope to generate more sympathy for female entertainers on the part of Egyptian as well as Western audiences.

In Egypt, singing and dancing are essentially regarded as expressions of rejoicing, and at many happy occasions people sing and dance. They often treat an honored guest with entertainment as well. In 1983, when, as an undergraduate, I conducted a study concerning the views of female students on education, labor, and motherhood and lived on the campus of Cairo University, the female students often treated me to singing and dancing. In a refugee camp on the West Bank where I visited a family, a young girl was asked to dance by her male relatives. They clearly took pride in their sister's dancing abilities. On another occasion, an Egyptian family wanted to treat me to dancing as well, yet, because nonrelated men were present, the girl was forbidden to dance and her brother danced instead.

Although Egyptians are very fond of singing and dancing, professional performers are regarded with ambivalence. Professional entertainers are central to the most important occasions in people's lives, such as births, engagements, and weddings. A celebration without performers is not a real celebration. Entertainers are necessary because they make people happy (*biyifraḥu innâs*)—they bring out people's happiness. Besides, performers are objects of prestige and competition. The more performers or the more expensive and famous the entertainers, the more prestige the host family gains. Yet, despite their importance, entertainers are generally not honored or accorded much prestige.

When I asked a female singer about her feelings regarding the view of society about her profession, she responded emotionally:

> Why do people talk about a woman who works [in this trade]? If they understood our circumstances, they would not talk like that. I support a house with this trade—I spend on my family. Why does society judge us so harshly? Entertainers want to live! But people do not know these things. They must be awakened. Take note of this topic! You must show the people that we work to support a family. You must write in your book that even the government now recognizes our trade and has given us a trade union. Why does society still condemn us so harshly? Words like this will benefit you and will benefit us as well. Even though you are not an Egyptian, you will do something for people like us. May God give you success!

Why does society judge them so harshly? Why does society condemn female singers and dancers? These questions intrigued me. It was unclear to me, nor did the female singer quoted make it any clearer, whether female entertainers are condemned because people talk about a *woman* who works in this trade or because society *generally* judges the entertainment trade harshly. I decided to investigate whether the low esteem of female performers is mainly related to the dishonor of the trade or to the prevailing gender ideology. Or, formulated in another way: Is the tainted reputation of female entertainers due to the fact that entertainment is a dishonorable profession or is it due to the fact that the profession is dishonorable for women?

DISHONORABLE PROFESSIONS

In many countries, and in different historical periods, entertainers have been held in low esteem. They have especially been regarded with suspicion by religious authorities. Since the first centuries of the church, worldly vanity and entertainment have been combatted. In Muslim countries, entertainers have also been outcasts and rejected by the clergy in the past. In more recent times, itinerant entertainers—those, for instance, of Gypsy descent—have ranked low on the social scale as well. Whether they roam around or settle down, they are perceived as outsiders and outcasts.[1] Although this outcast status allows Gypsies mobility in the larger social system, they represent a category that is looked down upon by members of even the lowest class or caste (Berland 1986: 4). Studies on female musicians document their low status as well. Female musicians, singers, and dancers in Algeria, for instance, are marginal women (W. Jansen 1987: 190–200). Although Moroccan female musicians who perform only for women have high status, female entertainers performing for men are held in low esteem, like their Algerian counterparts (Davis 1978: 422, 429).

There is thus ample evidence that entertainers had and still have low status. The question of how to account for this is, interestingly enough, rarely posed. The answer would seem to be self-evident. In general, there is a dearth of theory on the low status of professions. Such theories as those on honor and shame, developed in particular with respect to the Mediterranean (see Chapter 6), focus on the status of social groups—men, women, the young, the old, or individuals—not on the status of occupations. Studies on entertainers and those in similar occupations, such as Dalby 1985 on the Japanese geisha and G. W. Jansen 1987 on showmen in the Netherlands, hardly go into the topic of dishonor. Studies on peripatetic groups mainly focus on mobility and ethnic differentness, rather than on the status of peripatetics as a result of the profession they are engaged in (Berland 1982; Berland & Salo 1986b). My aim, however, is to examine the profession and its influence on the status of its practitioners. The focus is not on professions that are considered dishonorable because they are practiced by certain groups, but is on groups viewed as disreputable because they practice a certain profession (Blok 1981a: 121).

The only theories dealing with the dishonor of groups on account of their professions are those of the body of literature on "infamous occupations," mainly pertaining to the European Middle Ages. These studies center on why members of numerous trades are considered dishonorable on account of their activities while in their personal way of life they do not differ from other people (Kramer 1971: 855). These studies contain valuable suggestions concerning the nature of infamous occupations, although caution is called for, since they pertain to a different historical period and another cultural setting. Explanations for the dishonor of certain occupations in, for instance, fourteenth-century Christian Germany are hardly applicable to nineteenth- and twentieth-century Muslim Egypt. Yet the general structural characteristics of these professions can serve as a guideline to the study of the possible dishonor of Egyptian entertainers.

Among those considered infamous in fourteenth-century Germany were skinners, executioners, gravediggers, watchmen, jailers, field guards, barbers, surgeons, tooth pullers, lumbermen, foresters, shepherds, millers, latrine cleaners, refuse collectors, chimney sweeps, bath attendants, and prostitutes. Itinerant people such as peddlers, beggars, jugglers, musicians, singers, actors, dancers, acrobats, and magicians were also considered infamous. According to Blok, several categories of people with dishonorable professions can be distinguished. The first consists of people who came in contact with excreta of the human body or with illness, death, human remains, and dirt, such as skinners, chimney sweeps, barbers, and gravediggers. Another category viewed as dishonorable consists of people who publicly exhibited their bodies for profit, such as entertainers and prostitutes. A third category, overlapping the second group, consists of itinerant people, including beggars, peddlers, and roaming scholars. Finally, people who lived outside the towns and villages, such as shepherds and millers, were considered infamous (Blok 1985: 30–35).

In Muslim cities in the Middle Ages, several occupations were also infamous. On religious grounds, the usurers ranked first among the disreputable. Neither were traders of silver, gold, and silk highly regarded. Others who profited from transactions forbidden by Muslim law, such as moneylenders, slave dealers, wine sellers, and pork sellers, were also disapproved of. Professional mourners, too, were frowned upon on religious grounds. Prostitutes, dancers, and other entertainers, such as wrestlers, players, storytellers, and singing women, were suspected of a questionable morality and associated with vice and begging (Lapidus 1967: 82–83). Other despised occupations that were not forbidden (*ḥarâm*)[2] but that were blameworthy or rejected (*makrûh*) in Islam were those whose practitioners were defiled by dead animals or animal waste matter, including butchers, tanners, hunters, and waste scavengers. Camel and donkey drivers, shepherds, bath attendants, veterinarians, watchmen, and stablemen were considered to have low occupations and were looked down upon as well (Lapidus 1967: 82–83; Brunschvig 1962: 56).

These diverse professions exhibit common structural characteristics. First, members of dishonorable professions generally had strained relations with the religious authorities. In the eyes of religious authorities, entertainers were outside the community of believers. They were regarded as leading dissolute lives, unrestrained by religious and moral sensibilities. The casual and lighthearted nature of amusement was viewed as an impediment to serious devotion to God. For that reason, the clergy was strictly forbidden to associate with entertainers. Spending money on amusement was deemed to be a vice.

A second characteristic concerns the relations that members of dishonorable professions all had with the worldly authorities. Especially the lack of a permanent residence and a presumed lack of morality prompted the governors to undertake actions against entertainers. In the case of Dutch showmen, not only their itinerancy, by means of which they evaded control of the government, but also the popular recreation they provided at fairs were felt to be disorderly and unpredictable (G. W. Jansen 1987). Fairs and festivals were generally feared, owing to the frequent occurrence of drinking and fighting at them. The atmosphere of relaxation and freedom occasionally exploded into riots and rebellions (Burke 1978: 178–204). Attempts were made to reform or abolish fairs and festivals. Studies on prostitution in France also reveal the ways in which the government tried to control this infamous occupation. Several strategies were used, ranging from regulation and institutionalization to downright repression (Corbin 1978; Otis 1985).

A third characteristic of infamous occupations is that their practitioners in European as well as in Muslim countries had a weak legal status. Dishonorable persons were authorized neither to hold the position of a judge nor to act as a witness. Quite often they were not compensated for injustices done to them (Spruit 1969: 59–60; Al-Faruqi 1985: 22–23; Sawa 1985: 71–72). European sources document that members of infamous occupations were usually excluded from guild organizations and so were their children. They had no professional associations of their own. In the later Middle Ages, sedentary entertainers organized themselves into professional associations and their status rose considerably. The development of trade organizations with regulations, licenses, and examinations was an important factor in the professionalization of these occupations.

Other characteristics of infamous occupations might be useful to direct attention to the potential dishonor of Egyptian entertainers as well. Members of infamous occupations were often physically segregated as dishonorable persons and could be distinguished by their outward appearance. Usually they were not ethnically different from the respectable citizens, so the otherness of the infamous was created by artificial means—for instance, by prescribed clothes or colors. Chimney sweeps, for example, were usually dressed in either white or black. They were identifiable by their hat, a black cylinder, aptly called a stovepipe hat (Blok 1984: 668). Entertainers were recognizable by their colorful and varied attire. Usually they dressed in the clothes they received as payment (Spruit 1969: 100). Infamous people were also set apart in separate living quarters. Prostitutes are still a clear example of this, but other dishonorable activities were also carried out in special quarters, mostly located at the margins of the city.

It was not simply a matter of respectable people distinguishing themselves from infamous others; more crucial was the marginalization of the dishonorable. Entertainers were marginal to the community as a result of their mobility, which made them strangers and outsiders. They were not only spatially marginal, but socially and usually economically as well. Another aspect of marginality is described by W. Jansen (1987). She focuses on women without men and shows that they are socially, economically, and culturally marginal. Their cultural marginality pertains to the fact that they do not have the habits and qualities considered to be feminine, such as sitting at home, producing children, and avoiding contact with male strangers. These women without men—unmarried women, widows, or married women with disabled or absent men—are foremost among those who engage in livelihoods considered improper or regarded with ambivalence, such as working in a bathhouse, washing dead women, practicing magic, assisting in fertility and birth, and working as a prostitute or an entertainer.

Still two other notions, distilled from studies on infamous occupations, deserve attention. Medieval European entertainers were viewed as persons who sold their honor for money, who prostituted themselves. The expression "die gut für ere nement und sich zu eigen geben" was used in this connection in thirteenth-century Germany. "Sich zu eigen geben" means to exhibit the body in public for money, which was considered disgraceful (Blok 1985: 34). "Gut für ere nement" points to the fact that entertainers received money in order to praise the name and fame of the person who paid them (Spruit 1969: 62; Danckert 1963: 220). In the Muslim world as well, whoever paid was praised (Sawa 1985: 76–77). Because of this, entertainers had the unfavorable image of being dishonest and counterfeit. They were perceived as flatterers and hypocrites (Casagrande and Vecchio 1979: 915).

Entertainers and other dishonorable persons who either were itinerant or worked outside the towns and villages were stigmatized in still another way. They evaded the control of the worldly and religious authorities and were less subject to social control as well. For that reason, they were connected with heretical ideas, rebellion, frivolity, and illegal activities. They were seen as dangerous and receptive to unorthodox ideas (Ginzburg 1980: 120). W. Jansen as well notes that female entertainers in Algeria today are feared because they are perceived as disturbers of the sexual order (W. Jansen 1987: 160–200).

Several explanations are given to account for the infamy of certain occupations. For example, the handling of dirt is noted as reason for the dishonor of skinners, chimney sweeps, and refuse collectors. For other occupations, former bondage or serfdom is suggested (Blok 1985: 30, 31; Brunschvig 1962: 47). With respect to itinerants such as peddlers and entertainers, mobility is given as an explanation. As is the case with millers and shepherds, who worked outside the city walls, the fact that they evaded the control of worldly and religious authorities made them suspect.

A general theory to explain the infamy of all dishonorable occupations has been formulated by Blok (1981a, 1984, 1985), according to whom infamous occupations "bear a strong family resemblance: in one way or another they are involved with margins, thresholds, and boundaries—bridging the differences between clear-cut categories like self and not-self, city and countryside, man and animal, culture and nature, civilized and primitive" (1985: 36). Infamous people do not fit into these categories and are seen as "anomalous, ambiguous, liminal, betwixt and between." Because they are professionally involved with margins and mediate these basic oppositions, infamous people are taboo. The expectation of this approach is that stronger infamy occurs among those who mediate several oppositions, such as executioners, who mediate between life and death, illness and health, man and animal, this world and the next, and self and not-self.

Blok's structuralist theory contains a general claim, namely, that the structure of infamy of the dishonorable professions consists of their liminality. In entertainment, which can be defined as "publicly exhibiting the body for profit," the body is central. Could it be that the entertainer's body mediates between such binary categories as animal versus man or nature versus culture? Belly dancers, a small part of all entertainers, are associated with sexuality in the West and partly in the East as well. Could it be argued that "exciting the sexual instincts" makes belly dancers liminal and mediators between animal and man? In my opinion, this is a narrow view not only of sexuality,[3] but of belly dancing as well. As I have mentioned, dance is essentially an expression of happiness and only in certain contexts of sexuality. Besides, this argument does not equally apply to female singers and musicians, because they are associated to a lesser extent with sexuality. Moreover, it does not pertain to male entertainers. Thus, in the case of female entertainers, the explanation of their dishonor should probably be looked for in gender rather than in the liminality of the profession itself. This point is also hinted at by W. Jansen in her study *Women without Men: Gender and Marginality in an Algerian Town*. With regard to the marginality of female bath workers, she argues that though liminal characteristics such as their role as assistants in the transition from pure to impure are important, they do not provide a sufficient explanation in the case of women (W. Jansen 1987: 60).

A more general critique directed against the liminality thesis concerns its basic assumption of universal binary classification. As has been shown in the nature versus culture debate, this is unwarranted as a general assumption (MacCormack 1980; Brown and Jordanova 1981). Also concerning another putative dichotomy—man versus woman—several studies show the diversity, not only in the content of these cultural constructions, but in their presumed binary character as well (Ortner and Whitehead 1981; Wikan 1977; Nanda 1990; see Chapter 7).

Lastly, even if binary classification were demonstrable, this does not clarify the status of mediators. In his essay "Common Sense as a Cultural System," Geertz gives examples of the way three societies view intersexuality. Intersexuality in itself proves again that even biological sex is not a purely dichotomous variable. The point I want to make here is that whereas in American society intersexuals are regarded with horror, the Navaho respect them and regard them with wonder and awe. The East

African Pokot are neither horrified nor delighted by intersexuals, but simply see them as mistakes and as useless persons (Geertz 1983: 80–84). Whether people classify in terms of binary oppositions and what this means for the status of mediators should thus be the subject of study, not an unquestioned assumption.

I agree with Geertz that anthropologists should try "to see things from the native's point of view" (1983: 56). He introduces two valuable notions to this end: the "experience-near" and the "experience-distant" concepts. Experience-near concepts are defined as those which one "might . . . naturally and effortlessly use to define what he or his fellows see, think, imagine, and so on, and which he would readily understand when applied by others." People use them "spontaneously, unselfconsciously, as it were colloquially; they do not, except fleetingly and on occasion, recognize that there are any 'concepts' involved at all." He contrasts this with experience-distant concepts, defined as those which "specialists of one sort or another, . . . an ethnographer, even a priest or an ideologist, employ to forward their scientific, philosophical or practical aims" (1983: 57–58). These concepts should not be seen as incompatible. Anthropologists need both in order not to be confined to immediacies and vernacular on the one hand, or abstractions and jargon on the other. Yet experience-distant concepts should, in my opinion, be demonstrably founded on experience-near notions, whether distilled from words, sayings, proverbs, jokes, images, or behavior.[1]

Since I propose to take experience-near concepts as a guideline, I cannot begin my explanation by assuming the dishonor of entertainers. Instead, I should begin with a question: Are entertainers considered dishonorable and, in case they are viewed as such, for what reasons? The structural characteristics of infamous occupations should not be taken as assumptions; rather, they should be examined for Egyptian entertainers. In Chapters 2 and 3, I examine the nature of the relation of Egyptian entertainers with religious and worldly authorities. I also describe their legal status and the historical developments in their organization and professionalization during the nineteenth and particularly the twentieth centuries.

In Chapters 4 and 5, the notions of otherness, separateness, and the possibly resulting marginality are considered for Egyptian entertainers. Are Egyptian entertainers a distinct group or merely considered to be so? Are they mobile and, if so, what is the effect of their mobility on their status? Are they marginal either spatially, socially, or economically? Are female entertainers "women without men"?

Chapters 6 and 7 deal with the way entertainers are perceived by Egyptian society. Are they regarded as counterfeits and flatterers? Is the way in which they receive payment considered dishonorable and a way of prostituting themselves? Are they perceived as unorthodox, rebellious, or dangerous disturbers? These ideas are particularly examined with regard to female entertainers. In Chapter 8, I go into the self-presentation of female entertainers.

ENTERTAINMENT, ISLAM, AND GENDER

The study of the status of Egyptian entertainers should thus be carefully contextualized. An important element of the Egyptian context is related to Islamic views on music, singing, and dancing.

Although at the birth of Islam there was no animosity toward singing and music, the orthodox caliphs opposed indulging in them.[5] A discussion on the lawfulness of music ensued, which cast doubt on the permissibility not only of the performer, but of the listener as well.[6] Advocates and opponents alike traced the legitimacy of their position back to the Quran and the *hadîths*, the sayings of the Prophet. Although most law schools decided against the lawfulness of music and singing, this did not prevent the "forbidden pleasures" from flourishing in the palaces.[7]

According to the seventeenth-century Muslim scholar Chelebi, who summarized the religious views on singing and music, three categories of music can be distinguished: music coming from birds, from the human throat, and from instruments. He states that in Islam "the exponents of the sacred law have categorized it as perfectly permissible to listen to the melodies produced by birds, and have allowed those produced by human throats, subject to certain conditions and rules. But . . . to listen to instruments that are blown or struck is never permissible" (1957: 38). Certain instruments are forbidden because they are supposed to encourage drinking. The *kûba*, an oblong drum, for instance, is prohibited because of its association with drinking wine, licentious songs, and dissolute people. With respect to the human throat, if it produces songs about wine and debauchery, it is not permissible to listen to it (Chelebi 1957: 39).

According to the ethnomusicologist Al-Faruqi, religious opinion creates a hierarchy of music and singing that is expressed as forbidden, unfavored, indifferent, recommended, and commendable forms. The recitation of the Quran stands at the peak of the hierarchy, immediately followed by the call to prayer and religious chants. Also legitimate are various types of song connected to family celebrations, caravan chants, work songs, and the music of military bands. At the bottom of the hierarchy, we find "sensuous music that is performed in association with condemned activities, or that is thought to incite such prohibited practices as consumption of drugs and alcohol, lust, prostitution, etc." (al-Faruqi 1985: 12). This genre is clearly forbidden, *ḥarâm*. Most forms of music and singing, though, do not fit into these clear categories. Depending on the time, place, and person who is judging them, vocal and instrumental improvisations, accompanied songs, and instrumental music can be regarded as permissible, indifferent, or rejectable (al-Faruqi 1985: 1–13).

The approval or disapproval of performers is related not only to the genre but also to the context of the performance. Regarding the permissibility of the context, three elements are deemed important by the eleventh-century Muslim scholar Imâm al-Ghazâlî, namely, time, place, and associates. A performance is not acceptable if too much time is devoted to it, so that it interferes with higher Islamic goals and distracts believers' attention from their devotion to God. Full-time professional performers are accordingly less acceptable than nonprofessional amateurs. The acceptability of the place and occasion of the performance is also an important factor in judging the legitimacy of the entertainers and their public. Lastly, the type of people present during the performance affects the permissibility of the performers and their audience. A certain genre of music can thus be permissible in one context while it is rejected in another circumstance. Playing the tambourine is, for instance, acceptable if it is done by women at a wedding but forbidden if it is done by men in the context of homosexuality or prostitution (al-Faruqi 1985: 17–20; al-Ghazâlî 1902: 1).

The discussions on dancing are less detailed and mainly restricted to ecstasy. According to al-Ghazâlî, proper conduct during ecstasy and trance is also bound by the rules of time, place, and company. However, if ecstasy overcomes a person and makes the person move without volition, it is excusable. Yet when volition returns, stillness and restraint are preferred. The general rule is that "if the pleasure which causes dancing is praiseworthy, and the dancing increases and strengthens it, then the dancing is praiseworthy. . . . Yet it is true that the practice of dancing does not befit the station of notable people who set an example, because most of the time, it springs from play and sport" (al-Ghazâlî 1902: 9). In general, the suitability of dancing thus depends on the circumstances and the dancer. We should keep in mind, though, that al-Ghazâlî discusses the ecstasy of males dancing in a religious setting. Nothing is said about secular dancing by women. Maybe we can extrapolate that if female dancers are performing in front of a female audience and the pleasure which causes the dancing is praiseworthy—for instance, at a wedding—dancing is permissible. Yet we must first look into the different rules for male and female performers.

Although the impact of gender on the acceptability of performers has hardly received attention, it is a crucial factor. A well-known *hadîth* often cited to discredit female singers is "*sawt al-mar'a 'awra*," "the voice of a woman is a shameful thing." Imâm al-Ghazâlî explains this as follows: Music is allowed unless it is feared that the music might act as a temptation. The voice of women could seduce the listener. Looking at female performers is always unlawful. Listening to the voices of concealed female performers is still forbidden if it evokes tempting images. Al-Ghazâlî continues by stating that looking at a beardless boy is only forbidden if there is a danger of temptation. He then likens the lawfulness of listening to a concealed female singer to that of looking at a beardless young boy. Avoiding temptation is the rule which ought to be followed, and only if temptation is feared is music unlawful (al-Ghazâlî 1901: 235–237).

Women are thus generally perceived as more enticing than men, and the excitement aroused by looking is considered more powerful than the excitement aroused by listening. These observations have consequences for the lawfulness of the different forms of male and female performances. Female performances are more controversial, and their acceptability depends on whether they cause males to experience arousal. The fact that excitement is most strongly aroused by the eye rather than by the ear also affects the various categories of female performers. Female musicians are mainly listened to; female singers are both listened to and, at least at present, observed; while female dancers are solely eye-catchers. Female dancing is accordingly considered the most shameful form of entertainment. Yet if female dancing is performed in front of a female audience and no temptation is feared and the performance is in keeping with the limits of proper time, place, and company, it is probably permissible.

Many forms and contexts of entertainment are thus either controversial or forbidden, particularly for women. Yet we cannot solely rely on the opinion of Muslim scholars of the eleventh or the seventeenth century, but should also look at more recent views. According to the late Sheikh al-Azhar Shaltût, who wrote a *fatwa*—a formal ruling or opinion—on the issue in 1960, music is permissible under certain conditions. He argues that God is not against pleasure and that Islam seeks the Golden Mean. Yet pleasure should not take place under immoral circumstances or with dissolute companions (al-Faruqi 1985: 25–26). The Muslim scholar al-Qaraḍâwî states that music in itself is permissible, but also places several restrictions on it. The content of a song should not be against the morals and teachings of Islam or be accompanied by other things forbidden in Islam. Exaggeration is never desirable, and is especially undesirable in entertainment; thus a person who knows that entertainment easily excites him or her should keep away from it. According to al-Qaraḍâwî, Islam does not permit any kind of profession which might excite the instincts, whether through licentious songs, sexual dance, or other acts leading to the corruption of morals (al-Qaraḍâwî 1985: 139, 289). During my research, the leading television preacher, Sheikh Mitwalli al-Shaʿarâwî, stated that all female dancing is bad and that only music which does not "tickle the nerves" is permissible (*Economist* 21-5-1988). Recent religious views thus show similar arguments and points of divergence in the debate on the permissibility of music and entertainment.

Yet in order to understand the status of present-day performers in Egyptian society, we must go beyond religious opinion. The impact of Islamic laws and views on the thinking of present-day Egyptians cannot be assumed but must be investigated. Especially if we propose to use an experience-near approach, it is important to investigate people's own views, religious and nonreligious, on entertainment. During my research, it appeared that the form and context of entertainment and the sex of the performer were important criteria outside the religious framework as well. Literature on ethnomusicology in the Middle East has also shown that the musical aesthetics of different genres and contexts of performances and the competence of artists are important factors influencing the performer's status (Racy 1981, 1982). In order to examine the status of performers, it is thus useful to distinguish several forms and contexts within the trade and to compare their relative status in the eyes of the public.

The three main contexts of Egyptian entertainment are, first, the circuit of weddings and saint's day celebrations; second, the nightclub circuit; and, finally, the performing arts circuit, the performances in concert halls and theaters, on radio and television, etc. We should be careful, though, not to equate the Egyptian situation with the Western art scene.

The clear-cut Western division into a highly esteemed classical tradition and a popular tradition with low esteem does not apply to the Arab world (al-Faruqi 1979; Racy 1981, 1982). Although there is a distinction in contexts—that is, the most talented performers working in a theater have more esteem than those performing at a saint's day celebration or in a nightclub—the genre of songs and music might well be the same in all three contexts. The same famous songs of Umm Kalthûm or Muḥammad ʿAbd al-Wahhâb can be heard on the radio, at weddings, in nightclubs, and in concert halls.

The different forms of entertainment I studied are instrumental music, singing, and dancing (belly dancing and folk dancing). For women, singing and dancing are the most important activities. As will be described in Chapter 3, women have largely been pushed out of the domain of instrumental music. I often use the term "female entertainer" or "female performer" because most women in the past were, and to a lesser extent still are, singers and dancers at the same time. A good performer was supposed to be complete (*shamla*)—that is, competent in singing and dancing.

The sex of performers can also be a factor influencing their status as entertainers. Gender has only recently been introduced into the field of ethnomusicology (Koskoff 1989; Sugarman 1989). The main issues that have been investigated are the degree to which gender ideology affects musical thought and practice and how music reflects and affects intergender relations. I will deal with a more specifically anthropological issue: the relation between the social and cultural construction of gender and the status of performers.

In order to examine the experience-near views and evaluations of the Egyptian public, I interviewed many Egyptians of different socioeconomic backgrounds. In Chapter 6, I present their views on the various forms and contexts of entertainment for male and female entertainers. In Chapter 7, I specifically deal with the cultural construction of gender and the female body in entertainment. The main focus throughout the ethnography, however, is the views and experiences of the female performers I spoke with during my fieldwork.

FIELDWORK IN EGYPT

From September 1988 to April 1989 and from August 1989 to February 1990 I conducted fieldwork among female singers and dancers in Egypt.

In order to develop a better understanding of Egyptian dance and music, I participated in a belly-dancing course in Amsterdam. Muḥammad Ṭolba, an Egyptian choreographer, gave me the address of a music shop on Muḥammad ʿAlî Street, the Cairene entertainment street. Soon after I settled in Cairo, on a hot morning in September I took a cab to this music shop. It had just opened, and a man who repaired instruments was present. He indicated that the time was highly unsuitable for paying visits to entertainers and that I should return at 6:00 P.M., so I did. The oldest brother of the family that owned the shop, Sayyid, a small, resolute man in his late thirties, was waiting for me. He directed me inside the shop, where the rest of the family—his mother and younger brothers—and some curious neighbors crowded. I was asked the reason for my visit, and in broken Arabic I explained about my research. Sayyid said it was a great honor to his family that I came all the way from Holland straight to his shop. Since there were a number of similar shops along the street, my visit indicated the good reputation of his family. I was told that I was lucky to have chosen his shop, because not all families were as trustworthy as his. He was willing to make appointments with performers and to protect me as his sister. But, since I was under his aegis, I would have to inform him and consult with him before visiting other performers. To make sure I had understood everything, I had to repeat his conditions. Although I was a bit hesitant about the conditions, which could restrain my freedom, I decided to say what they wanted to hear. They nodded in agreement.

Sayyid then took me to the relatively quiet office of a friend. He introduced himself a bit more and told me that his family was well known in the entertainment trade. His late father had been an accordion player and in great demand at popular weddings. At the age of fourteen, Sayyid had started working with him, playing the accordion. Three brothers played the drum, while the fourth repaired instruments. Sayyid became the head of a music band and arranged weddings of the lower-middle class. He occasionally worked in nightclubs with a dancer, and for the past few years had also been employed by the orchestra of the national folk-dancing troupe.

Sayyid began to write down the topics I should pay attention to, the people I needed to meet, and the order in which we would proceed with the research. I was struck by the fact that although I had only given him a general outline of my research, he had very well understood what I wanted. He would first introduce me to performers of the older generation, so that I could collect historical material. In addition, he would take me to weddings. I was lucky, for he had a wedding and a private birthday party that week. Finally, he would arrange interviews with the female performers I saw at work.

Since I had the feeling that my Arabic was not yet sufficient to do interviews alone, Sayyid introduced me to a friend who spoke English and could act as an interpreter. A few days later, the interpreter, a curator of the Islamic museum, and I went to see Rayyis Bîra, an old singer and composer who was well informed about the trade. Unfortunately, he did not want his anecdotes to be taped and, since I had an interpreter with me, he spoke full-speed in Arabic. I could only write down some tidbits of translated information interspersed with my interpreter's own views, such as: "He's telling about one of his meaningless songs." I was not particularly happy about these first interviews with the composer and asked Sayyid to become my assistant. He agreed. Although he did not speak English, Sayyid was able to speak simple Arabic which I could follow quite well. He quickly grasped my vocabulary and translated difficult Arabic into easy Arabic or creatively acted out new words.

The next week, we met in Sayyid's regular coffeehouse on Muḥammad ʿAlî Street. It was a strange place for a woman to go, but after going there several times I became an accepted visitor, at least for the short time I had to wait for Sayyid to arrive or to finish playing backgammon. When I showed Sayyid an extensive questionnaire I had prepared in Arabic, to my annoyance he casually thumbed through the pages and then told me that he already knew what I needed. We went to two older female performers, and during the interviews I realized that he was right. I had neither the vocabulary nor the knowledge about the intricacies of the trade to pose meaningful questions.

The first interviews resembled a pleasant tête-à-tête between colleagues. I looked after the tape recorder and the batteries while Sayyid did the talking. Although it was not what I had anticipated a "real anthropologist" would do in the field, I found it very instructive. I sensed that it was the best way not only to learn the relevant vocabulary related to the trade, but also to gain insight into the subjects that performers themselves found important. I was more or less able to follow the discussions because Sayyid "translated" and explained at the same time, which could also be corrected and elaborated upon by the female performer we talked with.

Although Sayyid is a man, we had no problem visiting women at home. They were usually surprised but pleased to see him. To the older generation, Sayyid was like a son. They had known him from his childhood, when they worked with his father and Sayyid visited them to pay them in advance. To his own generation, he was like a brother. As children they had played together, and now they performed together. For the younger generation, Sayyid was a respectable head of a band who could provide them with work. Most of them liked to talk about their former glory or present fame and to recall common experiences. Sayyid's presence often brought back old memories, such as "Do you remember that as a child you fell asleep on my lap?" or "Do you remember that wedding when you did not give me my rightful share of the tips?" Their shared pleasant and unpleasant experiences at work were very fruitful and interesting to hear.

After some time, I felt confident enough to interview and to raise relevant topics myself. We developed a pattern in which the introductory interviews were mainly done by Sayyid. I had a good rapport with several women and I made appointments to visit them alone for further information. I visited a number of them regularly, just to chat, to drink tea, or to watch television. I also accompanied them to their work. Eventually I got to know other performers through the female singers and dancers with whom I had visited and become friends. Most of the female performers I was acquainted with were from Cairo, but later I also met performers from the Delta and witnessed weddings outside the capital. In summer, I went to Alexandria, like many Cairenes do. Sayyid and his family were present as well. They introduced me to performers from Alexandria, and Sayyid's wife joined me in visiting the many weddings in the "casinos" along the beach. I combined a holiday in Luxor with visiting the local dancers. I also visited a family who toured the saint's day celebrations of the Delta with a variety theater, in Ḥelwan, Ṭanṭâ, and Dessûq, and I stayed with performers in Mansûra and Ṭanṭâ. Although I increasingly went my own way, Sayyid remained a "key informant" until the very end of my stay.

Making contact with nightclub performers was more difficult. People who worked the popular circuit mostly live in the Muḥammad ʿAlî Street area. If someone was not at home, we just visited a neighbor to talk or we would find the woman at the house of a nearby relative. Nightclub performers live throughout Cairo. I thus had to visit nightclubs and try to make contacts during the entertainers' work time. I suspected that sitting alone in a nightclub would be a bothersome experience, so I looked for someone to accompany me in my nightlife. I was lucky to meet a young man, Târiq, who was a member of an association to aid tourists and eager to provide foreigners with a pleasant stay in Egypt. Because of his "respectable" upper-class background, he had never visited a nightclub before. Neither was he particularly interested in them, but he found it an amusing adventure to accompany and protect me in these "dangerous places." He even made several contacts for me through friends and friends of friends. We spent many pleasant evenings in all kinds of nightclubs, watching high-level and cheap programs and arranging appointments after the show. In addition to Târiq's assistance, Sayyid brought me into contact with the manager of a five-star nightclub, who introduced me to the female singers and dancers working there. Eventually I could go there alone, the waiters being instructed to ward off curious men.

Initially, I intended to include performers from the performing arts circuit of theaters, radio, and television as well. However, the information and studies available were mainly about famous singers like Umm Kalthûm, well-known actresses, and a few star dancers. The common performers in nightclubs and the circuit of weddings and saint's day celebrations had not been studied at all, so they were more interesting to me. Besides, I did not have time enough to study the performing arts circuit extensively.[8]

Although I met many nightclub performers, my contacts with them were less extensive than with entertainers working at weddings and saint's day celebrations. I spoke with thirty-eight female and ten male popular performers, and with fourteen female and five male nightclub entertainers.[9] In the second fieldwork period, I decided to focus mainly on the female singers and dancers of Muḥammad ʿAlî Street, not only because I had more and better contacts with them, but also because I was fascinated by the history of this branch of the trade and by their personal life stories. Many of them had started at an early age, around fifteen, and had worked for more than twenty years in the trade. Entertainment was thus central to their lives. Besides, the older generation, which had worked from the 1940s onward, was easily traceable and I could thus collect oral history that extended over at least fifty years. Moreover, this group formed a kind of community with shared codes and customs, which highly appealed to my interests as an anthropologist.

Nightclub entertainment is a separate branch and, for women, there is hardly any overlap between the circuit of weddings and saint's celebrations and the nightclub circuit. The performers of the two circuits have different socioeconomic backgrounds. Whereas many nightclub entertainers are from the middle class, most popular performers have a lower- or lower-middle-class background. Moreover, their customers and the style of their work also differ. Most nightclub singers and dancers work for a relatively short period. They start at around twenty, make money, marry, and after a few years disappear from the stages. Thereafter they are difficult to trace. The relatively short duration of their career ensures that they are less tied to their trade.

There were also more substantial reasons to concentrate on entertainers working at weddings and saint's day celebrations. They are not only the largest group of performers, but they also play a more central role in the lives of most Egyptians. Nightclubs, with the exception of the very cheap ones, are visited only by a small segment of society, the well-to-do Egyptians, whereas Egyptians of most classes have entertainers of Muḥammad ʿAlî Street at their weddings. Although members of the upper class usually reserve a five-star nightclub or hotel and celebrate with famous nightclub performers, most people of the middle and lower classes engage the cheaper performers from Muḥammad ʿAlî Street. Moreover, the circuit of weddings more closely reflects the fundamental meaning of singing and dancing in Egypt—that is, joy and happiness. With some reservations, it could be argued that whereas the circuit of weddings and saint's day celebrations represents the context of rejoicing, nightclubs are the domain of sexual excitement.

Although I mainly focused on the circuit of weddings and saint's day celebrations, nightclub performers were an interesting group for comparison. Despite the higher class background of nightclub performers, and that of their audience, they were more stigmatized than were entertainers of Muḥammad ʿAlî Street. In order to gain insight into the relation between dishonor and entertainment, it was thus illuminating to compare the two circuits.

Since I wanted to know the view of Egyptian society on the various forms and contexts of entertainment for male and female performers, I talked with fifty Egyptians of different socioeconomic backgrounds about these matters. Since my own network of acquaintances was small, I was happy to meet Shamiyya, an Egyptian woman with an extensive network of relatives and friends, ranging from chicken farmers and porters to housewives, government employees, physicians, and engineers. I had prepared a set of thirty-two cards, each with a different profession, among which, of course, were various forms and contexts of entertainment. I asked my informants to order the cards and to explain the order they chose. They usually found it an amusing game. In addition, we discussed their views on other topics pertaining to the entertainment trade and their own wedding celebrations. Our conversations were usually short and pleasant, although in the long run they became slightly boring to Shamiyya and to me as well. But Shamiyya liked to go out visiting friends and relatives, and the small sum of money she received for assisting me was always welcome.

Presenting gifts to informants was another amusing and instructive anthropological experience. For most, I had brought a typical Dutch present, a silver bracelet with a small charm, a pair of clogs, attached to it. My informants were genuinely happy with the bracelet, and it was sweet to meet them afterward at weddings wearing the bracelet. Another present I had brought, a brooch of delft blue, was not appropriate, as I was immediately instructed by Sayyid. He felt a bit embarrassed about the gift because it was too small. I was slightly surprised, since it had the same value and was bigger than the clogs. But Sayyid explained that the brooch could not always be worn and therefore its show-off value was less. This incident made me aware that with regard to money and presents, Sayyid's reputation was at stake. Since I was not part of the community, I had no reputation to keep or to lose. Accordingly, Sayyid indicated the form and amount of each gift to informants. Most people of his own or the younger generation were awarded a bracelet. People of the older generation usually received money. I totally agreed with this policy, not only because I had to give primary consideration to Sayyid's reputation, but also because some older performers were fairly impoverished. It would have been embarrassing to give someone two clogs if their value in money could have meant eating better food. How many pounds were given was dependent on the status of the people involved. The poorest were usually given less, rather than more. The former great performers who had worked above Sayyid and his father had to be accorded relatively more prestige. It was always interesting to see what and how much was given to whom. Usually Sayyid presented the money and I the bracelets. He gave the money in a casual way, and if the female performer politely protested, he sometimes jokingly tucked it into her dress "as a tip."

After the intense and interesting fieldwork period, sitting behind the computer was such a big change that it initially seemed boring in comparison. While reading and rereading the entertainers' life stories in Amsterdam, I was mentally still in Egypt. Yet as I worked, it increasingly became a challenge and another type of adventure to present as accurately as possible the history of the trade, the status of female singers and dancers in the eyes of society, and, last but not least, the life stories of the entertainers and their own views of their trade.

TWO

FEMALE ENTERTAINMENT IN NINETEENTH-CENTURY EGYPT

Female entertainers were one of the most important tourist sights of nineteenth-century Egypt. Many travelers preferred them to the pyramids and the Nile. Although female entertainers thus figure in many accounts, relatively little is known about their lives and profession. Only random and scattered descriptions of their performances remain.

Unfortunately, the only sources available are the largely unreliable accounts of travelers.[1] I traced the history of female entertainers back to the end of the eighteenth century. At that time, travelers did not ventilate their opinions as crudely as did their seventeenth-century predecessors, such as de Thevenot, who wrote: "The natives of Egypt, Muslims and Christians alike, are generally of a brown complexion and villainous character, weak-kneed, lazy, hypocrites, thieves, traitors and greedy to the extent that they would kill someone for a penny. To put it briefly, they are perfect in all shortcomings and the biggest funks in the world" (de Thevenot 1681: 420).

Nineteenth-century travelers also described Egypt as an imperfect and inferior place, albeit in a more sophisticated manner than previous visitors. "The East" as a whole was viewed as the negative mirror image of "the West." Cromer, governor of Egypt after the British occupation in 1882, for instance, stated: "It would seem . . . as if even in the most trivial acts of life some unfelt impulse, for which no special reason can be assigned, drives the Eastern to do exact opposite to that which the Western would do under similar circumstances" (1908, 2: 144).

The study of "the Orient" as a discipline, "Orientalism," began in the eighteenth century and flourished in the nineteenth century and the beginning of the twentieth. It gave the otherness and inferiority of "the East" a scholarly foundation. Edward Said, who sharply criticizes the mode of thinking and representation of Orientalists, characterizes Orientalism as: "a style of thought based upon the ontological and epistemological distinction made between 'the Orient' and (most of the time) 'the Occident' "(1979: 2). "The West" was depicted as changing, progressing, active, rational, and austere, "the East" as rigid, stagnant, passive, irrational, and sensual.

The Western expansion in the nineteenth century nourished the cult of otherness, particularly of the exotic and bizarre other. Eroticism was one of the main aspects of the exotic "Orient." Travelers were thus fascinated by the "licentious" female dancers, who provided them with a means to express the differentness and sensuality of "the East." The first European visitor who described the native dance was Lady Mary Montagu in 1717. The local dance was "very different from what I had seen before. Nothing could be more artfull or proper to raise certain Ideas, the Tunes so soft, the motions so Languishing, accompany'd with pauses and dying Eyes, halfe falling back and then recovering themselves in so artfull a Manner that I am very positive the coldest and most rigid Prude upon Earth could not have look'd upon them without thinking of something not to be spoke of" (1965, 1: 351). Most later travelers agreed with Lady Montagu on the effect of the dance upon the "rigid Prude," but rarely described it as "artfull." They characterized the dance as "voluptuous," "shameful," "stupid," "abject," or "savage."

Although travelers' accounts could easily be used to highlight the way Orientalists represent "the East,"[2] they also contain material which can shed light on entertainers and their profession. The descriptions of the "indecent dance" provide many examples of the prevailing prejudices and distortions, yet, between the lines, other details can be discerned. When the focus is turned away from the dance to the dancer's backstage and spectators, the travelers' accounts do contain observations of a more factual character. We have to limit the material we use, though, to eyewitness observations and small "facts" such as place and date of observation. For instance, three travelers visited Fûwa, in the Delta, respectively in 1777, 1798, and 1837. Whereas Savary (1787), the first traveler, witnessed dancing girls in abundance, Denon (1803) was only able to see them in 1798 because the French army forced the local authorities to show them the dancers. Pückler (1844), the third traveler, did not see any female performers at all in the Delta because they had been banned from the north. Information about presence or absence of performers in certain towns or villages, the amount and method of payment, the attire and the sex of the audience—all these small details can provide clues for a reconstruction of the historical developments in entertainment. In this chapter, it will become clear that drastic changes took place in nineteenth-century entertainment, changes for which the travelers themselves were crucial agents.

FESTIVE OCCASIONS AND TYPES OF ENTERTAINMENT

Around 1800, various entertainers, such as ropedancers, acrobats, actors, comedians, buffoons, conjurers, and snake charmers, amused people in public places, at coffeehouses, and at home. Singers, dancers, storytellers, poets, and minstrels were also popular at private and public festivities. Religious recitation of the Quran and the singing of lyric odes in praise of the Prophet were highly appreciated as well. Puppet shows mocking the "Franks" and monkeys dressed up as Europeans were other spectacles the native population enjoyed (Niebuhr 1776, 1: 181–183). Most travelers, however, preferred the performances of female dancers.

Most performances were held in the streets, especially in front of coffeehouses or at marketplaces where a large audience could be attracted. The day on which the Nile rose to a high level provided a special occasion for entertainment. The dams in the canal were breached and the flowing water filled the lakes of Cairo. The day before, the still dry bottom of the canal made a stage for buffoons, snake charmers, singers, and dancers. Afterward, people went out in boats, the rich with hired singers.

Several religious occasions provided opportunities for both religious and nonreligious entertainment. Saints' days, *mawâlid* (singular: *mûlid)*, such as the *mûlid* of the Prophet and *mûlid al-Ḥussein,* were celebrated with colorful fairs and festivals. The saint's day of Sayyid al-Badâwî at Ṭanṭâ was famous for its large-scale entertainment, sweetmeats, and traders. Traders from all over Egypt attended the *mûlid* to buy foodstuffs and cloth. In 1779, this celebration lasted for more than a week, during which time ten thousand small boats filled Ṭanṭâ's canal. Along the banks, small tents were pitched and their occupants provided music, trade, and prostitution (Savary 1787, 1: 236–237).

Another saint's day celebration that was much visited was the *mûlid* of Ibrahîm al-Dessûqî at Dessûq.[3] In 1798, Dessûq was deluged with about 200,000 believers and a large number of entertainers, particularly dancers, from all corners of Egypt (Denon 1803, 1: 180–181). The centrally located town of Maḥalla al-Kubrâ was the meeting place of singers and dancers, from which they dispersed to the *mawâlid* of the Delta (Dubois-

Aymé and Jollois 1822: 207–208[4]). Besides trade and entertainment, religious rituals of the various brotherhoods took place. The *zikr*, a Sûfî ritual based on the repeated mention of the name and epithets of God, and the *dôsa* were frequently described. During the *dôsa* ceremony, the *sheikh* of the Derwish, sitting on horseback, rode across several prostrated followers without hurting them (Lane 1978: 446–447).

Also in the evenings of the Ramadan, after breaking their fast, people went out into the streets and enjoyed themselves with *mûlid*-like spectacles and entertainments. It might be that female public dancing was considered incompatible with this holy month, since female dancers were forbidden in the streets during Ramadan (Jomard 1822: 441). But dancing girls seem to have appeared in the privacy of the harem (Chabrol 1822: 211–212).

At family celebrations, entertainers were also in demand. At weddings, in particular, they played a major role.[5] The wedding ceremony was conducted on Sunday or Thursday evening, just as at present.[6] For three days—or more in the case of rich people—the street was illuminated. Every night, entertainments, or *zikrs,* were held, especially during the Sunday or Thursday evening. Wednesday or Saturday at noon, the bride went in a procession to the bathhouse. This procession, which was called the *zaffit il-ḥammâm*, was accompanied by singers and dancers. Rich people hired the bathhouse and had female singers and dancers perform inside. Afterward, the bride was brought home, and preparations were started for the *lêlit il-ḥenna,* the dyeing of the feet and hands of the bride with henna, during which the company was entertained with songs. At the same time, separate entertainment was provided for the male guests in front of the house or in the court. Thursday was the day of the big procession, the *zaffit il-ʿarûsa*. Over a period of several hours, the richness of the bride's family was shown through the display of the furniture the bride brought with her and the number of singers and dancers accompanying her. The ensuing night was called the *lêlit il-dukhla*, during which the marriage was consummated. While the women were entertained upstairs, the male guests had their party downstairs (Niebuhr 1776, 1: 179; Savary 1787, 1: 42–44; Burckhardt 1972: 133–142; Lane 1978: 159–175).

It is obvious that the ceremonies of the lower classes were less expensive. According to Lane, the same customs were observed, but the processions were carried out with less splendor and fewer performers. Instead of singers and dancers, the lower classes had musicians with tambourines and conjurers or no entertainers at all. In that case, the invited people themselves drew attention to the wedding procession by beating on metal bars and by the sounds of *zagharît*, the joyous cries of women (Lane 1978: 168; Savary 1787, 3: 44).

The party for a seven-day-old baby, the *subûc*, and the circumcision were also celebrated with hired entertainment, particularly among the well-to-do. At the *subûc*, female singers and dancers performed, after which a ritual was conducted similar to present-day practices. First, someone took a brass mortar and struck it repeatedly with the pestle, close to the baby's ears. Then the newborn was put into a sieve and shaken. Next, it was carried by the mother, surrounded by friends and dancing girls, through the house, accompanied by loud music. Finally, someone carried a plate containing a mixture of several foods, such as salt, beans, and lentils, and threw some of it in every room. After the ritual, the entertainment was resumed (Chabrol 1822: 330; Lane 1978: 498).

The higher classes also gave parties for which there were no special occasions and hired singers, dancers, and reciters for entertainment during dinner. Women in the harem could entertain their female guests with female singers and dancers. Several travelers noted, however, that it was frowned upon to invite performers without an occasion such as a wedding (Chabrol 1822: 119–120; Lane 1978: 191, 496). Nevertheless, travelers' accounts indicate it happened on a large scale.

Travelers provided a new opportunity for entertainers, particularly female dancers, to earn a living. The travelers invited dancing girls to entertain them on their boats while they were anchored in one of the towns in the Delta or in the south (Henniker 1824: 184).

The entertainment activities of women were confined to singing, dancing, poetry, and music. All acting was done by men, even the roles of women (Niebuhr 1776, 1: 181). It is not easy to get a complete picture of female entertainment from travelers' accounts, since men—particularly foreign men—were not always allowed to be present at female performances. Niebuhr (1776) mentions female entertainers who performed in houses at parties which could not be attended by foreigners unless they were married. His company had to be satisfied with the public dancers who performed in the streets. Yet they were not very pleased with the dance performance: "Both because the instruments and the vocal music was very poor, and because the women assumed all kinds of highly indecent postures . . . we found them all equally ugly and unpleasant, with their yellow-dyed hands, blood-red nails, black and blue ornaments on the face, arms and chest and big rings round their ankles, in their ears and nostrils and the abundant pomade in their hair, which you could smell from a far distance . . . it was not our taste at all" (1776, 1: 177).

In some cases, even public dancers were not allowed to perform in front of the eyes of unbelievers. Denon, a painter who traveled with the French army during the short Napoleonic expedition from 1798 to 1801, related that a *sheikh* refused to allow the dancing girls to perform for the French: The eyes of the infidels would defile them. The superior strength of the army, however, forced the *sheikh* to relinquish his initial objections (1803, 1: 173–174).

In spite of the fact that the accounts of travelers usually described the more public forms of female entertainment, two broad classes of women performers can be discerned. Although there was confusion in terminology among the early pioneers, the following distinctions made by Chabrol (1822) and Villoteau (1822) were supported by later travelers.

In the first place, there was a group of *ʿawâlim* (singular: *ʿalma*), learned women or female scholars. Their main activities were writing poetry, composing music, improvising, and singing. According to Hamilton, they also danced, but only for women (1809: 342). They often played instruments to accompany their songs and they were greatly valued for their *mawâl,* or improvised songs. In 1777, Savary described them as follows: "They are called savantes. A more painstaking education than other women has earned them this name. They form a celebrated community within the country. In order to join, one must have a beautiful voice, a good possession of the language, a knowledge of the rules of poetry and an ability to spontaneously compose and sing couplets adapted to the circumstances. . . . There is no fete without them; no festival where they do not provide the ornamentation" (1787, 1: 124–125).

The *ʿawâlim* mainly performed for women in the harem. Inside the harem there was an elevation, protruding into the courtyard, from which the *ʿawâlim* sang. They were thus audible, but not visible, to men. Even the master of the house could not enter the harem while they performed (Villoteau 1822: 170). Or in case men were present in the harem, a screen of wooden latticework kept the *ʿawâlim* out of their sight. These educated *ʿawâlim* were highly appreciated for their art and probably respected as well, since they did not perform for men and did not break any rules of propriety.

The second group of female entertainers were the *ghawâzî* (singular: *ghazîya*). They were mainly dancers who performed unveiled in the streets and in front of coffeehouses. They were sometimes invited into a private house, but usually they performed in front of it or in the courtyard. The *ghawâzî* especially danced at saint's day celebrations and migrated from one *mûlid* to another. Most travelers described them as a separate tribe, as Gypsies or gypsy-type wanderers.[7] They were found in every town and large village, where they inhabited a special quarter. In 1817, their number was estimated at six to eight thousand. They were Muslims and Egyptian-speaking, although they had a secret language, a *sîm*, which was unintelligible to outsiders (Burckhardt 1972: 177–178; Lane 1978: 376; Burton 1898: 240–241).[8]

The description of their way of living by Burckhardt in 1817, faithfully copied by Lane, seems not very reliable. It is depicted as almost an inversion of the usual mode of life among Egyptians. The *ghawâzî* married only among themselves and, according to the two authors, the husband was never permitted to receive his bride as a virgin. She was offered by her father, assisted by a *sheikh*, to the stranger who offered the highest bid. After her marriage, she continued dancing and prostitution, while the husband acted as her servant, musician, and pimp. He was dependent on his wife for food, clothes, and protection, and could be repudiated by her (Burckhardt 1972: 174–176; Lane 1978: 375).

Most early travelers, however, did not describe the *ghawâzî* as prostitutes, but as dancers only. These dancing girls were the ones most accessible to foreigners, since they performed publicly. The most striking element of their appearance was that they were unveiled. Most descriptions of them were similar to Niebuhr's, depicting them as having tattoos and nose rings. Their dress was like other women's, except for the girdle and the lack of a veil. It is possible that during performances in houses their dress was of a lighter, semitransparent material (Savary 1787, 1: 126). They had an extensive repertoire. Besides the native dance, which earned them the amazement and sometimes admiration of travelers, they performed dances with all kinds of objects, for instance, with scarves, sticks, and sabres, and with vases or lighted candles on their head. Several travelers remarked that the *ghawâzî* used to smoke the water pipe and drank considerable amounts of brandy. Due to this and the fact that they danced in public for men with unveiled faces, they were generally not regarded as decent women.

There was also a category of female entertainers between the *ʿawâlim* and the *ghawâzî*. This group consisted of lower-class singers and dancers, common *ʿawâlim* who performed for the poor in the working-class quarters. Some *ghawâzî* were also singers and thus resembled the common *ʿawâlim*. This caused the confusion of the early travelers between the *ʿawâlim* and the *ghawâzî*. Prostitutes were registered as having a separate profession. Yet public dancers could be found who, to use a phrase of Sonnini, combined dancing with activities considered, insofar as possible, even more indecent (1798, 2: 374). Starting with the beginning of the nineteenth century, this group of common *ʿawâlim* and the number of dancer-prostitutes seem to have increased as a result of socioeconomic circumstances that I shall shortly deal with.

PAYMENT, TAXATION, AND TRADE CORPORATIONS

Many travelers observed that female singers and dancers were well paid. The higher class of *ʿawâlim* who performed in the harem received their money from the men through an intermediary. He collected the money from the male guests. Sometimes guests were so enchanted that they lavished upon an *ʿalma* sums which they could ill afford to lose (Lane 1978: 355). In case there was personal contact between performer and audience, the method of payment was also more direct. At private parties, men sometimes wet gold coins and stuck them on the dancer's body (Lane 1978: 495).[9] In the street, money was tossed in front of the entertainers. Dancers were said to know which persons had money and to dance in such a way in front of them that they received large tips, *nuʾûṭ* (singular: *nuʾṭa*) (Seetzen 1854, 3: 229–230). Accordingly, the Egyptian proverb "The fly knows the face of the milk-seller" was chiefly applied to dancers (Burckhardt 1972: 21–22).

There were still other methods of stimulating the generosity of an audience. Many female entertainers were accompanied by a buffoon—a *khalbûṣ*—who helped entertain the guests and collected the money. He praised the tipper in a song in which the amount of the *nuʾṭa* was considerably inflated in order to encourage competition. The *khalbûṣ* called: "shobash ʿalêk, ya ṣâḥib il-faraḥ," translated by Lane as "A present is due from thee, O giver of the entertainment [on a similar occasion and in the same way]," which hints at the reciprocal character of tips (1978: 495).[10] It seems that giving tips not only filled the pockets of the entertainers, but also heightened the interest and pleasure of the audience.[11]

Several systems of payment existed at private parties. Usually, a *nuʾṭa* was given at the parties of all classes, not just those of the poor, as Seetzen thought, although sometimes the host did not allow this custom to be observed (1854, 3: 256). The general practice was to engage the dancers for a certain sum. The host received the tips, which could fall short of or exceed the fixed amount. In the former case, the host paid the difference from his own purse; in the latter, he often pocketed the surplus. Another possibility was for the dancers to receive all the *nuʾṭa*, with or without an additional sum from the host (Lane 1978: 494).

Many female singers and dancers were probably well paid, although not the ones who performed in the street. At any rate, they were certainly assessed sizable taxes. Around 1800, they were under the protection of a *sheikh* and subject to the control of a police officer. This person derived a part of his emoluments from the general licenses he gave the female entertainers and from the permissions he issued for them to perform at parties (Hamilton 1809: 343).[12] Besides obtaining the permissions, they had to pay a weekly or monthly tax.[13] Taxes were extracted through trade organizations. These "guilds" were not voluntary associations, but were mainly imposed by the government in order to facilitate taxation.[14] Probably due to the same need for fiscal control, entertainers were further subdivided into seven guilds, based on sex and type of entertainment.[15]

The rate of taxation on female entertainers is indicated by Browne's account of the wedding party of Bey Ibrahîm's daughter in 1792:

> No occasion to satisfy their penny-pinching, even in the moments of relaxation and enjoyment, is left unused by the Beys. Ibrahîm Bey, after hearing that a group of female singers had not only sung during all the days of the wedding party, but also during the following night . . . and had thus earned a great deal of money, sent for the woman who was the head of the group. This woman had no other thought than that she was going to receive a reward. . . . But the first question the Bey asked her was how much money she had earned the day before. "Ten thousand half sequins," she answered in her innocence. "Well," said the Bey, "give me eight thousand of them." (1800: 142)

The reason for the high taxes on entertainment and other trades should be understood in the light of political events at the time.

SOCIOECONOMIC AND POLITICAL DEVELOPMENTS

At the end of the eighteenth century, Egypt was politically weak and divided. Although formally part of the Ottoman Empire, in practice Egypt was ruled by several Mameluke beys, who rapidly succeeded one another. All of them had weak internal power bases and consequently had to depend on their own militia. In order to finance their armies, they levied heavy taxes. The increasing taxes exacted by the clashing Mameluke factions caused a sharp decline in the economic and social living conditions and resulted in a series of urban revolts. The Napoleonic expedition of 1798 took place during this period of internal weakness. The existing state control—mainly fiscal regulation—of public entertainers, prostitutes, and other trades and services was extended under the French occupation (Tucker 1986: 141; Sayyid Marsot 1985: 50–53).

As soon as the French army entered Cairo, the bulk of higher-class *ʿawâlim* left the capital because of their contempt for the French. Only toward the end of the French presence did they return, although they remained hidden and refused to perform for the French (Villoteau 1822: 169). The French encouraged the *mawâlid* festivals in order to get women out of their houses and into the streets, where they could approach them (Gabârtî in Tucker 1986: 110). The women they had access to were the heavily taxed, poorer female singers, dancers, and prostitutes. For them the French were a source of income. DuBois-Aymé and Jollois, who were members of the French army of scholars Napoleon took with him, wrote: "More than once in our campaign, we saw these girls walking in front of our battalions, mixing the sound of the tambourine and castanet with our battle music, using all the cleverness of coquetry to seduce our soldiers, and putting their tents in the center of our bivouacs" (1822: 208).

The French as well as the Egyptian civil and religious authorities tried to keep the dancers and prostitutes away from the army. The women were accused of being a source of infection. The number of French soldiers with syphilis was considerable, so that it became necessary for the French to establish brothels in order to facilitate control and medical examination (Larrey 1822: 195–196).[16] The women were also accused of being a source of pestilence. In 1799, in order to combat a plague, the French issued the following regulation: For a period of thirty days, every person who took a public woman to Cairo, Bûlâq, or old Cairo would be killed. Public women who entered the army encampment of their own accord would meet the same fate (Gabârtî 1983: 29).[17]

In 1801, the combined efforts of the English and Ottoman armies forced the French army to retreat. In 1805, Muḥammad ʿAlî, commanding officer of the Albanian contingent of Arnaut soldiers, filled the power vacuum. With the support of the religious authorities, he put an end to the remaining power of the Mamelukes in 1811. He tried to gain strength and independence for Egypt, still part of the Ottoman Empire, by increasing state revenues. Opening to the West, new taxes, control of agricultural production, state monopolies, and state factories were started to achieve this end. A more active and interventionist state thus emerged under Muḥammad ʿAlî and his successors.

The government's control over female entertainers encouraged many heavily taxed common *ʿawâlim* and *ghawâzî* to leave Cairo, since state control was less effective outside the capital. Once more they mingled with the fighting armies, this time those of the Mamelukes and Ottomans. Mengin attributes the weakness and defeat of the Mameluke soldiers to their licentiousness, stating that the soldiers spent their nights in drunkenness with singers, dancers, and prostitutes (1828, 1: 295). The Ottoman army and Arnauts were flooded with impoverished dancers and prostitutes as well.[18]

Besides the armies, foreigners, who came in increasing numbers to Egypt, provided another, safer opportunity for employment. Foreigners, mainly interested in dancing, were often entertained with female dancers at parties given by consuls and governors. On other occasions, the dancers performed on the foreigners' boats. The *ʿawâlim* were increasingly described as singers and dancers, the *ghawâzî* as dancers and prostitutes. It is not clear whether higher-class *ʿawâlim* added dance to their repertoire to be more attractive to foreigners, or if women from outside the profession started dancing and singing to earn a living.[19] At any rate, the number of female entertainers who danced and sang for foreigners at the time was considerable.[20]

This new development met with fierce opposition from the religious authorities—the *ʿulamâʾ*. Female dancers were still Muslims and ought not to perform in front of foreigners. The religious authorities were against female dancers, "not on account of their impropriety, but on the plea that the profane eyes of the 'Infidels' ought not to gaze upon women of the true faith" (Warburton 1864: 295). Already during the French occupation this was a source of dispute, but now it happened on a larger scale and resembled a foreign monopoly on female entertainers (St. John 1852: 29).

Despite the trouble with soldiers and the growing resentment from the religious authorities, no measures were taken against female entertainers until 1834. This delay was probably due to a profitable tax being levied on them.[21] Religious opposition to a tax on vice—on prostitution and public female dancing—was a recurrent issue which was strengthened by an incident in which a tax farmer had added several honorable women to his list of prostitutes in order to increase his revenues (Tucker 1986: 151–152). This resulted in public protest under the leadership of the *ʿulamâʾ*. In order to end the public protest and satisfy the religious authorities, with whose support he had gained power, Muḥammad ʿAlî had to take steps against public women.[22]

It was thus probably a combination of internal and external factors which resulted in the 1834 measures against public women. Muḥammad ʿAlî's opening to the West attracted a growing number of European visitors to Egypt. Muḥammad ʿAlî tried to reform Egypt on the basis of Western models; he did not want the image of Egypt to be largely determined by dancers and public women. In addition, many female entertainers, impoverished by taxation, had become dancers. This lowered their status and caused growing resentment from the religious authorities. The *ʿulamâʾ* had always been opposed to public performances by female entertainers, but when the dancers increasingly started performing for the "infidels," they could no longer tolerate it. The excessive European interest in female dancers, and the fact that Europeans monopolized the dancers' services, intensified the dissatisfaction of the *ʿulamâʾ* and caused a more general Egyptian protest. Quarrels and collisions occurred until the government assuaged religious and public opinion by an edict (St. John 1852: 29). The tax advantages thus no longer outweighed the disadvantages of public protest.[23]

THE BANISHMENT

In June 1834, Muḥammad ʿAlî issued an edict forbidding public female dancers and prostitutes to work in the capital. Women who were detected violating this new law were punished with fifty lashes for the first offense and with hard labor for one or more years for repeated offenses (Lane 1978: 566). This meant in practice that most public women were banned from Cairo. After being punished, they were deported to the south of Egypt, particularly to Esna, Qena, and Luxor.

It was not a total ban but an attempt to marginalize most public women by pushing them to the periphery of Egyptian society. It is not clear whether the edict was applied solely to Cairo or if it also was enforced in the area surrounding Cairo, that is, from as far south as Minyâ to Alexandria in the north.[24] The ban seems to have been most effective in Cairo, but was less closely observed outside the capital. Although Pückler was very disappointed that he could not find dancing girls in the Delta to perform on his boat, the *mûlid* of Ṭanṭâ and Dessûq abounded in female entertainers (Pückler 1844, 1: 145; St. John 1845: 88; St. John 1852, 1: 28). At the *mawâlid* of Cairo, however, female entertainers were absent and the festivals were less merry than they had been. Also, at the *mûlid* of the Prophet, although there were storytellers, conjurers, buffoons, ropedancers, and sellers of sweetmeats, the main attraction was missing (Lane 1978: 449, 453, 461).

The higher-class *ʿawâlim* could continue their usual activities, to wit, singing and making music in the harems. Ṣafia, one of the *ʿawâlim* who was "too much of a lady" to be affected by the general proscription, performed in Cairo around 1837 (Pückler Muskau 1844, 1: 263–264). Yet a few years later she too was banned and had to perform in Esna.[25] It is possible that singing and dancing on special occasions such as native weddings was still allowed in Cairo. Dancing at ordinary private parties, however, particularly in front of foreigners, was closely watched by the police. Only in secrecy outside the city could the curiosity of travelers be satisfied (Hackländer 1842, 2: 238–245). Female entertainers and prostitutes had to be on their guard lest they be deported. In the brothel Flaubert visited, the girls were afraid to play the *darabukka*, a small earthenware hand drum, for fear the noise would arouse the suspicions of the police (Flaubert 1979: 39–40). Some female entertainers tried to continue performing in Cairo; they dressed as washerwomen and beggars when they visited the houses of foreigners (Burton 1857: 134).

The most striking side effect of the ban was the replacement of female dancers by men. Although dancing boys had existed before 1834, their number increased. Lane mentions that from a religious point of view it was preferable to engage male dancers (Lane 1978: 376–377). Two types of male dancers performed, native *khawal*[26] and non-Egyptian *ginks*.[27] The appearance of the *khawal* was similar to that of female dancers. This sometimes caused confusion among the spectators, as happened to the French author Nerval. He thought he was looking at three beautiful female dancers, "their eyes brightened by kohl and their full yet delicate cheeks lightly painted," but the third dancer "betrayed the less gentle sex by a week-old beard." After discovering the betrayal he decided on a new course of action: "I was ready to place upon their foreheads a few pieces of gold, in accordance with the purest traditions of the Levant. . . . But for men dressed up as women this ceremony may well be dispensed with, and a few paras thrown to them instead" (1980: 199–201). These dancing boys substituted the female dancers at *mawâlid*, weddings, and processions. They also performed for foreigners—for instance, in the dining room of the hotel Flaubert stayed in. There he enjoyed the dance of two "rascals, quite ugly, but charming in their corruption, in their obscene leerings and the femininity of their movements, dressed as women, their eyes painted with antimony. . . . From time to time, during the dance, the impresario, or pimp, who brought them plays around them, kissing them on the belly, the arse . . . and making obscene remarks in an effort to put additional spice into a thing that is already quite clear in itself" (1979: 83–84).

The purpose of the ban was to marginalize public women and to keep them out of the sight of foreigners. It proved, however, to be counterproductive. European eyes followed them to the south, where they became the center of attention. There, as well, tourists were the main source of income. The native population was too poor to pay for dancers at weddings (Balen 1884: 92; Davenport 1894: 277). Only the *mawâlid* in the south provided a small source of income. The *mûlid* of Sayyid ʿAbdelRaḥîm at Qena, for instance, was celebrated with singers, dancers, and *zikrs*, and showed the "usual mixture of holy and profane" (Duff Gordon 1902: 255). The government also provided them with a meager living and a shelter,[28] yet the main part of their livelihood was gained by performing for foreigners.

For several travelers, the main purpose of their journey to the south was to see the celebrated dancers. When they still performed in Cairo, the entertainers were relatively anonymous and scattered. In Upper Egypt, they were brought together and thus became visible and conspicuous. The names of famous performers—Kuchuk Hânim and Ṣafia of Esna, Ḥosna il-Ṭawîla of Luxor, and ʿAzîza of Aswan, for example—circulated among the travelers. They visited the entertainers' establishments on their trips to the south and back (Scherer 1848: 71–72, 116–117, 123–124; Curtis 1860: 90–101; Fromentin 1881: 282–283, 140–141, 295, 303). The English, French, and German consuls also entertained their guests with female dancers. Several tourists, after obtaining permission, had the dancers perform on their boats. Some female entertainers walked about the boats, offering their services on the spot. Although the few famous ones were probably well paid, those who were less well known were now and then dismissed with a few piasters and brandy.

The European gaze was sometimes very obtrusive. In her letters, Lady Duff Gordon, who lived for seven years in the south for health reasons, described the way the Europeans misbehaved. An Egyptian friend wanted to give a party with female dancers in her honor, but was afraid she would take men with her. At the previous party, some Englishmen had caused problems by insisting that the female dancers at the party perform naked. They had refused to do so, and the Englishmen had to be thrown out of his house (1902: 100). Other travelers, however, wrote that some dancers gave in and performed naked. This performing act was called the "wasp" or "bee dance" and was very popular among tourists. Some tourists described it discreetly. According to Villiers Stuart, for instance, the bee, hidden in the dancer's clothes, was found before the last garment was parted with (1883: 304). In Warburton's version, the dancer discovered in time that it was all a mistake (1864: 296). Yet Flaubert was explicit in its content, to wit, a striptease. He asked Kuchuk Hânim and ʿAzîza to strip. Albeit reluctantly and after blindfolding the musicians, they granted his request (1979: 117, 122, 153).

Besides working as dancers and singers, a number of entertainers became prostitutes as well. The word *ʿalma* completely lost its original meaning of learned woman. At the beginning of the nineteenth century, its meaning had changed to singer-dancer, and by the 1850s it denoted a dancer-prostitute.[29] Dancing became stripping, and dancers increasingly worked as prostitutes. The travelers' descriptions of, for instance, Kuchuk Hânim and Ṣafia reveal that the two were gifted singers, dancers, and musicians. They had probably belonged to the group of higher-class *ʿawâlim*. The fading of the distinction between *ʿawâlim* and *ghawâzî* in an earlier period, as well as the growing number of common singer-dancers, led to the expulsion of all to the south. The banishment further erased the distinction among entertainers and between entertainers and prostitutes as well.

The move to prostitution was not due solely to the requests of foreigners. It was also caused by the insecure and unsafe existence entertainers had in the south. Esna and Luxor were regularly terrorized by bands of Albanian soldiers.[30] Ḥosna il-Ṭawîla and her group were forced to perform for them without payment (St. John 1852, 2: 70–72). The governor of Esna received orders before the arrival of the Arnauts to send the *ʿawâlim* with a strong escort into the desert because it was feared the soldiers would create problems. The Arnauts were so enraged on finding Ṣafia and her colleagues gone that they burned her house and destroyed her property (Warburton 1864: 291). Several entertainers were regularly robbed. To avoid theft, Kuchuk Hânim stored her jewelry with the sherif (Flaubert 1979: 157–159). She also had a pimp for protection, a practice in strong contrast with entertainers' conduct at the beginning of the eighteenth century, when public women exercised considerable control over their own professional lives (Tucker 1986: 154–155).

Not only did thieves and soldiers make their lives unsafe, but they were also at the mercy of the police. Although most of them could hardly earn a living, once again they had to pay taxes to the police, certainly after Muḥammad ʿAlî's reign in the 1860s. In 1866, Lady Duff Gordon wrote from Luxor: "In Egypt we are eaten up with taxes. . . . The taxes for the whole year *eight months in advance* have been levied. . . . I saw one of the poor dancing girls the other day, (there are three in Luxor) and she told me how cruel the new tax on them is. It is left to the discretion of the official who farms it to make each woman pay according to her presumed gains, i.e. her good looks . . ." (1902: 322). This new tax once more met with religious and public protest because "the wages of prostitution are unclean, and this tax renders all Government salaries unlawful according to strict law" (1902: 323). By instituting this tax, the ruler Ismâ'îl earned himself the nickname "Pimp Pasha" (Duff Gordon 1902: 323; Tucker 1986: 153). As a result of the new tax and their lack of income, a number of female entertainers fell into the hands of moneylenders (Davenport 1894: 277). The resulting impoverishment forced some to give up the trade and to earn a living as, for instance, bread sellers; others went into prostitution (Flaubert 1979: 153; Combes 1846: 222).

RETURN TO CAIRO

The ban was apparently lifted by ʿAbbâs Basha (1849–1854), probably for the same reason that delayed its implementation—that is, the profitable tax.[31] Female entertainers were allowed to return to Cairo, but not to practice their occupations publicly. Many female entertainers tried their luck again in Cairo. Rapid urbanization in the second half of the nineteenth century increased the demand for women who performed services for other women, such as hairdressers and female entertainers (Tucker 1986: 101). In Upper Egypt, on the other hand, except for the tourist winter season, there was hardly any employment. Although a certain number of entertainers remained in the south—they were witnessed there by twentieth-century travelers—entertainment in Upper Egypt slowly withered.

The ban on public performances in Cairo was never an obstacle to well-known singers, since they mainly performed in the harems or behind screens. Two such famous rival singers at the end of the nineteenth century were Sakna and Almâz. Sakna was "fifty-five—an ugly face, I am told (she was veiled and one only saw the eyes and glimpses of her mouth when she drank water), but the figure of a leopard, all grace and beauty, and a splendid voice of its kind, harsh but thrilling. . . . Sakna was treated with great consideration and quite as a friend by the Armenian ladies with whom she talked between her songs. She is a Muslimeh [Muslim] and very rich and charitable; she gets £50 for a night's singing at least" (Duff Gordon 1902: 20). Almâz was of poor descent. She started in Sakna's performing group, which she later left to form her own. After her marriage to the celebrated singer ʿAbdel Ḥamûlî, with whom she had sung duets in harems, she had to give up her career (Buṭrus 1976: 61–67; ʿArafa 1947: 40–41). Two female observers of singers and dancers were shocked by the free and friendly association in harems between female entertainers and harem women. They shared conversation, jokes, and even the water pipe (Romer 1846, 1: 330–331; Duff Gordon 1902: 136, 141, 268). Egyptians seemed to have had a relatively tolerant attitude toward harem singers and dancers, especially after they repented and became respectable housewives (Romer 1846; Duff Gordon 1902).

Famous singers were probably no longer called *ʿawâlim*, since the word had become too tainted in the course of the nineteenth century. This word was now used for the group of common singers and dancers who performed in working-class quarters.[32] At weddings of the lower middle class the *ʿawâlim* sang from behind a window, closed with a thin curtain, while the men were sitting in the street or alley (Leland 1873: 120). Common dancers could also be invited at weddings to perform in the court,[33] a celebration which could easily turn into a (forbidden) public spectacle (Budge 1925: 111–112).

Although public singing and dancing were prohibited except on special occasions, female entertainers were abundant, as the following conversation of Leland with a "natural linguist" indicates. Despite the denigrating tone, it is instructive about the availability of female entertainers: "You likit 'Gypsian sing-music? You go garden Esbekiah—You hear much fine sing-girls; his name Bulbul, You know Bulbul—Almah, kwaiz. One piastre to hear sing. Ghasie, she one dance-girly, great beautifuls. . . . Si paga telata shillin' for see dance filbayt. Thirteen shillin' for *tutto insieme*, all together. That nuf; you not *paga piu*" (1873: 13–14). On special occasions, such as the opening of the Suez Canal in 1869, the ban on public performances of female entertainers was lifted (Keer 1870: 36).

After the British military occupation in 1882, Egypt became a veiled protectorate. Although Egypt remained formally an independent state, British officials effectively directed the government (Tucker 1986: 78). During the last decades of the nineteenth and the beginning of the twentieth century, control over entertainment was increased—by regularization, not by repression.[34] The *mawâlid* were reformed and the amount of celebration on saints' days restricted. The *dôsa* and other spectacles such as flagellation and the eating of live coals, frowned upon by the orthodoxy and the British, were prohibited. In an attempt to separate the holy from the profane, activities not conducive to moral behavior were forbidden on *mawâlid;* coffeeshops and cabarets, for example, were not permitted to open (de Jong 1978: 97, 197–200, 213). The *mûlid* of Ṭanṭâ, after Ṭanṭâ was connected to the railway network in 1856, grew into a mass spectacle with half a million visitors. Although Ṭanṭâ was in 1878

FIGURE 1

A café-chantant around the turn of the century.

still the gathering place of all entertainers from as far as Luxor, at the turn of the century the government suppressed the festival "for sanitary and other reasons," presumably fear of disorder (Ebers 1879, 1: 91; Baer 1969: 138–139, 145; Mitchell 1988: 98). The smaller saints' days probably kept their secular entertainment tents at the religious celebrations (Charmes 1883: 179–180).

For entertainment without special occasions, such as the former singing and dancing in the streets and markets, a new opportunity was created, in the form of the café-chantants. Female entertainers who previously had sung and danced in the streets or in front of coffeehouses were now concealed inside music halls. In the café-chantants there was a round stage for the musicians, and at the back of it was a curtain behind which the female singers performed (Leland 1873: 128–129). They also increasingly performed in hotels for foreigners. The places where entertainment was allowed were thus increasingly institutionalized and regulated.

The Ezbekiyya Garden became the center of "Cairo by night" (Baedeker 1885: 22; Kemeid 1898–1899: 46; Aegypten 1908: 28). Ezbekiyya had been a place for entertainment from the time it was still a lake. In 1837, it had been turned into a garden by Muḥammad ʿAlî in order to provide the public, and particularly the Europeans, with a promenade and pleasant garden (Linant de Bellefonds 1872–1873: 595–603). Later, theaters, the opera, restaurants, coffeehouses, and café-chantants were built in the neighborhood. In several music halls—particularly in Eldorado, the first nightclub in Cairo—shows with native dancing were offered. At the turn of the century, the local dancing, for the first time, was called belly-dancing.

THREE

FEMALE ENTERTAINMENT IN THE TWENTIETH CENTURY

The main twentieth-century developments in entertainment had already started at the end of the nineteenth century and merely crystallized into laws and regulations at the beginning of this century. The reason for dealing with the twentieth century in a separate chapter is thus not so much dictated by a break in history as by changes in the sources of information about entertainment. Travelers' accounts had run dry as a source at the end of the last century. Due to the opening of the Suez Canal and the improvement of its infrastructure, Egypt became an attraction for mass tourism. Instead of individual scholars, romanticists, and authors and painters, groups of tourists now visited Egypt's antiquities. Their shorter stays and widely shared experiences made their accounts less valuable for publication than the adventures of earlier travelers (Carré 1956, 2: 355). Although a number of travelers' accounts and memoirs of British officials do exist, newspapers, magazines, and interviews with performers of the old and present days form my main source of information concerning entertainment in this century.

In the course of the twentieth century, two different entertainment circuits developed. First, nightclubs and variety theaters imitated their Western counterparts. Second, performances at weddings and other festive occasions continued the tradition of the *ʿawâlim*. The first circuit was aimed mainly at Arabic and European tourists, although numerous Egyptians frequented nightclubs as well; the second provided diversion for the native population. The description of the nightclubs of the early period is based mainly on newspapers and art magazines,[1] which mushroomed in the 1920s and 1930s. Journalists visited nightclubs and commented on the programs, performers, and morals. "Virtue commits suicide" was a regularly used expression in characterizing the entertainment places.[2] The magazines, although they do not present a value-free account of entertainment, provide useful and well-documented descriptions of the nightclubs. The developments in the wedding circuit are based on oral history, since the art magazines and other Arabic sources hardly touch on this irregular form of entertainment for the common people. The older generation I spoke with had worked from around the 1940s, and most had performed at saint's day celebrations as well as in other entertainment areas.

The recent circuit of radio, television, and national theaters is an important field of art. Orchestras, ballet companies, and folk-dancing troupes, as well as film and theater productions, are outside the scope of my research. Yet this institutionalized circuit, with its schools and certificates, increasingly serves as a standard by which the less-recognized singing and dancing in nightclubs and at weddings are judged. I briefly describe its developments and its impact on nightclubs and entertainment at weddings and saint's day celebrations.

WORLD EXHIBITIONS AND NIGHTCLUBS

In the first decades of the twentieth century, nightclubs and variety shows sprang up to meet the demands of the colonial rulers and Western tourists. The "Oriental" shows, featuring a *danse du ventre,* belly dance, contained many show elements imported from the West.

During the last decades of the nineteenth century, belly dancers were exported in the flesh to the numerous world exhibitions in the West. The world exhibitions, for instance, in London (1851), Paris (1855, 1867, 1889), and Chicago (1893) were linked to the massive industrial developments in the Western world and to colonial expansion into Africa, Asia, and Latin America. Western goods as well as native art and entertainment were on display. The 1889 Paris Great Exposition had a coffeehouse in the Egyptian or Algerian style with dancers.[3] Due to their financial success at the Paris show, the Egyptian dance troupe appeared at the 1893 International Exposition in Chicago as well. The entertainment section, the Midway Plaisance, consisted of colonial villages arranged in evolutionary lines, leading to the White City (Rydell 1984: 65–68). Little Egypt, a Syrian dancer, was the sensation of the Midway and attracted more visitors than the seventy-ton telescope (Buonaventura 1989: 102).

The audience received the dancers in an atmosphere of expectancy, created by the descriptions and images of travelers and painters. Yet their appearance was disappointing and their *danse du ventre* was not appreciated by all on account of the "boldness of its pelvic movements."[4] During the dance, Little Egypt occasionally lifted her skirt above her left knee, an outrageous act in the still-puritanical American society. Yet Little Egypt inspired a host of imitators, who introduced the dance into burlesque shows. The American "Little Egypts" presented an even bolder version of belly dancing. They exaggerated to the extent that the original Little Egypt, who stayed behind in the United States, was regularly forced to protest against the "lewd acts" attributed to her (Buonaventura 1989: 103). This vulgarized version of the hootchy-kootchy dance became the stock-in-trade of amusement parks such as Coney Island and of music halls (Kasson 1978: 53–54; Badger 1979: 161).[5]

The Egyptian dance troupe returned home from the six-month trip to Chicago with five hundred dollars. It was an enormous sum in those days and prompted other Egyptian dancers to set out for Europe and the United States. Western dancers, in turn, set out for the East. Dancers plying East and West probably brought Western dance innovations to the Middle East.

The development of the Western cabaret costume was one of the most striking changes to influence belly dancing. The Egyptian dance costume of the nineteenth century consisted of a simple wide skirt or trousers, an undershirt, and a waistcoat. According to Buonaventura, Western belly dancers embellished this rather ordinary dance outfit. "Eastern" elements found missing were added. The costume was thus "orientalized" with glitter, beads, and pearls in a style that owed its inspiration largely to Hollywood. The veil, preeminently "Oriental," was introduced to heighten the mysterious vamp image of the dancers. In the 1920s, the Western cabaret show attire had developed into the present-day presumed Oriental dance costume, to wit, a spangled bikini top, low-slung gauzy skirt with side slits, and bare midriff. The orientalized version, introduced into Egypt by dancers and early American movies, greatly influenced the Egyptian film industry in the 1930s and was gradually introduced into Egyptian nightlife (Buonaventura 1989: 148–152).[6]

Several music halls and theaters existed in Cairo at the turn of the century. Nightclubs, which combined food, drinks, and entertainment, were a later development. In 1910, only three nightclubs existed in the neighborhood of Ezbekiyya Square, but their number gradually increased in the 1920s and 1930s. Entertainment also spread to Rod al-Farag, northwest of the Ezbekiyya area on the banks of the Nile. The first regulation of theaters and other entertainment places dates back to 1904, when the Theater Act was passed. This act regulated in detail the number and width of doors (based on the number of visitors), the lighting, and the availability of fire extinguishers. The presentation of immoral pictures was strictly forbidden by the act. The police were required to inspect the places two or three times a week to enforce these provisions. The 1911 amendments to the Theater Act further regulated the inside of entertainment places and stipulated that an appropriate place should be made available to the police where they could watch the performances. Names of performers and new acts had to be passed on to the police in advance, and plays contradicting public order and morals were forbidden.[7]

According to a description in the art magazine *Rûz al-Yûsif*, the entertainment program of the early nightclubs first featured a second-rate dancer and next the star attraction. The latter part of the evening was filled by a female singer, the high point of the program. In later times, the program became more varied. Singing, dancing, acts, jokes, and sketches were alternated (*RY* 30-12-1936: 34). In spite of the bad reputation of most nightclubs, the artistic level of many performers was high. Since there was hardly any alternative, talented artists had to work in the cabarets.

Shafîʾa il-Ibṭiyya was a legendary dancer in the 1920s. According to a romanticized story, she was born in a working-class quarter of Cairo. Her parents died when she was young and she got married to an assistant train conductor of humble means. Forced by economic circumstances, Shafîʾa started to work with the *ʿawâlim* at women's parties. She did not have the consent of her husband and eventually left him. Dissatisfied with the work with women, she started performing at the Eldorado nightclub. She was the star performer, and like other stars she managed to open her own nightclub, Alf Lêla. She introduced the *shamʿidân* dance, in which she balanced a candelabra with lighted candles on her head while doing the splits. Her *ṣâla*—a neutral term for nightclubs, often contrasted with *kabarêh*, the negative expression used in the early days—was mainly visited by the aristocracy. Shafîʾa became famous for her wealth. She went to the Paris Exposition in 1920. Yet, at the summit of her fame, she became addicted to cocaine. A few years later, she died in poverty (Bindârî 1962).

This romanticized picture does not give insight into the events going on inside the *ṣâlas* of the 1920s and 1930s.[8] The main task of female entertainers was to sit and drink with customers. Usually they first sang or danced on the stage, and if they were admired by a client he ordered them to sit at his table and opened bottles of champagne, whiskey, or beer for them. Some walked around and asked clients if they could join them for a drink. This system of sitting and drinking with customers was called *fatḥ,* from the Arabic verb "to open." It was the most profitable part of the job, for the nightclub owner as well as the women. Therefore some female entertainers mainly engaged in drinking with customers and were reluctant to leave the tables for the stage. These women were called *fâtiḥât* (singular: *fâtiḥa*). One of the nightclub owners had to hire four new entertainers to fill the stage because his regular entertainers refused to perform (*MF* 24-7-1933: 20). Sometimes they were said to be too drunk to dance. The female entertainers received a percentage of the profits made from the drinks they and the customers consumed. Their salary as performers was low, since it was expected that they would supplement it with gains from drinking. Probably at least half of their income was earned from *fatḥ*.[9] The dancers Leila and Afranz developed a strategy in order to increase their income. They first sat together with a rich customer. As soon as he ordered, one of them left and returned after a while. The customer was forced to open a new bottle for her out of courtesy (*MF* 20-5-1928: 12).

Competition among men stimulated consumption. A big order—for instance, a dozen bottles of beer—was brought in by a train of attendants, enabling the drinker and the *fâtiḥa* to show off. The competition among men provoked by the female entertainers and the high bills the men were presented with at the end of the evening regularly caused fights. Rich people had their own bodyguards who sometimes destroyed the *ṣâla*. Entertainers also had bodyguards, since they sat with different men during the evening and thus provoked conflicts and rivalries between admirers. These protectors, however, sometimes turned on the entertainers—the dancer Imtisâl Fawzi was killed by her bodyguard after a financial dispute. Much to the dismay of the Egyptian public, the police took over as bodyguards and escorted the entertainers from the nightclubs to their homes (*RY* 30-9-1936: 26).

It seems that prostitution was not necessarily part of the performers' job, although several probably engaged in it in order not to lose a wealthy customer. Yet dancers had diverse tricks to avoid sexual relationships with clients. An old story runs that in Manollî's Eldorado around 1910, various lovers were each secretly given a key at the beginning of the evening. In a state of happy expectancy, they each generously consumed drinks and bought drinks for the performer they all admired, only to find at the end of the evening that there were several of them trying in vain to unlock the same door (*RY* 8-7-1936: 30). Customers felt it was their right to take a performer home, but whether she went depended on her wishes. One dancer was rescued by the police when a pasha tried to force her to accompany him (*RY* 14-6-1937: 16). Another dancer left behind a wealthy man each night, even though he had spent a great deal on her over a long period, because she chose to join her poor lover (*RY* 23-12-1936: 33). Female entertainers were paid to sit, drink, and dance or sing, not to sleep with customers. Yet they were generally regarded by the public as fallen women. Whether they were, strictly speaking, prostitutes or not did not really matter to the public. The vice of *fatḥ* and dancing in a revealing costume was sufficient to earn them the title of prostitute.

PROSTITUTION AND CLEANING UP THE NIGHTCLUBS

Prostitution was a legal trade. The licensed Egyptian prostitutes worked in the Wasâᶜa area. Wish al-Birka was the tolerated, though not officially licensed, European prostitute quarter. Both quarters were in the Ezbekiyya area. The first law regulating the trade dates back to 1896. It established the licenses for brothels, the registration of prostitutes, and their weekly medical control. Prostitutes were forbidden to sit at the door or to lean out of the window at brothels. State regulation was limited to the protection of clients from disease; the working conditions of prostitutes were not their concern (Tucker 1986: 153). Russell, who worked in the Colonial Service in Egypt from 1902 to 1946, described the Wasâᶜa area: "Painted harlots [were] sitting like beasts of prey behind the iron grilles of their ground-floor brothels, while a noisy crowd of low-class natives, interspersed with soldiers in uniform and sight-seeing tourists, made their way along the narrow lanes" (1949: 179).[10] One of my informants, Rayyis Bîra, lived in the area between 1930 and 1958. He related that especially the area around Clot Bey Street was a neighborhood with its own rules, laws, and secret language. It abounded in coffeehouses, bars, and dens in which hashish, heroin, and cocaine were sold. The small alleys had many brothels, each of which was run by a *badrona* who had about five girls working under her (*ṣubyân il-maʾṭûra*). A network of pimps firmly controlled the women.

The Wish al-Birka area, with foreign prostitutes and their pimps, was under the protection of the Capitulations, that is, the legal agreement which gave foreigners the right to be tried in their own consular courts. Attempts to bring them to court or to close down their brothels were largely ineffective. When they were raided, they sometimes simply changed ownership or nationality, so as to transfer the proceedings from one consular court to another (Sladen 1911: 117).[11] Russell remarked:

> The native bully was subject to Egyptian criminal law and could be brought to book if he went too far . . . , but the European souteneur had little to fear from Egyptian law, being subject only to his consular jurisdiction with its feeble legislation and often indifferent officials. These lieutenants of the white-slave traffic were well organized with their headquarter offices in many ports and cities of Europe, and our police attempts to control them were made still more difficult by the refusal of their women to complain against them for fear of vitriol or the razor (1949: 181).[12]

Yet in 1924 the government cleaned up the unlicensed native and foreign brothels (Russell 1949: 178).[13]

Prostitution and entertainment were separate professions with regard to the law and licenses. Nevertheless, they were not only located in the same area, but had professional ties as well. Foreign women were suspected of using the profession of actress or dancer as a cover for illegal prostitution (*MM* 12-11-1931: 9). As stated above, some Egyptian female entertainers probably worked as prostitutes as well. In Alexandria, journalists wrote that for lack of dancers, the nightclub owners hired prostitutes (*MF* 19-2-1928: 12).

Badî^ca Masabni owned one of the most famous *ṣâlas* on ʿImâd al-Dîn Street in the Ezbekiyya area. She was born in Syria and started her career as a dancer and actress around 1921 in Egypt. Badîʿa was a specialist in performing male roles and became the star of Nagîb al-Rîḥânî's theater company. She married al-Rîḥânî, a famous actor, but left him and his troupe in 1926 and opened her own *ṣâla* in November of that year. Leading singers, dancers, and actresses, such as Fatḥiyya Aḥmad, Ḥikmat Fahmî, Beba and Samia Gamâl, worked in her nightclub. Every Tuesday, she had a six o'clock matinee for women only. She was described as a keen and tough business woman. Journalists wrote that she had no need of a bodyguard since she was one herself and had threatened intrusive journalists with a gun. She sold her *ṣâla* to Beba in 1950 and left for Syria (Bindârî 1958: 28–40; Graham-Brown 1988: 184; *AṢ* 21-12-1927: 4; *K* 13-3-1933: 4).

Her *ṣâla* as well as those of her female colleagues[14]—such as the sisters Inṣâf and Ratîba Rûshdî, Mêri Mansûr, and Beba—flourished in the 1920s and 1930s. During the First World War, Cairo became a war base and a garrison populated with British, Australian, and other troops. In the interbellum period, British troops remained stationed there in order to protect British interests, for example, in the Suez Canal. Cairo was thus full of soldiers and officers spending the evening on ʿImâd al-Dîn Street. Even during the depression of the 1930s, nightclubs thrived as a result of the foreign clientele and well-to-do Egyptians. The police made only minor attempts to restrict nightlife, forbidding dancers to dance "with their belly a vulgar dance" in 1927 (*AṢ* 19-4-1927: 4).

The continuing bad economic situation sparked criticism from the general public. Lavish spending in times of need came under attack (*MM* 22-7-1932: 7). The political crisis, due to the slow progress being made in obtaining independence from Britain, resulted in a drawing back from secular nationalism and a reorientation based on Islamic principles. Several movements appeared in the 1930s, foremost among them the Society of Muslim Brothers.

Against the background of the economic crisis and strong religious sentiments, a new attempt was undertaken to clean up the nightclubs. In 1932, the Ezbekiyya police briefly used the law against "scandalous acts in public" to prevent belly dancing (*MM* April 1932: 6; August 1932: 33). In 1933, they forbade belly dancing as well as sitting and drinking with customers in order to put an end to the "moral violations." Yet Badîᶜa and other nightclub owners of ᶜImâd al-Dîn Street became very clever at evading the new laws. The bodyguard of the nightclub would signal a dancer to leave the stage as soon as he noticed a car belonging to the police. After the police walked around in plain clothes, dancers would introduce a "foreign" dance strikingly similar to belly dancing. However, foreign dancers—European nationals and women belonging to the Greek, Levantine, and Italian minorities who were protected by the Capitulations—could continue their performances of belly dancing and dances "which would cause the forbidden dance to blush" in foreign and Egyptian nightclubs. Egyptian owners and journalists, for once united in a nationalist spirit, strongly opposed the legal inequality (*MF* 1933 10–12: 13; 17–12: 15; 24–12: 13; *K* 1-1-1934: 3). The patriotic protest was short-lived, though, since soon the owners and performers began evading the regulations once again. Because compliance with the regulations was heavily dependent on the vigilance of the police, periods in which dancers openly sat and drank with customers alternated with times when they sat together in back rooms or when the dancers drank whiskey in teacups (*RY* 12-3-1934: 32).

The Second World War brought another boom to the *ṣâlas*. Several dancers set out for Europe and "Herr Ahmed Bey" arranged contracts with cabarets in Austria.[15] Ḥikmat Fahmî is said to have danced for Hitler and Mussolini and Amîna Muḥammad for Goering in Libya.[16] In Egypt, the nightclubs were filled with British officers. In order to please the officers, the dancer Shûshû Barûdî renamed belly dancing "the dance of the Allies and the success of democracy" (*RY* 12-9-1941: 32). Pyramid

Street, the street built by Khedive Ismaʿîl during the opening of the Suez Canal in order to transport his important guests from Cairo to the Pyramids, became a new and more luxurious area for nightlife. Journalists criticized the officers for their lechery, gambling, and drunkenness. This resulted in repeated attempts to restrict the opening times of the *ṣâlas* and serving of alcohol (*RY* 12-3-1939: 48; 16-11-1940: 23; 14-5-1942: 20). Despite these regulations, the war brought employment, and many new girls temporarily worked in the nightclubs. Girls from the countryside and former domestic servants started to perform as "war artistes" (*RY* 2-12-1943: 18). As during the First World War, the sight of soldiers searching for bars, nightclubs, and brothels was a thorn in the side of the population; in particular, members of the Society of Muslim Brothers, an Islamic fundamentalist movement that was founded in 1929 and became powerful in the 1940s and 1950s, "were outraged that their poorer women were opting for a life of sin through the lure of British gold" (Sayyid Marsot 1985: 100).

The period between 1945 and 1952 was a time of political activity and unrest marked by anti-British demonstrations, riots, and strikes and the growing influence of the Muslim Brothers. After the war, a new campaign was launched against prostitution and nightclubs. In 1949, prostitution was made a criminal act.[17] Prostitutes and brothel keepers could be imprisoned for a period ranging from three months to three years. Accordingly, they had to work clandestinely and spread throughout Cairo. Several prostitutes started to work in the *ṣâlas*. Yet nightclub owners who employed prostitutes or provided opportunities for soliciting faced closure of the *ṣâla* and one-year imprisonment. In 1951, a new article was added to the law on public places, which stipulated that "it is not permitted for women who are employed in a public place, nor those who perform theatrical acts, to sit with the customers of the shop nor to eat, drink or dance with them."

On Black Saturday, during the revolution of 1952, supporters of the Wafd Party, Communists, and Muslim Brothers demonstrated and set fire to British and French cultural centers. Shepheard's Hotel and the former nightclub of Badîʿa Masabni were also burned down. Cinemas decorated with half-naked women that the demonstrators associated with the British and the corrupt King Farûq[18] were sent up in flames as well (Mostyn 1989: 167–171). Nasser's postrevolutionary Arab nationalism and Islamic socialism prompted a reappraisal of Arabic culture. Folk art, folk music, and folk dance, all of which glorified traditional Arabic culture, were revived. Belly dancers were seen as a bad advertisement for Arabic Muslim womanhood. Arabic dancers were required to wear at least a modest costume. A naked midriff was no longer permitted; it had to be covered with material (Buonaventura 1983: 108–109).[19] The new regulations were generally evaded once more. The belly was covered with skin-colored chiffon and later with net leotard, a token piece of material. *Fatḥ* went on, with red lamps and ringing bells warning the women of a vice-squad raid.

Fatḥ was eventually abolished, under Sadat. In 1973, a new system of registration and licenses was initiated. The *muṣannafât*, the department for censorship and supervision of theaters, films, music, and dance, is currently responsible for granting permits. The present head of the *muṣannafât* explained that in order to receive a license to work in a nightclub, the female performer first has to pass an examination, in which she proves to be a real dancer or singer. Before she can enter the examination, her record with the police and tax department is checked. An examination board of four persons usually sits in the audience to watch the candidate's artistic level, costume, and behavior with clients. This certificate, together with papers from the Ministry of Tourism and the vice squad, permits her to work in nightclubs. On her identity card is written *fannâna*—artist—which facilitates her being in the street in the middle of the night without being taken for a prostitute by the police. Dress prescriptions have been sharpened; today side slits can only start at the knees. Behavior with customers is restricted. Not only are sitting and drinking with customers things of the past, but the government has made dancing, laughing, and talking with customers punishable as well. Tips have become the most profitable source of income for performers and owners.[20] It is the major way a customer can express admiration for a performer and show off as well. Although the new regulations are not airtight, sitting and drinking with customers no longer occurs.

THE ERA OF THE *ʿAWÂLIM*

The heyday of the *ʿawâlim* was at the beginning of this century. They performed on festive occasions, particularly for other women, as they had done in the nineteenth century. In contrast to that period, however, at the turn of the century they increasingly sang and danced for the lower and middle classes, although some famous *ʿawâlim* performed in the houses of the pashas as well. The Westernized elite mostly invited nightclub entertainers to perform at their weddings. Yet the provincial upper class was entertained by the *ʿawâlim*. Bamba Kashshar and Amîna il-Ṣirrafiyya were among the well-known performers; most others were common singers and dancers and performed in working-class quarters. The profession of the *ʿawâlim* was mainly restricted to the Delta and Cairo. In the south male entertainers and *ghawâzî* performed (Buṭrus 1976: 123–126; *DF* 9-3-1948: 19).

At the beginning of this century, wedding celebrations were still segregated, and for that reason women were prominent in the entertainment market—female singers, dancers, and musicians were in great demand. Women played the lute, drum, tambourine, and *qanûn*, a zither-like instrument. They formed groups that regularly worked together under the leadership of an experienced performer, the *usṭâ* (plural: *usṭâwât*). She taught the trade to family members and new girls. After a long period of training and experience with customers and the market, a woman could establish herself as an independent *usṭâ* with her own performing group. Female performers often lived in the same house, and most *usṭâwât* clustered together in one neighborhood of a town. In Cairo, the entertainers lived together on Muḥammad ʿAlî Street. This boulevard, which cut diagonally across the old city, was made by Khedive Ismaʿîl to connect the citadel with the palace of Abdîn and led to Ezbekiyya Square. Muḥammad ʿAlî Street consisted of music shops that specialized in copper instruments for the many brass bands of that time, coffeehouses, and agencies for parties. The performers lived in the small back streets, while the *usṭâwât* resided in a separate alley, the *ḥârit il-ʿawâlim*. The houses of the *usṭâwât* were decorated with signs advertising the leading lady. Their offices were downstairs, since no male customer could enter their houses. The *usṭâ* or her male assistant (*muṭayibâtî*) received customers in the office, and the latter also negotiated in the coffeehouses on the main street. The *usṭâ* sometimes went to the coffeehouses in order to learn the latest songs and to meet customers herself (*DF* 9-3-1948: 19).

The *ʿawâlim* usually went veiled on a cart to their work. Their servant, the *ṣabî il-ʿalma*,[21] brought their costumes and instruments in advance. The *usṭâ* arrived a bit later, and her performers received her like a bride with a procession. If the wedding lasted several days, the performers stayed the night at the house of the bride and performed during the *lêlit il-galwâ*, the night the bride showed all her finery to female visitors; the *lêlit il-ḥenna,* when the bride's feet and hands were dyed; and the final night, when the marriage was consummated, the *lêlit il-dukhla*. The procession of the furniture and trousseau the bride had brought in, the *zaffit il-gihâz*, was accompanied by a brass band. The most famous band was called Hassaballa, which later became a general name for brass bands. The bridegroom walked around different neighborhoods in a procession, accompanied by a band of musicians that played popular songs (*ṭabl*

FIGURE 2

A former usțâ.

FIGURE 3

The mother of the groom shows the gold of the bride.

baladî) and stopped at coffeehouses to play and to receive tips. The procession lasted for several hours and went through a number of neighborhoods. Although it was protected by *fitiwwât*, neighborhood strongmen, fights regularly ensued when the parade entered other quarters. When the procession arrived home, the *ʿawâlim* brought the groom to his bride. Then they performed for the new couple, the female musicians and sometimes blind men playing music while the female singers and dancers took turns performing.[22] The *usṭâ* was usually a very fat lady because obesity was a sign of beauty and wealth. She remained seated on a cushion while singing special wedding songs. She lay back and danced with the upper part of her torso while balancing objects on her head and belly. A handkerchief was spread on the lap of the bride in which the tips for the performers were placed. The mother of the bride and groom also paid money and danced out of happiness. Besides the tips, the *usṭâ* received cigarettes, coffee beans, and sugar. The *ʿawâlim* were always offered food before their performances and before they left as well.

The party for the male guests was held outside the house. Rich families erected tents of multicolored cloth, sometimes with separate viewing boxes for the diverse pashas and their families, and offered an extensive show to the invited men. Most weddings, however, were celebrated on a modest scale, with chairs for the guests and a wooden platform for the musicians. Sometimes the guests simply sat on reed mats and the entertainers on chairs. In the country, the show mostly consisted of the horse dance—the guests competed to make a horse move to the rhythm of music played by a small band.

At the beginning of this century, there seemed to have been a distinction between the performers for the women's party and those for the men's party. The men's party was usually not attended by *ʿawâlim*, since they mainly performed for women. Although they sometimes left the women's party and performed downstairs with a veil, I was told that in the past this was not common. During the period my informants worked—from the 1940s onward—however, there existed a difference between the two, but merely in name. The performers working on women's parties and the party itself were called *ʿawâlim*, while the entertainers at the *sahra*, the men's party, were called *artistes.*[23] Most of the older performers I spoke with were both *ʿawâlim* and *artistes*, that is, they first performed for the women upstairs and then they sang and danced for the men until the early morning. They usually added that they did not like the *ʿawâlim* and left for the *sahra* as soon as possible because the women had little money. In the late 1940s, the *ʿawâlim* vanished from urban weddings because the weddings became less segregated and less extravagant. Separate women's parties lingered on in the countryside, but by the 1960s they had disappeared there also. People either abolished professional entertainment at the women's party or allowed female guests to be present at the men's party. Women then usually sat apart with the bride and groom and left early, after which the male party continued until early morning.

According to an article in the art magazine *Dunyâ al-Fann*, many *ʿawâlim* started out by working in the *ṣâlas*, initially veiled and fully dressed (*DF* 9-3-1948: 19). Yet my informants categorically denied this. With the exception of a few performers who said that they did work in nightclubs but never sat with customers, which is supported by the abovementioned article, most claimed that they had never worked in nightclubs at all. In general, singing and dancing at weddings seems to have been more in line with working at saint's day celebrations than with performing in nightclubs. Cairo abounded in *mawâlid*, and several saint's day celebrations in the Delta formed regional circuits and went well together with performing at weddings. There was a group of people, the *mawladiyya*, who only worked at the *mawâlid* and attended all saint's day celebrations from north to south. The female performers were usually called *ghawâzî* or gypsies, yet many Muḥammad ʿAlî Street performers worked at least occasionally on *mawâlid* as well; some even devoted the bulk of their career to *mawâlid*.[24] The older generation commented that the *mûlid* was a school of art and that a performer who did not work at saint's day celebrations was not a real artist.

In order to have a theater at a *mûlid*, one needed permission from the Ministry of Interior, which also fixed the duration of the festival. MacPherson, who lived in Egypt for forty years, visited many saint's day celebrations in the mid-1930s. He gave a lively description of the gay and secular side of the *mûlid*, with its sugar stalls, variety theaters, shadow shows, swings, merry-go-rounds, fire-eaters, snake charmers, gambling, tattoo and circumcision booths, processions of brotherhoods, and *zikrs* (1941: 76–83). According to Muḥammad ʿAlî Street performers, the variety theaters ranged from a platform outside a coffeehouse to a vast, circus-style tent. The small coffeehouses that had some singing and dancing were called *ghuraz*; the big ones, *teatrât*. In the coffeehouses, the tent owners sold tickets and paid the performers a fixed sum. In addition, performers collected money from the visitors in tambourines. The program of the small theaters usually included singing, dancing, acrobatics, and magical acts. A program lasted for about half an hour, after which new tickets were sold and the same program started again.[25] Most tents had a wooden platform on which performers gave samples of their art, so as to incite people to buy tickets. Dancers were sometimes rivals in how high they lifted their skirts in order to attract customers. In the most famous *teatro* of ʿAida Ṣâbir, a well-known female performer and theater owner, there was an extensive program of three hours with acting, singing, dancing, and literary recitations.

In the late 1930s, political and economic crises resulted in a religious revival. The government, probably motivated by the religious outlook of the public, attempted to restrict the secular side of festivals. The spaces for religious and secular activities had been separated some years before, but now the authorities limited the duration of saint's day celebrations and suppressed several *mawâlid* entirely on account of their lack of "morals and religion" (MacPherson 1941: 5–16, 37). Concerning the moral side, according to MacPherson, it was true that some years before, the dancers had adopted "less laudable classic steps . . . , but they always danced fully dressed and never with men" (1941: 84). In 1933, while visiting the big *mûlid* of Ṭanṭâ, he witnessed a *zaffit il-sharamît*, a procession of gaily decorated carts bearing the town's prostitutes and their admirers, accompanied by music and songs (1941: 286). Religious suppression was due to a more fundamental reason. *Mawâlid* are not regarded as Islamic because they did not exist in the time of the Prophet. The celebration of saints' days in Egypt dates back approximately to the twelfth century and is accordingly considered *bidʿa*, an innovation, which should be banned (Biegman 1990: 22).

At the end of the 1940s, the heyday of the Muslim Brothers, fundamentalists attempted to ban the Sûfî brotherhoods and their saints' days. Under the reign of Nasser, however, there was a revival of the festivals (de Jong 1980: 750–751). The Muslim Brothers were severely repressed and the regime tried to gain religious legitimacy by sanctioning the official Azhar orthodoxy and the mystic brotherhoods. The government's policy was aimed at gaining control over the popular festivals. Tents of the Arab Socialist Union were pitched beside the booths and theaters with "lavish spectacles promised by huge posters of incredibly-endowed belly dancers" (Gilsenan 1973: 50).

From the 1940s through the 1970s, women of Muḥammad ʿAlî Street families, although they lost an important market with the disappearance of the *ʿawâlim*, remained active at saint's day celebrations, at weddings, and occasionally in nightclubs. At weddings they were not only important as singers and dancers, but several women managed to build up a male clientele as well. They once more undertook the organization of wedding parties, bargained with customers, and brought a group of performers. Female performers no longer worked with one specific *usṭâ*, but started working with several female and male employers. Yet entertainers still formed a relatively small society of loosely related groups. During the 1970s, however, political and economic developments, together with changes in the way weddings were celebrated, had a profound impact on all Muḥammad ʿAlî Street performers and employers, especially the women.

THE DECLINE OF MUḤAMMAD ʿALÎ STREET

During Sadat's reign (1973–1981), Egypt adopted an open-door policy in order to attract foreign investments. With the changes in the economy, a middle class consisting of prerevolutionary businessmen and newcomers emerged and exploited the new situation. The journalist Haykal branded them a "parasite class . . . with a high pattern of vulgar consumption" (in Hopkins 1982: 166). This class of newly rich spent part of their wealth on recreation and brought about a flourishing period for entertainers. Weddings and other festive occasions were celebrated on a large scale. Wedding processions gained new vigor. Although the brass bands that had been used in the "procession of the furniture," the *zaffit il-gihâz*, had fallen into disuse and did not reappear, the procession of the bride was enlarged. It was supplemented with dance performances, mostly male folk dancing, although sometimes women performed the candelabra dance, the *shamᶜidân*.

The growing demand for entertainers resulted in higher wages. Prices had been on the rise from the 1950s, but under Sadat they increased tenfold. The oldest of my informants had worked for less than a pound, including both their wages and tips. Around the 1960s they earned five pounds, during the 1970s it became around fifty pounds, and today one hundred pounds a performance is not a high offer for a dancer. Not only the wages but also the tips rose. In the past, only the village headman could afford to show off by tipping a pound; most men gave a piaster or two, while women could afford only a few millimes. Now a man usually tips ten pounds, which is matched by other men, so that the total can amount to a thousand pounds.

The growing profits have led to changes in the system of payment. At the beginning of this century, the performers received no wage but shared all the earnings (*ḥeṣaṣ*). Around 1950 the performers got advance payment and half of the tips. Nowadays, they usually agree upon a fixed sum (*ḥa*ʾ, literally a right) and receive no share of the tips. People sometimes refuse to include the tip-giving ritual at all for fear of quarrels. They pay all the needs of the performers. If tips are given, they usually disappear into the pockets of the person who arranges the wedding.

The changes in the system of payment mirror the growing individualization of performers. Entertainers no longer formed separate groups with fixed membership that were headed by specific *usṭâwât*.[26] From the 1970s on, the groups were increasingly composed of mere individuals working for the highest bidder. The individualization is related to the end of the monopoly of the Muḥammad ᶜAlî Street entertainers. The increased profits attracted many people from outside the profession. They started working not only as musicians, singers, and dancers, but also as impresarios[27] and employers. The newcomers are called intruders (*dukhâlâ*ʾ or *khashânâ*) by the Muḥammad ᶜAlî Street performers, who refer to themselves as "the people of the trade," *awlâd il-kâr*. They view the trade as an "inn without a doorkeeper" (*wikâla min ghêr bawwâb*).

Anyone can enter the profession and contract to provide the entertainment at weddings.

During the late 1970s and the 1980s, when the boom came to an end, the original performers found that where the hogs are many the slop is poor. The open-door policy was not very effective. Not only did it open the country to Western corruption, according to fundamentalist Islamic critics, in economic terms it benefited but a small segment of society. For most people of the lower and lower-middle classes and those living on fixed salaries, such as government employees, the growing inflation and rising food prices proved a hardship. When Sadat, seeking loans from the World Bank, ended subsidies on such basic food items as flour, rice, sugar, and oil, many people took to the street. As in 1952, demonstrators attacked hotels and nightclubs. The economic recession has continued up to the present (1991), and has negatively affected the entertainment business.

The heritage of the 1970s—that is, the end of the monopoly of the Muḥammad ʿAlî Street performers and their growing individualization, combined with the recent economic recession—has affected the entertainment market in several ways. First, people presently economize on parties and entertainment by inviting professional performers only to weddings. They celebrate other festive occasions such as engagements and birthdays privately, replacing live entertainment with cassettes and radios. Some people only hold a long, extensive wedding procession (*zaffa*) with some folk-dancing performances, without a program afterward. Others go with a small company to a respectable nightclub. If they give a wedding party, some people rely on tips to defray their costs. Tip giving always reduces the cost for the host, since if the performers take the tips the basic wage he gives them is low. Other people may decide to give the entertainers a fixed sum and to pocket the tips themselves. Because tip giving is reciprocal and people know who gave what amount, they are morally obliged to match or exceed the sum on a party of the tipper.[28] Thus, if the host calculates that he has tipped a lot at the celebrations of his guests, he may decide that it will be more profitable to pay the performers wages only and to take the tips himself.[29]

Second, the end of the Muḥammad ʿAlî Street performers' monopoly eventually pushed many women out of the market as employers. The market, dictated by supply and demand, became impersonal and hazardous. The system of profit and risk-sharing disappeared, and women became reluctant to undertake weddings. The financial hazards were aggra-

FIGURE 4

A wedding procession.

vated by the increased problem of drugs, alcohol, and quarrels, which today can cause a wedding party to break up before enough tips have been gathered to cover the basic costs. Due to the increasing financial risks, many women decided it was better to be a mere employee.

Third, bands of criminals and a lack of protection are another problem. Hard drugs, which were introduced in the early 1980s when Egypt became a transit country for heroin and cocaine, caused rising criminality. Currently, gangs sometimes wait for entertainers after a wedding in order to steal their earnings or to kidnap female performers. This has made the role of male employers as protectors more important. Yet the growing number of outsiders and the individualization of the entertainers' groups have made protection by male colleagues less than guaranteed. Some "intruding" employers are said to disappear with the money. Due to the risk of theft and kidnapping, most women say they prefer to work with the familiar and trusted *awlâd il-kâr* only, although several have been tempted by—and some have accepted—attractive offers from outsiders. Due to the lack of safety and protection, some female entertainers from Muḥammad ʿAlî Street have left the trade altogether, and most have kept their children out of it.

Fourth, the circuit of saint's day celebrations and weddings lost esteem. As a result of the restrictive government policy, secular entertainment at *mawâlid* is limited and the big *teatrât*, which provided artistic programs, have largely disappeared. At the larger saints' days, these coffeehouses have been replaced by national theaters and other tents promoting "art, crafts and culture." In the countryside and the less strictly supervised places, however, only small variety theaters of a low or mediocre level remain. "Intruders" entered this branch of the trade as well, and Muḥammad ʿAlî Street performers accuse them of causing the low esteem for entertainers working at saint's day celebrations. Entertainment at *mawâlid* is presently considered the cheapest form of amusement. According to some performers, if it is known that someone works at saint's day celebrations, the performer will not be asked to entertain at weddings. The person who is paying for a wedding would feel that he was getting low-quality entertainers if they "belonged to *mawâlid.*" Thus, in contrast with the past, most Muḥammad ʿAlî Street performers claim that they do not work at saint's day celebrations anymore.

Muḥammad ʿAlî Street entertainers complain that professional ethics have also been abandoned at weddings since their monopoly was broken. Proper conduct of female entertainers with male customers and colleagues used to be maintained by the *usṭâ* and their relatives who also worked in the trade. The older generation claims that presently the women's success is mainly based on going with customers and wearing scanty costumes, not on their artistic level. Yet whether the costumes are more revealing now than in the past is not clear. The performers of the early 1940s who worked at weddings and saint's day celebrations (*mawâlid*) probably wore dresses (*tôb* or *talbîsa*). Because they had to leave the stage in order to collect tips, they had to cover their bodies more than nightclub dancers. Those who worked a decade later confessed that they wore a costume (*badlit ra'ṣ*) with a naked midriff until this was forbidden, at which time they started to cover their bellies with tulle and later with net leotard (*shabaka*). Ten years ago, long side slits had to be eliminated as well.[30] The claim of the older generation that the female "intruders"—the newest entertainers—earn money only through wearing revealing costumes may be unwarranted. The assertion that the artistic level has been lowered, though, may be more justified. In the past, performers had to be *shamla*—complete—that is, good singers and dancers. The new entertainers have hardly any training and most are only dancers. Yet they are not the only ones to blame because, as one performer put it: "riz' il-hibl ʿala il-maganîn," "The fool is provided for by the madman." That is, the taste of the audience seems to have changed as well. In the past, singing was the most important art at weddings. Nowadays, singing has been replaced by dance that is indeed not always of a very high artistic level.

Because of the present low esteem of weddings celebrated in the streets, wedding hosts are choosing to celebrate them in clubs. Since the late 1970s, the government has built a growing number of clubs for sports and festive occasions. It has partly been an attempt by the authorities to restrict the uncontrolled weddings in the streets. Not only fights but also salvos fired out of happiness—particularly popular among people from the south—have been a source of casualties.[31] Weddings limited to a number of invited guests, without alcohol being served and finished by midnight, have replaced the disorderly and unpredictable happenings of the street. At present, weddings in many towns of the Delta, and increasingly in Cairo as well, take place in clubs. The Cairene lower and lower-middle classes living in working-class neighborhoods, though, still prefer the freedom of unlimited parties. Middle class people never held their wedding parties in the street. However, they have shifted the location from homes to army and sports clubs or, less commonly, to respectable nightclubs. Upper-class persons celebrate their weddings either in the better nightclubs or in the prestigious five-star hotels.

Finally, the performers relocated their sphere of activity as well. In order to perform in an army or sports club they must be registered with an agent and obtain several papers. Several performers who obtained the requested papers started working in clubs. In former times, the women remained the whole evening at one party and alternately worked as singers and dancers. Some women still work like this, but others have adopted the *nimar* system prevailing in nightclubs. That is, they only drop by for half an hour to do their show and then leave for the next wedding in a club or in the street. Several opted for this system after they incurred troubles with drunken customers and criminal gangs. They prefer to leave as soon as possible with a male protector, who drives them to the next appointment. A few female entertainers have decided to work in nightclubs. Former performers of Muḥammad ʿAlî Street were insulted when I asked them whether they had worked in nightclubs in the past. But now, with the loss of esteem and safety in the circuit of weddings and saint's day celebrations, a number of them have been trying their luck in nightclubs. The *maḥallât*—literally "shops," as performers euphemistically call the nightclubs—provide a steady income and higher than they could make at weddings or saint's day celebrations. Moreover, since sitting and drinking with customers is no longer part of the job, their main objection to this work has been removed.

RECENT DEVELOPMENTS: PROFESSIONALIZATION AND ISLAMIC FUNDAMENTALISM

A third entertainment circuit that provides employment opportunities is the patronized arts. Theater, film, records, radio, and television are the most respectable media for transmitting art and entertainment. Theater groups already existed during the reign of the Westernized ruler and builder of the national opera house, Khedive Isma'îl, and during the British protectorate, but the opera house was only visited by foreign nationals and the Egyptian elite. After the First World War, musical theaters and public concerts emerged as a new mode of entertainment. Many companies started performing in nightclubs and theaters. Because their programs were less varied and the tickets more expensive, theaters met with fierce competition from nightclubs. Since nightclubs paid three times as much, apart from the profitable *fatḥ*, many actresses left to act and dance in the *ṣâlas* (*MM* 15-10-1931: 6; *RY* 25-12-1933: 33). There was thus an overlap between the art circuit and the better nightclubs of the Ezbekiyya area. Famous performers such as Munîra al-Mahdiyya worked both in theater companies and in nightclubs. She was among the first women to make commercial recordings (Danielson 1991: 296).

The film industry provided entertainers with a new opportunity for stardom and high salaries on top of that. Early American movies flooded Cairo during and after the First World War, and the number of movie theaters gradually expanded. The first Egyptian studio was begun in 1934. The films of the 1940s and 1950s invariably starred belly dancers and singers. Acting was of secondary importance, and most famous actresses were actually well-known singers and dancers (Landau 1958: 155–205). The radio and recording media were yet other roads to fame and prestige for singers. After the revolution, these media and arts were controlled by the state (Shawan 1980: 86). Then TV, which made its debut in 1960, became the most powerful medium for propaganda, education, and amusement. The Ministry of Culture encouraged Western arts such as ballet, opera, and classical music, as well as expressions of the Arabic heritage, especially Arabic music and folk dance. Cassettes, introduced in the 1970s, became a cheap way to make recordings.

The new media provided performers with a more respectable context. In the beginning, the new options were open to many. Umm Kalthûm, born in a small village in the Delta, started her career as a singer in small nightclubs, slowly moved on to performances between acts in larger theaters, and later performed in the major music halls in the

Ezbekiyya area, including the large Ezbekiyya Theater, which seated about eight hundred people. In the 1920s she started recording and became extremely successful. In the 1930s she also worked in films created around her songs, which were very popular (Danielson 1991: 297–301; Graham-Brown 1988: 189–192). Some of my informants from Muḥammad ʿAlî Street had minor film roles as dancers. A few had done work for radio and some had made cassettes. There was no distinction between the classical or serious art heard and seen in the media and the lighter entertainment at weddings. Belly dancing was prominent on the screen, and the songs of respected singers could be heard in the street.

Yet from the 1960s onward, due to a process of professionalization, star performers have ceased working in the less prestigious popular performing arts circuit, after they reach the higher echelons of art, and many common entertainers have been barred from the state-controlled radio and TV. Due to the growing number of art schools and institutes, a distinction has been created between institutionally trained artists and those without formal training. In order to obtain a job in an orchestra or a music ensemble, it has become necessary to have a certificate. Singers and musicians who are not graduates from the Institute for Arabic Music cannot perform on radio or television (Shawan 1980: 96).[32] One of my informants, for instance—the late Khadra il-Bakhâtî—had once sung for radio but later was not allowed to do so because of her lack of institutional training. Professionalization of the performing arts circuit thus established a rift between high and low art. In addition, due to the increasing number of separate training institutes, the unity of the performing arts—a performer could be an actor, singer, dancer, and acrobat at the same time—has been broken up. The Institute for Arabic Music (1929) produces trained singers and musicians, while the School of Dramatic Arts (1930) turns out actors and actresses. In the film business, actors and actresses are still occasionally asked to sing and dance, but acting has become their main job. Entertainment can thus no longer be considered one profession with the same status for all performers. The status of entertainers became increasingly determined by the form and context of their performances.

Professionalization has influenced the status of the various branches of the performing arts in different ways. For actors and actresses it has generally resulted in increased esteem for them and for their profession. All have had formal training; nongraduates have no access to theaters, TV, and films. In the world of musicians, professionalization has had a two-sided effect. It has led to a split between those with a certificate who worked in ensembles, orchestras, radio, and TV, and those with lifelong experience but no formal training who work at weddings and in nightclubs. It has brought esteem to some at the expense of others. For dancers, professionalization has generally had an unfavorable effect. From the 1960s, the Ministry of Culture has patronized ballet and folk-dance groups, such as the Reḍa Troupe and the National Troupe of Folk Arts. Belly dancing has been left without any form of schooling or recognition. It is not allowed in theaters and, as a result of growing religious opposition, is refused on TV as well.

These tendencies are reflected in the policies of trade unions. Actors and actresses have a recognized trade union. Dancers have a union, but in reality only those with training are admitted. Most dancers are refused; it accepts only folk and ballet dancers, who form a relatively small group. Musicians and singers are united in another trade union. Beside payment in case of illness or retirement, the union's policy aims at keeping unqualified people out of the trade. The second man of the trade union and director of a music ensemble, Ṣalâḥ ʿArrâm, disclosed that in the future membership will be based on a certificate from the Institute for Arabic Music or a vocational training course the union itself plans to set up. The training course would include not only rules of music but reading and writing as well. Most musicians from Muḥammad ʿAlî Street approve of this policy if it will keep out unqualified applicants, although they would prefer to be examined only on their skills in music.

Most dancers are thus left without legal protection or pensions. Recently, their situation has been aggravated by the actions of the agency that provides them with licenses, the *muṣannafât*; it has closed its doors to new dancers. Only dancers who belong to the dancers union and have at least five years of work experience in ballet or folk dance can receive a permit to dance for the public. This means in fact that only folk and ballet dancers can engage in the more profitable belly dancing. When I discussed this situation with ʿAida Nûr, an experienced and talented dancer working in five-star nightclubs, she mentioned that one alternative dancers have available is to organize a strike. She thought one could have a considerable effect, but she did not think that dancers have sufficient unity to be successful—joining forces is hampered by competition and rivalry. The action of the *muṣannafât* in denying new licenses is largely a response to the growing pressure of Islamic fundamentalists.

Religious agitation against public entertainment is not a recent phenomenon. As mentioned above, around 1830 and in the early 1930s and late 1940s, Egypt also witnessed religious revivals unfavorable to entertainment. Although the al-Azhar orthodoxy and Sûfî brotherhoods were merely controlled and hedged in by the state under Nasser, active Islamic fundamentalists and Islamicist groups were severely repressed. However, during the Sadat period, the Islamic fundamentalists regained their freedom. Sadat installed Islamic committees in the universities to counteract atheistic Marxists and Nasserism. Yet after the Camp David agreements, the Islamicists turned against Sadat, and an extremist group killed him in 1981. Under President Mubarak, a multiple strategy is being followed. The extremists are being repressed and imprisoned, while the moderates are given the opportunity to voice their opinions. The government is attempting to Islamicize its policy in order to take the wind out of the sails of Islamic fundamentalists. Consequently, the effects of growing religious pressure are discernible in all fields of art and entertainment.

Nightclubs have recently endured yet another attack. As in 1977, when twelve of the fourteen nightclubs on Pyramid Street were burned down, corruption and wealth have again provoked anger. On 25 and 26 February 1986, poorly paid soldiers who were quartered nearby sent several nightclubs up in flames. Recently, closing or relocating the Pyramid Street nightclubs has been under debate. When the street became an entertainment area in the 1940s, it was at the city limits. Today, as a result of the population boom, Cairo has expanded enormously and the nightclubs are situated in a new residential quarter. The governor of the area would prefer to relocate the nightclubs far off in the desert (*al-Wafd* 10-9-1989).

Religious influence on the wedding circuit is most strongly felt in the south, particularly in Minyâ and Asiyûṭ, the Islamicist strongholds, where fundamentalists succeeded in banning female entertainment and alcohol from weddings. Wedding parties are held in clubs, and young men provide the singing and accompaniment. Occasionally a dancer is brought all the way from Cairo, but then refused entrance to a city. ʿAbîr, a folk dancer from Minyâ whom I met in Luxor, left her town in 1984 because her work had become intolerably dangerous. She now tries her luck in the tourist towns. In Cairo, a few neighborhoods are effectively controlled by Islamic fundamentalists. They manage to keep unwanted female entertainers out of their areas. Islamic fundamentalists occasionally disturb weddings, break the musicians' instruments, and chase the female performers from the stage. This sometimes leads to fights with the party goers, who defend the entertainers' and their right to merriment (*NRC Handelsblad* 9-6-1988). As a result, female entertainers now refuse to perform in Islamicist bastions such as the Cairene neighborhood ʿAin Shams. The Islamic fundamentalist alternative is a segregated wedding with religious songs accompanied by the tambourine, the *duff*, one of the few lawful instruments according to strict opinion.

The larger saint's day celebrations are affected as well. The Sûfî brotherhoods are used by the state to counterbalance Islamic fundamentalism and are thus free to execute their *zikrs* and to listen to religious singers. Secular entertainment, however, is restricted, and belly dancing is sometimes forbidden. The amount of lighthearted entertainment available depends largely on the presence of government supervision and state theaters, which are usually confined to the larger *mawâlid*. For instance, at the *mûlid* of the Prophet in Ḥelwân, a suburb of Cairo, I witnessed belly dancing in revealing costumes as well as gambling. In the town of Dessûq, *teatrât* were allowed to operate for a week and dancing in a more conservative dress was permitted. At the large *mûlid* of Ṭanṭâ, however, entertainment was restricted to three days and dancing had been banned for several years.

The theaters and media are under stricter religious censorship as well. Belly dancing has been banned from TV, although old films—invariably with scenes from nightclubs and wedding parties featuring dancers with the scanty costumes of the early days—are allowed. Videotapes with belly dancing are available. A recent song by Muḥammad ʿAbd al-Wahhâb with the line "We come to the world not knowing why" is considered blasphemous by Islamic fundamentalists, who are attempting to ban the record. Yet the Azhar ruled that the song does not clash with Islamic law (*Middle East Times* 19-12-1989). At the University of Minyâ, riots occurred as a result of the traditional music and theater program at the end of the academic year. Yet a popular actor, ʿAdil Imân, challenged the Islamic fundamentalists by going on tour through the south, performing a farce with many puns. He drew a large audience (*NRC Handelsblad* 9-6-1988).

From these examples, it is clear that although Islamicist pressure is strong, there are forces counterbalancing it. The government tries to moderately implement some of the fundamentalists' proposals, but ignores the more fundamental issues. Islamic fundamentalist influence, although strong in the south, should not be overestimated. Most people still enjoy art and entertainment and invite performers to their weddings. If they forego these pleasures, it is mostly because of economic rather than religious reasons.

FOUR

LIFE STORIES OF FEMALE ENTERTAINERS

This chapter presents the life stories of the female entertainers I know best.[1] These accounts are their initial responses to my request to tell me something about their backgrounds and, especially, how they started to work as performers.

I describe four clusters of related female entertainers. In the first section, I introduce Umm Muḥammad, the oldest female performer of Muḥammad ʿAlî Street, and Ibtisâm, who belongs to the present generation. These life histories illustrate the developments in the profession during the last fifty years. In the second section, I present the Madbaḥ family, a family of former *usṭâwât* working at weddings of the lower-middle class. Their careers illustrate one of the patterns by which women start and leave the profession. It will be followed by a general discussion on women's careers in the entertainment business. Bûḥa and her family, who work at weddings and saint's day celebrations, are introduced in the third section. Their family enterprise is an example of the close relation between family, marriage, and work. It is followed by a general analysis of the socioeconomic and professional background of entertainers' parents and spouses. The last section presents Karîma, a dancer working in cheaper nightclubs, and the sisters Imân and Yasmîn, performers in the more expensive nightclubs. Their backgrounds and careers illustrate the differences and similarities between the nightclub circuit and the circuit of weddings and saint's day celebrations.

LIFE HISTORIES: UMM MUḤAMMAD AND IBTISÂM

Muḥammad ʿAlî Street still has the reputation of being the street for performers and wedding agencies, albeit for the lower classes. Yet the character of the street has changed considerably over the past three decades. Only a few music shops have survived—most of the shops selling copper instruments have been replaced by furniture firms. The signs and offices of the *ʿawâlim* have disappeared. Male musicians no longer work solely at weddings, but combine this circuit with the world of nightclubs. During the day, the coffeehouses are thus still busy with musicians waiting for wedding customers. In the evening, though, the musicians sit in black suits and white shirts, their work clothes for the nightclubs. Thursday is the peak day for weddings and the place where people gather on Muḥammad ʿAlî Street, ʾArḍ Sharîf, is so crowded and chaotic that it is nicknamed *mûlid* ʾArḍ Sharîf. Big Peugeots come and go, carrying performers to weddings all over Cairo and neighboring villages.

Older performers still live in the back streets, but many of the younger generation have saved enough money to move out to new living quarters in the district around Pyramid Street. Newcomers from the provinces find refuge with older performers or stay in a nearby hotel. In one of the huge buildings on Muḥammad ʿAlî Street, old and new performers live together. I was introduced to several by my assistant, Sayyid. Samîḥa il-Urashî, a well-known female musician and singer of an old *ʿawâlim* family from Ṭanṭâ, is presently working in a five-star hotel and lives on the fourth floor. The couple Ḥummuṣ and Ḥalâwa, "Chick-pea and Sweetmeat," who sing *munulôgs*, humorous songs, and perform sketches together, live on the third floor. A retired singer and dancer from a well-known performer's family lives on the second floor. The back entrance on the first floor leads to a long, narrow corridor with little rooms on both sides. One belongs to Umm Muḥammad, while other cubicles are occupied by several new performers. Ibtisâm, although she lives with three of her children in the district around Pyramid Street, retained a larger room at the end of the corridor. Two of her children, whose school and work are near Muḥammad ʿAlî Street, stay in this room with an older, childless widow, Zûba, who rents the room opposite.

Zûba, an old performer herself, knew of my interest in the history of the profession and introduced me to the oldest of all, her neighbor Umm Muḥammad. She was a thin old woman dressed in a frayed black gown. She sat on a bench beside me and started coughing loudly which, as obese Zûba gesticulated from her bed behind Umm Muḥammad, indicated that she wanted a cigarette. She related her story, now and then accompanied by the soft tones of Zûba's snoring:

> In the year 1938, the time of King Farûq's wedding party, I married a certain Aḥmed. I was fourteen. He married many women and took me as a bargain and taught me the trade. He was a singer, a clown, a comedian, a *munulôgist*—anything you wanted him to be. My father was a farmer in Zaqaziq [town in the eastern Delta]. Of course, after my marriage, I followed my husband's lead. My father had nothing to do with this profession; it all happened through the father of my son. I started in order to help him. I also liked the profession because of all the good artists I saw during the wedding of King Farûq. . . . When I found that he had three wives and I was number four, the youngest, life was difficult, I became pregnant and life messed me up. There was little money, we ate beans, but to put him to shame, no! I kept silent and the older artists told me to be patient.
>
> We went to saint's day celebrations and worked there. We'd leave the stage of a wedding and run back to a *mûlid.* We worked everywhere. Why? Because that is the way you build a house, stone by stone. We would work in a *ghuraz*, a tent or shop with electricity and a stage. Sometimes we worked on a bench and sometimes barefoot on the floor, such is a *mûlid*! At the end of the evening, the coffeehouse owner profited, the musicians profited, and we as well. We did *barrâda*, that is, we stood at the door of the shop with the castanets in our hands and played them to get the men to enter. When the shop was crowded we worked inside, *matinêh, soirêh.* Sometimes we went around the village to announce the group, and we visited the village headmen in order to ask permission. When the ticket was one piaster we sold it for five and to the well-to-do for fifteen. We did duets like this one [starts singing a duet admonishing a man to feed his wife and children instead of drinking the little money he earns]. I would go to a wedding and returned to a *mûlid.* Why? Because a *mûlid* means many days of work, eighteen or ten days. Is that the same as a wedding party of one day? No, I wanted to work many days. In Cairo, at the *mûlid* Sayyida Zeinab, instead of the square where the police were, we worked in the small alleys like the one you just came through. We traveled everywhere—to the south, the Red Sea, the countryside, anyplace where we found work and food. A wretched life! We sang songs like this one [song about the wretched life of a prostitute]. The group belonged to me. My husband went away, but there were other men [who could sing]. When my husband left me, for instance, if I was working at a *mûlid*, then I would just take one of my colleagues and teach him the duet . . . .
>
> At weddings, the women were upstairs. There was a group for women

and a group for men. We went upstairs and performed for the bride. After that her face was taken—do you understand? That is, her virginity. Then we went downstairs and performed the rest of the wedding for the men, until two, three o'clock in the morning, as long as there was money. Why should we leave if there was still money? We wanted to earn money, didn't we? . . . I remember another song [she sings a little love song]. I did not like the *ʿawâlim*, the tambourine by the women was empty. We wanted to earn for our children. If there was no money, we stopped working and went to the men.

When I first started working, I sang a *munulôg* about marrying seven men [she sings the first couplets of the song several times and explains the text]. The first man I lived with was a greengrocer, but he was not able to feed me; he gave me only salads, no meat or chicken. The second was a fruit merchant. The third couplet, God be praised, my husband did not allow me to sing. It was about a fisherman, but also about him. Like a fisherman who cleans a fish, after I married him, he cleaned me of my gold bracelets. The last marriage was to a rich man—I repented and stopped working. . . . In real life? No, that subject is not important. My husband left me, he had five children. I had one son, but he died four years ago.

I undertook weddings, *mawâlid*, worked alone or organized a group, and if I had no work I looked around for work with others. I was clever. I had a lot of work; I did not sleep. I stopped working when the trade became naked. My dresses covered me up to here, nothing was visible. We wore three or four skirts, the belly and breast were covered with spangles and beads. When it changed, I had had enough of it and stopped. My generation was pushed aside by the next. This generation wants nudity. When I found that the trade had changed and did not want dancers to be covered, I fell ill. I was in the hospital for a year. I thought, "Before the trade rejects me, I better reject it myself," and so I stopped. I was fifty-five. Now, I am eighty-five [probably around seventy]. I started selling everything I had and after that, what could I do? I don't know how to work as a charwoman or washerwoman. I shall leave it to God and he will protect me. Now, I am waking people for prayers five times a day. Just as my father did in Zaqaziq—he went on a donkey through the village and announced prayer time. . . . I went to Mecca two times, *uʾbâlik*! [wishing me the same happy occasion]. If you'll excuse me, it's prayer time—I have to go.

Umm Muḥammad receives little money from passersby for her religious calling and leads a meager existence. She is well liked by others and respected for her religiosity.

Ibtisâm started in 1963, around the time Umm Muḥammad stopped working. Sayyid introduced me to her toward the beginning of my first stay. I often accompanied her because I enjoyed watching her cheerful dance, particularly the show in which she balanced a water pipe on her head. I visited her many times at her place in the district around Pyramid Street, and sat chatting and watching TV with her and her two daughters while she was busy repairing costumes. The vicissitudes of her career illustrate the developments of the last twenty-five years. I have selected parts of her long story:

> I left my mother, she was married to someone else than my father. He was ruthless, cruel. He wanted to do things with me, he wanted to take me. I was a child and I did not know anything. Instead of telling my mother, I left the place [Maḥalla, town in the northern Delta]. I wanted to go to a female singer who had been in our shop while arranging a wedding. She had given my mother her address. I left with only ten piasters. I bought grapes and took a taxi to Ṭanṭâ. I had golden earrings and went to a jeweler. I exchanged them for smaller ones and received $2\frac{1}{2}$ pounds. I bought a sandwich and went to the mosque to say the *fatḥa* [the opening chapter of the Quran] and left for Cairo. I told the driver to take me to Muḥammad ʿAlî Street where the singer lived. But she was not in Egypt. I sat on the pavement until people took me to a drummer. I stayed with him until the singer came back. She wanted to inform my mother, but I told her I would disappear and no one would know my whereabouts. I stayed three months at her place. Then I married someone. I was fourteen, but they raised my age in the marriage contract. He was a tambourine player. . . . Once, my husband had to arrange a wedding on a Thursday but he could not find any dancers. And so I started. Most dancers were old and I was young, therefore they were happy with me and paid me three pounds. After the first wedding I was satisfied and happy. I liked it and wanted to continue dancing.

Yet soon after it became clear that her husband, the tambourine player, was always drunk or stoned, had many women, and gambled away her money. She had a daughter and a son. She asked for a divorce, which he initially refused. After some time, he gave her the choice of keeping the children or the house. Ibtisâm left with the children and started once again to build a home through dancing and singing. Another musician proposed to her. He promised that he would take care of her and her two children and that she could stop working. She agreed, but after a few months it turned out that he was married and had two children. Besides, he lived off her money instead of providing for her so that she had to continue working. She gave birth to a third child. Her husband repudiated her, according to her wish, but a few months later he insisted on remarrying her. He promised that everything would be different. She initially refused, but after he threatened her with a knife she returned to him. Ibtisâm gave birth to another son and daughter. After she found out that nothing had changed, she asked once more for a divorce. He refused to repudiate her, but she eventually managed to divorce on the grounds that he did not fulfill his duty of supporting the children. Her professional career was not easy either:

> In 1964, I started working in a nightclub. But I found out that there was *fatḥ*. I said: "I shall only dance." When they tried to force me to sit with a customer and said, "That customer ordered two bottles of champagne for you; if you don't sit with him we'll put it on your tab," I left the place. I returned to the weddings. I worked in *teatrât* [at saints' days] and traveled with a circus. But weddings were not as good as before. In the past, people had respected us and treated us as stars. They had invited us into their houses and offered us food. But now the artists were no longer the same and people would not let them in their houses. . . . After the problem at the wedding I told you about [she was almost robbed and kidnapped in 1973], and after they abolished *fatḥ*, I took the examination for the *muṣannafât* [censorship and licensing department]. I started working in a nightclub, but they behaved as if it was a coffeeshop. It was gloomy like a seedy bar and there were girls, hostesses, standing with the customers or waiting for them downstairs. I told them: "There is still *fatḥ*." But they said: "No, they are hostesses and they are different from artists." But the managers of the clubs were used to the old system and wanted me to enter into relations with customers so that my admirers would sit in the *ṣâla* every night. I left the place and went to another nightclub. The same story. They said: "We want you at 12:30 with your customers." I was the best *nimra* [act], but because I did not bring customers they put me at the beginning of the program, the warm-up part. Dancers who were not as good as I was, but who had customers, worked after me.[2] I make jokes and laugh with customers when I am on the stage, from a distance, but why should I have to get to know them afterward? . . . People say I am complicated, but I am just normal. Because of this my work stopped. So I returned to weddings, but as a *nimra*. People phone that they want me and give me the address. I go there and after my *nimra* I say good-bye and go home. Although I like

> dancing, I want to leave the trade because of all I've seen and experienced in it. I'll leave it, but what can I do? First I have to give my children a good upbringing.

Some years ago, Ibtisâm tried to leave the trade. She opened a grocery, but for lack of customers she had to close it again. Presently, besides working as a *nimra*, she is trying to open an agency for weddings.

These two careers illustrate in a nutshell the historical developments of the last fifty years. At the time of Umm Muḥammad, weddings were celebrated separately by men and women. She worked at weddings and saint's day celebrations, and it was an entirely different field of work from nightclubs. About thirty-five years later, Ibtisâm entered the trade and witnessed the developments in the wedding and nightclub circuits. Due to a lack of safety, she left the street weddings. Although *fatḥ* had been eliminated, nightclubs were not a suitable place to work either. Accordingly, she decided to work independently as a *nimra* at weddings.

CHOSEN CAREERS: THE MADBAḤ FAMILY

This family was given the nickname Madbaḥ, or slaughterhouse, because they are among the few of the older generation who do not live on Muḥammad ʿAlî Street. They live near a slaughterhouse in another working-class neighborhood. I was introduced to them by a friend who is related to them by marriage. Although she likes them, it was difficult to visit them because her husband is unwilling to acknowledge that they are his relatives. She was allowed to take me to their home on the condition that she would introduce them as former neighbors. They told their children the same story when they went to a family reunion. Although she confided the true relationship, I had to act toward her husband and children as if I had visited former neighbors.

The Madbaḥ family lives together in a dilapidated house. Sayyida is the oldest. She occupies a dark room. Her pots and pans are piled up against the wall. A beautiful picture, portraying her past glory, decorates the opposite wall. In winter, she usually sits in the window and looks out at the big square adjacent to the new metro and the last remnants of the old houses like their own. Next to her lives her younger sister, Zeinab, who has a two-room apartment. Their brother Muḥammad, his wife, Samîra, and their three unmarried children live upstairs. The ground floor is occupied by an unrelated former singer and dancer and her husband and children.

Sayyida started working in the early 1940s, when she was twelve years old. She was attending school, a sewing class. As a child, she visited all the weddings in the neighborhood and loved singing and dancing. She wanted to work at weddings. Her father had a coffeehouse, where her mother occasionally worked as well. The field of public entertainment was not far removed from their own business, and although not pleased with her plans, Sayyida's parents did not try to thwart her ambitions. Relatives on her mother's side, farmers who lived in the countryside, however, seriously opposed her choice. They set her brother Muḥammad against her by pushing him to guard the family honor. Initially, he tried to keep her out of the trade and even threatened her, but later Sayyida and Muḥammad's family broke off all ties with the farmers' branch of the family. Muḥammad eventually accompanied her to weddings and thus protected her respectability and safety.

Sayyida was in demand and worked at many towns outside Cairo. At sixteen, she worked for a few days in the *ṣâla* of Badîʿa Masabni, but the police prohibited it on account of her age. After reaching the required age of twenty-one, she occasionally worked in nightclubs, but as she stated: "I never sat with customers or opened bottles. I did my work and went home." She had roles as a dancer in seven films. The greater part of her work, however, was at weddings. By the time she was eighteen, she had built up a reputation and established herself as *usṭâ*. She clearly liked her work, and related with nostalgia how she worked with a candelabra on her head or in a man's long, flowing gown (*gallabiyya*) with a stick: "I put the stick here on my gown [her belly]—I was fat!—together with my colleague and we turned and turned. I worked with the stick until six o'clock in the morning, the men with hash and such things and I as a bee working amid them." She worked until shortly after her second marriage, stopping when she was thirty-eight. She summarized her married life and the end of her career as follows:

> Then there was a groom. Of course I listened to the words of my mother and agreed. He had a piano—it was the size of a bag[3]—and used it for work. I divorced because he ran after another woman. Then Morsi came, the father of my children. He was mad. He saw me at a wedding and went to my father. My father said: "He is a taxi driver; he has a car. He will be good." I said: "OK father, I'll stop working; I've had enough of it." I took him and gave birth to Amîra, Niʿma, who died, Aḥmed, Ḥasan, Fardûs, and Samîr. I kept on working a short while and then I stopped. Also be-

> cause I got older. This work wants young girls. Although they don't know how to work, as long as they are young they are in demand. Then he married someone else, a nursing assistant, and I left him [without formal divorce], now twenty-three years ago.

Her sister Zeinab followed in her steps.[4] She started working with Sayyida when she was thirteen. After ten years, she established herself as an independent *usṭâ*. She married a taxi driver, who accepted her work. They had no children but instead raised the two youngest of Sayyida. Zeinab signed a contract with a nightclub, but when it became clear that she would be expected to sit and drink with customers, she tore up the contract in front of the owner. She said: "Go to hell! You want me to be drunk the whole evening. I come to dance. I don't want this *fatḥ*. I belong to weddings." She worked at weddings for more than thirty years. Five years ago, after her husband died, Zeinab left the trade because, as she said: "The weddings are not like they used to be. In the days of beer and hash everything was fine, but now with the new generation and hard drugs, I don't like it anymore."

Muḥammad, who after his initial opposition played a drum himself, soon left the trade. He became a *fitiwwa*, a neighborhood strongman, and worked as a mechanic. Samîra married him in order to be able to enter the trade. She related her beginning as follows:

> I loved the profession when I was young, I was fourteen, fifteen years old. I started at weddings. We sang and danced, worked with open costumes,[5] everything. I started with Sayyida's group. I saw them at a wedding in my neighborhood and I admired them. I said, "Let me work with you." They took me with them one night. My parents did not agree. My father was a conductor, he worked for the railway. They were not happy with the field I chose. They tried everything to make me leave it. They were *baladî*, conservative.[6] They prayed and were religious. They thought that artists were bad people. Sayyida told me: "Since your parents object, why don't you marry my brother and work with us?" So I married her brother behind my parents' back. I married him so that my parents could not stop me from working anymore. After marriage my life started. We worked every day, we had good work. And we had fun together.

Samîra was offered work in nightclubs but, like her sister-in-law Zeinab, she felt that she belonged to weddings and not to the field of *fatḥ*. "We are *baladî*," she said. They saw their work as more respectable because they did not lose their dignity for the sake of money. "Otherwise we would not live in a place like this but have an apartment on Pyramid Street!" After ten years of working with different *usṭâwât*, she had sufficient knowledge, experience, and customers to undertake weddings herself. She worked until five years ago.

> We liked each other. We never quarreled about money like they do today. If we collected money, fine; if not, we went home in good spirits anyway. We were equal, we shared what we collected. Now even if I earn only two hundred pounds at a wedding, the dancer still wants her one hundred pounds, the drummer wants fifty, the accordionist wants seventy. I have to pay them from my own pocket. Therefore I don't want to work anymore. If there is a quarrel at the wedding and the party is ruined, where am I supposed to get the money? Now the girls drink wine or beer on the stage and there are many troubles and quarrels at the weddings. There used to be good singers and dancers, but now it is rubbish, *issaḥḥ iddaḥḥ umbû!*[7] What's that?!

She was almost kidnapped and robbed of her gold bracelets. The musicians had left her alone. She was rescued by a butcher, who took her to his place and brought her home after the gang was gone. Another reason she quit the stage was her age: "Now we are old, and with all the young beautiful people it is shameful. My children are grown up and one of them is married. If I work on the stage now, the young men start yelling, 'Hey, Grandma!'"

Sayyida, Zeinab, and Samîra chose their careers as performers. This is not always the case. There are four main ways in which women start working as entertainers. First, as is illustrated by the Madbaḥ family, the profession has strong powers of attraction. Glittering costumes, gold ornaments, songs, music, and applause have a powerful effect on many young girls. Most girls are well acquainted with the profession; they often witnessed several weddings in their neighborhood as they were growing up. Children are often put on the stage with the performers to sing and dance. In conservative families, this is less common for girls after they reach puberty. Yet in many families, particularly at the weddings of their own relatives, singing and dancing are an expected expression of happiness. In the days preceding the consummation of a marriage, there are also gatherings of women in which girls are encouraged to exhibit their singing and dancing talents. Several entertainers started their story by relating how much they had liked singing and dancing as young girls and saying that they had sometimes visited weddings in their neighborhood without the consent of their parents. One of them said that she had once used the family's food money as a tip in order to dance and sing at a neighborhood wedding. Others, particularly those from the countryside, were inspired to become performers after visiting a saint's day celebration. Although talent and attraction can be the sole motives, they are usually combined with other reasons.

In many cases economic reasons are decisive. Most entertainers are from the lower or lower-middle class and have hardly any schooling. They have no other options but factory work, cleaning, or other low-income and unskilled jobs. Two former entertainers first worked in a textile factory and left for the field of entertainment because of the higher earnings. Others have no choice and are simply forced by necessity—their father is dead or unable to provide for the family. A dancer I met in Mansûra, a town in the Delta, said: "I never liked the trade. In the past, I had to work so that my brothers and sister could attend school. And now I have to work so that my children can go to school."

A third pattern of entrance into the profession is by way of birth or marriage. Several are born into the trade. For some it is thus neither a choice nor compulsory, but a normal way of living. Others, such as Umm Muḥammad and Ibtisâm, marry entertainers, sometimes at a fairly young age, and work with their husbands, willingly or unwillingly. The link through family and marriage is also illustrated by Bûḥa's family, whose life stories are presented below.

Last, a few girls start because of bad situations at home, usually due to living with stepmothers or stepfathers. Bad treatment, child abuse, or incest can cause children to leave home, and a few of them end up as performers. The accounts of the entertainers show that most became performers for a combination of the above-mentioned reasons. The motives quite often changed during their careers. The initial attraction usually decreased and changed into economic necessity.

If girls become entertainers because of family background or economic necessity, there is usually not much resistance from their families. If they are talented and attracted to glamor or the economic gains, many of them meet with fierce resistance, as initially happened to Samîra and to a lesser extent to Sayyida. Both were then left in relative peace by their families, in Samîra's case due to her marriage strategy, and in Sayyida's case because her parents' social environment was not very different from that of entertainers. In other instances, parents beat, imprison, or even burn their daughters. Several entertainers described how their parents shaved them so that they could not perform. A few escaped from their parents' place and sought temporary refuge with entertainers. In some cases, contact with relatives is permanently severed. Those whose families object usually do not perform in their natal village or neighborhood. Some said that their relatives threatened to kill or slaughter them.[8]

Most former performers started at a relatively young age, particularly if they were born into an entertainer's family or married a performer at a young age. Many started their careers at fourteen. At present this is less common and most young women start around twenty, after finishing or dropping out of secondary school. The legal minimum age for females is twenty-one, or eighteen if the parents or legal guardians approve. At the time of my research, there were only two dancers under fifteen on Muḥammad ʿAlî Street. This was not only due to criticism of child labor but also, according to Sayyid, because most party goers prefer to watch mature women.

The age at which women quit the trade depends on several circumstances. Several female performers stopped working regularly after marriage; they worked occasionally in times of need. Many of those whose husbands did not object worked until forty. After that age dancing becomes shameful and sometimes embarrassing, as Samîra explained. Generally, dancers are less in demand at an advanced age. Singing is less dependent on physical attractiveness and is sometimes done after forty. Several entertainers thus changed from *shamla*, singing and dancing, to exclusively singing later on in their careers. Several kept on working as impresarios after they left the stage.

The careers of most female entertainers, although many work for twenty-five or thirty years, thus end at a relatively young age. Just as they begin the profession, without qualifications, they also leave it. They generally have few options for other work. Some of the older performers were reduced to poverty. Umm Muḥammad, for instance, sold her gold bracelets and necklaces, which she had bought as both decorations and provision for her old age, and ended as a quasi-beggar. The proverb Sayyida once used, "ṭiliʿt min il-mûlid bala ḥummuṣ," "I left the fair without any chick-peas," usually said of one who gets nothing out of something from which she might expect profit, held true for her as well as for Umm Muḥammad. Sayyida is supported by her children. Zeinab works as a cleaner, and Samîra recently followed her example. The achievements of the trade unions were too late for the older generation. The present generation of singers or *shamla* performers are better off. If they pay the monthly contribution, they have the right to a pension. Some of them are saving in order to have at least a house for their children or, like Ibtisâm, are planning for another income-generating project. Yet most merely cover the daily expenses and have little left for the future.

FAMILY ENTERPRISE: THE RELATIVES OF BÛḤA

Two weeks after my arrival, I met Zizi, a housemate of Bûḥa's relative. Sayyid was in charge of entertainment at a wedding in a lower-class neighborhood and took me with him. The wedding was in a blind alley. Red lights were hung up between the houses, and chairs and tables were put in the street. A wooden platform enclosed by multicolored cloth served as a stage. The program started after the wedding procession at eleven at night. The bride was inside her apartment, and women leaned over the balconies to witness the show downstairs. Children were running and playing among the crowd. I was put on the stage next to the musicians. I looked into curious brown eyes which expected me to be one of the *nimar* for that evening. Soon their attention was drawn by the performers. ʿAida, a blonde girl originally from Dumyât, started singing. Next, Khadra il-Bakhâtî, a popular singer wearing country-style ornaments in her hair, briefly performed. She was in a hurry to be on time for her next *nimra*. Sayyid was asked to play a *tôba*, an improvised solo, which was followed by a dance rhythm, the *tit*. Large quantities of beer and water pipes filled with hashish were available. The atmosphere was cheerful and the money was pouring in.

Every two or three minutes, the entertainers were interrupted by tippers. They came onstage and yelled their congratulations to the family of the bride and groom in the ear of the man with the microphone.[9] They continued, while waving ten-pound banknotes, to greet their friends, neighbors, and colleagues. The ritual was concluded by a *salâm*, a musical salutation consisting of a popular song, while the money quickly disappeared into the bag of the musicians. The *salâm* was interrupted by the next tipper who wanted to give his greetings and congratulations. As guests arrived, they also had a right to be announced and greeted by a short musical salutation. Accordingly, the party was rather hectic. People jumped on and off the stage and tried to grab the microphone. Now and then they quarreled about the lack of respect paid to their tip or the length of time spent on the salutations of others. Suddenly a fight occurred in the alley, which was settled as quickly as it broke out.

For the entertainers, it was absolutely impossible to perform until late at night, when the party had calmed down. When Zizi and ʿAida danced, several men tried to dance with them, a privilege usually reserved for

FIGURE 5

A Muḥammad ʿAlî Street singer with country-style adornments.

FIGURE 6

A Muḥammad ʿAlî Street dancer balancing a water pipe on her head.

the men of the bride or groom's family. At two o'clock a *nimra* arrived, Magda, an experienced dancer. At four o'clock, there was another disturbance which was so serious that the female performers were taken to a safe area. After half an hour, Sayyid came to pick me up. The police had broken up the party. But considering the short duration of the party, the profits were quite satisfactory.[10]

Zizi had hardly worked that evening. I met her again more than a year later when I visited Baṭṭa. It turned out that Zizi had just started at the wedding where I met her and was still inexperienced. She came from Dumyât and was vague about why she became an entertainer. Her choice probably resulted from a combination of lack of schooling, problems at home, and attraction to the financial gains that were possible. She said that she married a taxi driver who found it convenient for her to support herself. She lived with Baṭṭa, Baṭṭa's husband, and their two children. The more experienced Baṭṭa had taught her the essentials of the trade.

I was first introduced to Baṭṭa by Sayyid. I had seen her perform several times. She was much in demand. Although we visited her in winter on a Monday afternoon at six o'clock, she was eating and preparing for work. Meanwhile she related self-confidently:

> Five years ago, I started as an acrobat. I worked in Jordan in a variety program. For an acrobat, dancing is easy. I changed to dancing because I was beautiful. And indeed I succeeded, even more than in acrobatics. I started in this profession because I liked it, but also because of our financial circumstances. I wanted to stop because of my parents—they don't like this field. I am from Dumyât, and dance is shameful there. . . . I met my husband [Ṣalâḥ, a drummer] in Dumyât; he was working in a variety theater. I was not yet in the field of art. I was shy and embarrassed when I saw a dancer at that time. He came and talked to me and I looked at him. [Sayyid: "He flirted with you?"][11] Well, we liked each other. My parents did not agree, but I chose him and married him. I gave birth to Morsi, and thereafter I started working. He did not want me to work. He wanted me to be a housewife. He said: "If I had intended to marry a dancer, I would have married one." But I told him: "Let me work in order to improve our financial situation. I want to give Morsi a good education and send him to the best school." And so I started. My parents were furious and I did not see them for some time. But blood is thicker than water; I am still their daughter and they cannot do without me.
>
> Of course there were times when I wished I had never entered the trade and I came home crying and told Ṣalâḥ: "Look what you did to me." For instance if someone wanted to dance with me . . . and grabbed me as though we [dancers] are not human beings. At such moments I feel that people despise a dancer, that they do not consider her a normal woman, a housewife. They view her as a bad person. Afterward I quarreled with Ṣalâḥ. Well, he really did not want me to work in the beginning. . . . But now I know how to handle every situation, I have everything under control. I am nice and sweet to all, so that even the toughest bully is embarrassed and will protect me. . . . Dancing is in my blood.

I was somewhat surprised to learn from Sayyid that she was Ṣalâḥ's second wife, since she did not mention it at all. Later on it became clear that the situation was more problematic for the first wife, Bûḥa. We visited her the next day, and she talked at length about her wretched married life. Because of the winter season, Bûḥa hardly had any work.[12] She was bored and happy to have some company. Sayyid prepared her water pipe, from which she was inseparable, and she told us the following.

> Our father died. We [children] were three; I am the oldest, then Nagâḥ and Aḥmed. Then our mother married someone else, a musician. He took us out of school and taught us acrobatics. Stepfather! He had us work at saint's day celebrations. Then my husband, Ṣalâḥ, came along. I was fourteen. He taught me how to sing and dance at weddings. He took me to Damanhûr [town in the western Delta]. We started from scratch. We slept on a reed mat. Whether we found something to eat or not, I struggled alongside my husband because I did not want to return to my stepfather's family. He was a tyrant—he beat us and burned our hands. So I accepted the poverty. . . . I stayed two years without giving birth, and the third year I was pregnant. We were doing a little better; we had a bed. I gave birth to two other sons. . . . We went to Cairo. We were doing well; we had some money and bought a piece of land. But then my husband married a second wife [Baṭṭa]. He took her from the countryside and taught her dancing. He wanted to take my money and to employ the children in the trade. But I refused. I needed the money for the education of my sons. . . . I suffered and experienced calamities, but I bore it all because of my children. I wanted to give them the best education, because I was afraid that they would turn out like me—ignorant. I am forty-one and I cannot write my name. . . . After all my suffering, they would be unsuccessful as well? That would be a shame!
>
> Well, he married her. They stayed with us here, in this room. She said: "I am poor and unfortunate, I shall be your right hand." I was not that angry, but my children started to have emotional problems. They were angry and depressed. They did badly at school. So I told [Ṣalâḥ and Baṭṭa] to leave. Ṣalâḥ started to cause problems, so I went to court to get a divorce. But he came again and said that he wanted me back. He said that he would divorce the other girl. I agreed because of the children. There was someone else who wanted to marry me. The devil was tempting me and said: "Why don't you do the same to him. You suffered poverty, you had only one dress while all the other girls had many. He took your money and you had nothing." . . . But finally I said no and returned to him. If I had married someone else the children might have been homeless. I was afraid that the same thing would happen to my children that happened to me [having a stepparent]. So I returned and he immediately married the other

> girl once more. He told me: "I shall neither repudiate you nor visit you; I shall make you *bêt il-wa'f*" [unused property].[13] I went to the court to get a divorce. But they said: "You returned to him by your own volition, so you have to endure the situation." He does not give us money and it is winter. I have worked only once during the last three months.

Usually Baṭṭa and Ṣalâḥ work together. Yet despite the problems and quarrels between Baṭṭa and Bûḥa, all three occasionally cooperate. During the *mûlid* of the Prophet, Ṣalâḥ rented a tent and they performed together in a suburb of Cairo.[14] I visited them on several evenings. There were four theater tents next to each other, each trying to outdo the others in producing the most noise to attract customers. Ṣalâḥ and some other musicians constituted the band. Bûḥa started the program, which lasted for twenty minutes, with some songs. Zizi danced for a short time, followed by a clown. Baṭṭa was the next *nimra*, and finally some acrobats performed tricks. Thereafter a new group of people elbowed their way to the front in order to have the best view of the dancers' legs. Zizi and Baṭṭa wore very revealing costumes which completely showed their legs. They did the same program six times that evening. During the *lêla il-kibîra*, the last and climactic evening of the *mûlid*, they performed eleven times. After the second time I watched the program, I decided to make myself useful and helped Bûḥa's son sell tickets. The tickets cost one pound, a considerable amount for many visitors. Since their show offered one of the few possibilities to watch singing and dancing, people were eager to enter.

At one point Bûḥa took a rest to smoke her water pipe in front of the theater. Baṭṭa slapped her wrist and lectured her, saying that it was not proper to smoke in front of people. By reprimanding the first wife in public, Baṭṭa touched on a sore spot. Although Bûḥa kept silent at the time, as soon as we were in the car on our way home her anger came out as an outburst. The following evenings Baṭṭa stayed at home with her baby.

Two weeks later, Ṣalâḥ and Bûḥa left for the big *mûlid* of Ṭanṭâ. Dance was forbidden, so Zizi and Baṭṭa remained in Cairo. I was there five days before the *lêla il-kibîra* in order to avoid the crowd of pinching men. Since, as it turned out, secular entertainment was restricted to three days, I missed Ṣalâḥ and Bûḥa. In Dessûq, I ran into them again. There were two small tents with magic acts such as flying ladies and two variety theaters. One of the variety theaters was run by people I had met three weeks before in Mansûra, the other by Ṣalâḥ and Bûḥa. Zizi was dancing in a dress because two-piece costumes were forbidden. Baṭṭa did not come along because of the baby. I was asked to sell tickets since, as Bûḥa said, I brought them good luck.

While Bûḥa was out of town, I visited her sister Nagâḥ several times. Like Bûḥa, she had grown up at *mawâlid*. She had worked as a flying lady and explained this magical act to me. As a flying lady she was wrapped in a white sheet and laid on a wooden bed. A man "hypnotized" her and she started rising. He put a hoop around her body and drew it from one end to the other to convince the spectators that she was not being moved by threads or other tricks. Laughingly Nagâḥ explained the trick. Behind the curtain someone jacked up the metal plate on which she lay, which was concealed by the white sheet. The hoop was equipped with a sliding section which was opened to avoid the jack.

Nagâḥ started, like Bûḥa, as an acrobat in her stepfather's theater. She met her second husband, an acrobat, at the *mûlid* of Ṭanṭâ, where they both worked in the big theater of ʿAida Ṣâbir. At that time, she worked not only as an acrobat but also as a singer and a dancer. He proposed that they work together because together they could produce a complete variety show. They married and taught their three children acrobatics as well. They were proud of their work at saint's day celebrations, although they left the field due to the present low artistic level. Nagâḥ mainly works alone at weddings, while her husband works at the national circus. Last winter season they tried to find employment with a folk-dance show for tourists in the south.

Baṭṭa, Bûḥa, and Nagâḥ are members of a family enterprise; all three work with their husbands. Bûḥa and Nagâḥ had already worked with their stepfathers, while Nagâḥ employs her children as well. Although several female performers work with parents or husbands, it is not the most common pattern.

Only about one-third of the older and younger generations of my Muḥammad ʿAlî Street informants are from an entertainment background. Daughters of performers, in particular, do not automatically work as singers or dancers with their parents and brothers. A former female entertainer related that although her father was a musician and regularly undertook weddings, she had to work in a textile factory for a meager salary. She could not convince her father to let her work in the trade. Sayyid's father, although he employed his sons, kept his daughters out of the trade. When I asked Bûḥa's brother, a drummer, why he did not work with his sisters, he replied that he would feel uncomfortable if they danced in front of him. Since it would be known that it was his sisters who were dancing and talking with strange men in front of his eyes, he would suffer loss of face.

Samîḥa il-Urashî, a female musician and singer from an old family of *ᶜawâlim*, related that in the past, when they only performed in front of women, it was more common to employ daughters. Hers was a family enterprise comprising father and son and mother and daughter. In the middle of this century, although the members of many families on Muḥammad ᶜAlî Street worked together in family enterprises, daughters and sisters were not always employed. The present generation mostly keeps daughters and, increasingly, sons out of the profession due to the changed conditions of the trade. Sons are occasionally sent to a conservatory. Yet parents prefer that their children get enough education to pursue a career with higher esteem.

Two-thirds of my informants from Muḥammad ᶜAlî Street are accordingly from a nonentertainment background, mostly from the lower or lower-middle class. Although in a few cases the father is a peasant or a low-ranking civil servant, most parents have enterprises such as milk shops and coffeehouses, work as shoemakers and tailors, or are self-employed as tradesmen and taxi drivers. This class of independent small crafts and businesses, economically speaking, is comparable to the entertainment enterprise.

A family enterprise in which the husband and wife work together is more common than one in which parents and children work together. Two-thirds of my informants from Muḥammad ᶜAlî Street married entertainers. It would be incorrect, though, to assume that all male entertainers consider it normal and desirable for their wives to work as entertainers. Although it is definitely more accepted for a man's wife to be a performer among entertainers than it is in the larger society, many men share the wider society's ideal that wives should be housewives. Sayyid, for instance, married a dancer but insisted that she be a housewife, as did most of his brothers. Sayyid's family, accordingly, has high esteem. Teaching the wife the profession upon marriage and employing her stains a family's reputation. In particular, a man who works with his wife risks loss of face. If they do sketches or sing together and the man jealously guards his wife, as Ḥummuṣ did Ḥalâwa, he is respected. Yet when he allows his wife to dance in a revealing costume, and to smile and make small talk with other men in front of his eyes, he suffers loss of face. Ṣalâḥ is thus not a highly respected person. Baṭṭa's contradictory statements that he taught her to work but did not want her to work and her later blaming him for employing her should be seen in this light. Accordingly, many musicians and dancers who are married work separately.

Although many of my female informants married performers, more than one-third married outside the entertainment field. Their husbands usually belong to the same class of independent trades as their fathers. Many married taxi drivers. People of these two mobile professions often meet. Several taxi drivers first worked as drivers for their future wives and later married them. Some take their wives to work, drive through the city looking for customers, and later pick their wives up. They thus earn money and partially protect their wives without being confronted with the less desirable side of the profession. Although several female performers who married persons outside the entertainment field have had to stop working—for example, Zûba and Sayyida—many continue performing. Some keep on working full-time, while others perform only in the case of financial need.

In general, most female performers are married, either to entertainers or nonentertainers. The profession does not make them nonmarriageable. They are not "women without men," that is, unmarried women, divorcees, widows, or married to disabled or absent men (W. Jansen 1987). Although some are divorced, this is usually a transitional state leading to a new marriage. For none of them has divorce been caused by their work, and only a few women started working after being repudiated. Performing is thus usually no obstacle to marriage, and in many cases marriage did not end their careers as performers.

This can be understood in light of the fact that most are married to entertainers. Yet, as has become clear, being a married female performer is neither necessarily acceptable to entertainers nor totally unacceptable to men outside the profession. This is mainly related to family finances. Although most men can provide for their families, their standard of living would be considerably lower if they were the sole breadwinners. Most female entertainers, especially after several years of work experience, would prefer to be housewives, and most husbands would prefer their wives to be at home as well. Yet financial considerations often override the ideal, a situation which is not unique to entertainers.

NIGHTCLUB LIFE

Târiq, my chaperon for nightclubs, introduced me to Karîma. Her driver was a neighbor of his. The four of us met in a coffeeshop on a Thursday evening. She told me that she used to work as a waitress in a nightclub. Four years before, she had met a singer who arranged her work permit through his contacts. They split up after a short while, because of a financial dispute. She married and her husband made her stop dancing. She gave birth to a son. Her husband left them after a few months, and she started working again as a waitress in order to provide for her unemployed father, mother, brother, and son. After she was officially divorced, a few months before I met her, she returned to the more profitable dancing. She was in demand and could afford a driver and a boy to carry her bags.[15] She developed a liking for the driver and almost married him—Târiq and I were to be their witnesses—when it came out that he was already married.

We accompanied Karîma to her work on the evening I met her. First she had a *nimra* in an army club. Thereafter she started her tour of five nightclubs. She worked in two cheaper clubs adjacent to each other in the Ezbekiyya neighborhood. The entrance fee was small and the profits were earned by drinks and tips. The program consisted mostly of a new dancer every twenty minutes. Karîma managed to create a lively atmosphere with her suggestive dance, in which she mainly moved her pelvis and eyebrows. We had to hurry in order to be in time for her next *nimra* in a hotel, at half past twelve. This was a more expensive place where people were having dinner while watching the program. At two o'clock, Karîma was expected at one of the most notorious nightclubs downtown. Waitresses walked around and made appointments with customers. Her last *nimra* was in one of the nightclubs on Pyramid Street, the more expensive entertainment area which is mainly visited by Arabs. The entrance fee is usually at least fifty pounds and includes dinner. Some of these nightclubs have good programs with well-known performers and are also visited by families when they have weddings to celebrate. The place we visited with Karîma, however, was less respectable. She danced on the tables until half past four. A drunken Saudi showered banknotes on an Egyptian visitor who enjoyed himself dancing on the stage. This condescending show-off gesture by the Saudi—Arabs from the Gulf States and Saudi Arabia being generally despised—angered the Egyptian. The Saudi ended up penniless and could not even pay for a taxi. For us it was not yet the end of the night because Karîma wanted to have breakfast near al-Ḥussein Mosque. Like most entertainers, Karîma thought five o'clock was still too early to sleep.

For Karîma it had been a profitable night. She has a right to one-third of the tips, beside her basic salary, which is usually low. The musicians and the owner of the club are entitled to the remaining two-thirds of the *kît*, as tips are called in this circuit, in order to distinguish them from the *nu'ṭa* of the popular weddings. The tips vary according to season, time, and place, ranging from twenty to sometimes a few hundred pounds. A dancer of a high artistic level with whom Sayyid worked once received five hundred pounds from one Saudi. The largest amount of money Karîma has ever received in tips in one night was six hundred pounds, but usually she does not receive more than one hundred pounds, and in the slack season not over fifty pounds. Occasionally the competition among men results in quarrels like those at weddings of the lower-middle class. But usually the waiters and bodyguards calm everyone down before a big fight breaks out. Karîma does not have contracts with nightclubs, because most owners prefer to change the performers regularly. Only the famous dancers contract with five-star hotels.

Afterward, I went to several of the downtown nightclubs we had briefly visited with Karîma. Some of the cheapest still resemble the old days of the *fâtiḥât*. The difference is that the socializing is done by hostesses or waitresses instead of performers, who are not allowed to sit with customers at their tables—they must walk around and talk to them while standing. In most nightclubs, though, it is still the task of performers to please customers, albeit from the distance of the stage. Female entertainers are still supposed to make long-lasting contacts with customers but, in contrast to the past, mainly after instead of during working hours. They are expected to have their own customers and bring them to the club. If they do not have high-spending admirers, they can be fired or assigned the less-profitable hours of the program, as Ibtisâm related. The lack of personal clientele can be compensated for by laughing and flirting with the customers present in the clubs. This behavior, in combination with drinking alcohol, is supposed to "bewitch"[16] the customers and to put them in the right mood to give generous tips. Customers still try to make contacts with female entertainers. Because they can no longer invite them to their table, they sometimes write their name and address on a tissue and give it to the performer with a tip.

In contrast to the past, entertainers are now no longer supposed to make customers consume, but rather are expected to provide the best ambience for giving tips. The giving of tips is officially forbidden, but it happens on a large scale and the police turn a blind eye to it. Good performers manage to bewitch the customers by their good voices, stirring melodies, or passionate dances. Yet particularly the less-talented entertainers working in the cheaper clubs use their time onstage for holding hands, talking, joking, and making dirty remarks to persuade the men to take out their purses. Several performers know which men are generous tippers and devote their attention solely to these happy few, mostly Arabs from the Arabian Peninsula. Many men dance onstage, which is also forbidden, and the performer has the choice of dancing with them or standing back by the musicians. Some men try to put the tip in the performer's costume, and again the entertainer can allow them to do so, or grab the money and turn away with a sweet smile. These forbidden activities cease as soon as the police enter.

Karîma managed these demands of her job more easily than Ibtisâm. She said:

> Onstage I am a different person. I do all kinds of impolite things. I act spoiled and make certain movements like this [moving her eyebrows, while having one hand on her hip and sensually moving her pelvis]. I tease and flirt with men. If someone says while giving me a tip, "I want to meet you," I tell him, "OK, I'll meet you tomorrow." Another says: "I'll buy you this and that." I answer: "Fine." . . . They want to see meat, they want to see movements that can make them imagine they are sleeping with you. That's part of the job; it's business. After I finish my *nimra* I leave immediately. I have my driver waiting for me outside and I see them the next day on the stage.

In the better nightclubs the entrance fee and the wages of the entertainers are much higher. Owners and performers are therefore less dependent on tips. The talented and successful women who perform in five-star nightclubs are in a strong position. They can refuse money offered in an impolite way by throwing it on the floor. In five-star hotels, the ban on tips and other prohibitions are observed. Men are removed from the stage if a woman is performing. The atmosphere is quiet and the artistic level considerably higher. Most *nimar* have an extensive show, which usually lasts an hour, with a small folk-dancing group. Many dancers change their expensive costumes halfway through their show. Artists known from radio and television perform in these five-star nightclubs and hotels.

The sisters Imân and Yasmîn perform in the better nightclubs, although they have not yet reached the echelon of five-star hotels. I visited them in their luxurious apartments on Pyramid Street. They came originally from Mansûra. Imân started ten years ago. The resistance of her family, with the exception of her mother, was fierce. They eventually left for Cairo. Even today one strict brother does not enter their house because it is supported by "illicit" activities. In Cairo, Imân started to make a name for herself and had her own music group. Yasmîn joined a

FIGURE 7

A well-known dancer working in a five-star hotel.

folk-dance company after secondary school. The fixed movements of folk-dancing did not suit her temperament and she changed to belly dancing. Her first performance was as a substitute for her sister. She is a good singer as well, and has a singing and dancing show. Imân is divorced, while Yasmîn is married to a tradesman. He is convinced her artistic level is high and therefore does not mind that she continues performing after marriage.

We mainly talked about the organization of their work and the present state of the art in nightclubs. They complained that currently only the *nimra zibâla,* the "garbage acts," are successful and the good performers stay at home. Despite the new restrictions on permits for dancers, many women manage to enter the profession. The sisters have never performed at weddings of the lower classes. Yasmîn commented on that

FIGURE 8

A singer and dancer of the cheaper nightclubs.

type of work: "It is *baladî* work and it has its own performers. It is different from a *nimra* in a nightclub. Just like there are different classes in society—poor, middle class, and rich people there is a group of people from Muḥammad ʿAlî Street for the people in the street, and there are nightclub performers for the other classes. At weddings of the lower classes, people drink and make problems. The performers usually do not care about their appearance and the dancers are often very fat. They have no official papers. It is not possible for such a person to work in a nightclub."

Yasmîn, to a large extent, is right in that many of the women working at weddings have a different style of presentation. They are used to creating an atmosphere rather than giving a show. Usually their costumes are less chic and, according to the standards of beauty among the lower-middle class, they are more voluminous than the norm. They risk being out of place when they work outside of the popular circuit. Sayyid took me to several birthday parties of an upper-middle-class family. At one, they wanted to have an unusually jolly party so that they could record it on video and send the video to relatives in the United States. Baṭṭa was the dancer for that night. The guests, comfortably seated on couches, were eating sweets and drinking tea or expensive whiskey. Baṭṭa tried to create the atmosphere she was used to by getting an old man to dance, but he refused. She tried the next one, who only danced for a short while, then wiped his jacket with a satin handkerchief where he had been touched. Although Baṭṭa was proud that she had performed at such a "refined place," another Muḥammad ʿAlî Street dancer, who had met the same fate two months before, felt insulted by their attitude toward her. She said that she liked weddings with hashish and quarrels a thousand times better than stiff upper-middle-class parties.

Most women of the popular circuit have ambivalent feelings about work in nightclubs. Many of them, particularly the older generation, say that they are more respectable than nightclub performers because they do not go with customers. Yet at the same time, many of them feel that work in nightclubs is more desirable. Bûḥa's sister Nagâḥ, for instance, despite her earlier remarks that she belonged to weddings and saint's day celebrations, seized the opportunity to do a test nightclub work when a singer asked her to appear with him. Her initial ambivalence and uncertainty were strengthened while we were watching the program and waiting for her turn. The vice squad entered and stopped the program because the performer onstage, instead of respectfully greeting the authorities, continued singing. This frightened Nagâḥ, and we hurriedly left the nightclub.

As Imân and Yasmîn expressed it, most nightclub performers could not imagine working at weddings of the lower-middle class. One of the few exceptions was Magda, the *nimra* I saw at the first wedding I visited during my fieldwork. She started as a folk dancer and had her own performing group with which she worked in nightclubs. She liked her work and refused to stop after marrying a well-to-do businessman, who consequently divorced her. Her family actively tried to destroy her career in order to keep her from working. Her religious brother, whose education at the Azhar university had been paid for by Magda's dancing, spread the rumor that she had stopped working because of her age. Due to this, Magda lost some of her customers. Because she is less in demand, she presently works as a *nimra* at weddings, clubs, and occasionally in nightclubs. Together with a few other girls, she waits for work in her car near a coffeeshop downtown.

The difference between the wedding and nightclub circuits to a large extent is a class distinction—that is, between lower or lower-middle and middle or upper-middle class. This holds true with respect not only to the audience but to the entertainers' backgrounds as well. Popular entertainers and those working in the cheaper nightclubs have a comparable lower-class or lower-middle-class background.[17] The performers at the better nightclubs—like Yasmîn, Imân, and Magda—are usually from middle-class families and live in well-off neighborhoods. Their level of education is usually much higher than that of wedding performers. They have at least secondary school education, and many had training in art, folk dance, ballet, or music. Their reasons for entering the trade are, accordingly, slightly different from those of the wedding performers. Many, particularly those working in higher nightclubs, start because of their love of and training in ballet or folk dance, which enables them to enter the more profitable field of belly dancing. They rarely enter the trade through marriage or birth. Although financial necessity caused several performers in the cheaper nightclubs to enter their trade, those working in the better nightclubs are not forced by circumstances but choose their careers, possibly attracted by money and stardom.

As a result of their upper-middle-class background and, usually, marriage into a family of the same standing, many performers at the better nightclubs experience tougher familial resistance than their Muḥammad ʿAlî Street colleagues. Parents often totally reject the role of performer for their daughter, as do most husbands. Several nightclub entertainers have been forced to stop working after marriage, and some have resumed their careers only after divorce. If they insist on continuing their career, as Magda did, they face repudiation. There is usually no compelling financial reason for them to keep on working, and most of their husbands thus prefer to keep them at home. Only a few husbands are so convinced of their wives' artistry that they allow them to perform. Dancers in particular have to choose between marriage or work. Many female performers working in nightclubs are thus "women without men."

With regard to one of the structural characteristics of dishonorable professions, that of being "women without men," female nightclub entertainers seem to be more consistent with the expectations of the literature. Is this solely due to class differences, in the sense that, compared with men of the middle classes from which most nightclub performers come, lower-class men are forced to accept more readily that their wives work as singers or dancers? Or is it also related to the fact that, despite the more affluent family background and better educational level of nightclub performers, nightclubs are more reputable than the circuit of weddings and saint's day celebrations? In the next two chapters, I examine the status of performers working in the different contexts and forms of entertainment.

FIVE

MARGINALITY

In this chapter, I investigate whether entertainers working at weddings and saint's day celebrations constitute a marginal community. Do they form a distinct social group whose members are set apart from other social groups? Members of dishonorable professions usually live at the margins of towns, and mobility sometimes makes them total strangers and outsiders. They are thus socially marginal to the community and economically belong mostly to the lowest strata of society.

Egyptian entertainers do not differ from other citizens with regard to nationality or ethnicity. Members of minority groups—Jews, Levantines, Greeks, and other European nationals—played a role in the nightclubs of the beginning of this century, but most entertainers were nonminority Egyptians. According to some nineteenth-century travelers, *ghawâzî* entertainers were Gypsies, but as mentioned before, this is far from definite. It might have been the case in the past. Presently, however, the word *ghawâzî* is loosely applied to a type and place of work rather than to ethnicity.[1] Present-day entertainers at weddings and saints' day celebrations, as well as performers in nightclubs, are thus mainly Egyptians. With respect to religion and language, entertainers do not constitute a separate group either. All my informants are Muslims,[2] and they speak Egyptian Arabic with the accent of the town they live in. Their possible separateness as a social group is thus mainly related to the entertainment profession. Mobility, for instance, is for many entertainers part of the trade, and most of them leave the community for certain periods. Performers in the circuit of weddings and saint's day celebrations also share an extensive professional argot, which makes it possible for them to communicate privately among nonentertainers.

In the first section, I discuss the secret code of popular entertainers and its relation to marginality. Mobility and the effect of this spatial marginality on the status of entertainers is the topic of the second section. In the third section, I focus on whether performers are socially marginal—that is, whether they are avoided and stigmatized by other people. I also examine whether economically they belong to the lowest strata of society. Cultural marginality—that is, whether entertainers lack the habits and qualities of "the real Egyptians" and are consequently considered "others"—is dealt with in the last section. I thus distinguish marginality according to its spatial, economic, social, and cultural aspects. Together, these facets should provide insight into whether performers are stigmatized, rejected, and perceived as others by the larger society. In view of the central theme, I chiefly investigate whether they are disregarded and shunned on account of attributed dishonor.

SECRET COMMUNICATION

Several professional groups in Egypt—for example, gold- and silversmiths, entertainers, thieves, money changers, hashish dealers, and pimps and prostitutes—make use of a secret language or argot (*sîm*). According to Rowson (1983), there are two main secret languages that have long been in existence, the *sîm* of gold- and silversmiths (*sîm il-sâgha*) and the *sîm* of entertainers (*sîm il-fannanîn* or *sîm il-ʿawâlim*). Several secondary argots are to a large extent based on a mixture of these two *sîms*. For example, *sîm il-kartiyya*, the argot of men who perform all kinds of services for tourists, is a variant of *sîm il-sâgha*, and the secret language of homosexuals is a variant of the entertainers' *sîm*. The argot of the gold- and silversmiths was greatly influenced by Hebrew, while that of the entertainers was modified by Romany[3] and, in the late nineteenth century, by Italian through the commedia dell'arte troupes who were touring throughout Egypt. For example, *biano* is the word for "slow" or "shut up," *furti* for "hurry up," and *salûti* for "leave-taking."

The entertainers' argot, especially that of those performing at weddings and saints' day celebrations, is known by entertainers all over the country. With the exception of a few words, the same secret vocabulary used in Alexandria and Ṭanṭâ is spoken in Cairo. The sharing of a special language over a wide geographic distance can be explained by the former and present mobility of entertainers. According to Rowson, the *sîm* is used by a variety of entertainers, not just those who perform at weddings and saints' day celebrations. Since the social status of musicians has changed in the course of this century, Rowson claims that knowledge, if not use, of the *sîm* goes fairly far up the social scale in musical circles as well (1983: 17). The last remark, in my opinion, is partly inaccurate. I met several entertainers fairly far up the social scale, particularly those who had graduated from music institutes and theater schools, who did not know a word of argot. Most entertainers performing in nightclubs are also ignorant of this *sîm*. For example, Magda, a dancer who has been performing in nightclubs for fifteen years, turned to dancing at weddings in the last two years. Only then did she become aware of the *sîm* used by her colleagues in the circuit of weddings and saint's day celebrations. Members of the younger generation who have recently entered that circuit and do not belong to the original families or the *awlâd il-kâr*, people of the trade, know only a few words. In short, the *sîm* is mainly used by the *awlâd il-kâr* who perform at weddings and saint's day celebrations. They learned the profession through experience, not at schools or institutes. Rowson is right in the sense that some of the entertainers working at weddings and saint's day celebrations have moved up on the social scale. But only those who started in the popular circuit know the argot.

Unfortunately, the article by Rowson contains only a few words of the entertainers' argot. I collected some 120 words and expressions, but I am not sure that all of them are part of the entertainers' *sîm*. Some may be ordinary slang, and for some I obtained very different definitions. Also, a few of the ones I wrote down in Alexandria are unknown in Cairo, and vice versa, and there are a few words which some entertainers say belong to the *sîm* of performers and others say belong to the argot of thieves and pickpockets.

The secret language mainly consists of words which do not bear any resemblance to Egyptian Arabic. For example, "wedding" in Egyptian Arabic is *faraḥ*; in *sîm* it is *bilbil*. Some words, especially in Cairo, are formed by inverting the consonants. For example, Cairene entertainers use *rafaḥ* instead of *faraḥ* for "wedding," *labda* instead of *badla* for "belly-dancing costume" and *raḥamiyya* instead of *ḥaramiyya* for "thief." There is a tendency, according to the older performers, among the younger generation to create a whole language in which the first letter of a word is changed to an *s* and a second, meaningless word beginning with the original first letter is affixed to it. For example, I was called Karîma, which in this type of *sîm* would be S̱arimaḵirkir. I am not sure whether this belongs to the real argot of performers or only represents a recent invention by the newcomers. Although a few older performers claimed it was part of the *sîm*, most of them said it was nonsense. The old *sîm*, which still resembles a list of the secret vocabulary of shadow players Kahle collected (1926–1927: 313–323), mainly consists of incomprehensible words, existing words with a different meaning, and some loan words. I confine myself to the vocabulary which, with a few exceptions, is shared by the entertainers in the circuit of weddings and saints' day celebrations all over the country.

The importance of the use of secret vocabulary should not be overestimated. Usually entertainers do not speak in *sîm* except at work in specific circumstances. Yet an analysis of the argot gives insight into aspects of central importance to the trade. The following are the main categories of words in the entertainers' *sîm*, together with examples.

Money

It is not surprising that performers have a secret vocabulary for money, since money is the main objective in the entertainment profession. In *sîm* there are two words for money in general, *ubeiyig* and *ḥiwa*. In addition, all the coins and banknotes have individual names which, in order not to bore the reader, I shall not list. Also, there is a terminology with regard to the division of money and tips. *Tashnîb* is a kind of "begging." It is a way of behaving on the part of the entertainer which more or less forces the audience to give money—for example, by emphatically congratulating the groom or dancing at great length in front of a spectator. The leader of the band can order the women to do *tashnîb*, which means they have to descend from the stage, dance among the guests, and collect money.

Barrâda is also a way to collect money or to attract an audience. For example, if people at a wedding party are not inclined to be generous, entertainers can give tips themselves to inspire the guests to do the same. At saint's day celebrations, as Umm Muḥammad explained, dancers also engage in *barrâda*. Usually there is fierce competition among the many small entertainment shops adjacent to each other. In the past, women used to stand in their belly-dancing costumes with castanets in front of their shops to attract customers. Since this practice is now forbidden by the government, the women sometimes do *barrâda* but without their costumes and castanets.

Flirtation, *amarûz*, is a way of earning money by pleasing customers or employers. *Amarûz* pertains to admiration, smiling, looking, and talking, which usually results in an effort on the part of the admirer to arrange a rendezvous. It is considered an improper word and some entertainers refuse to use it or to admit that *amarûzât* plays a role in their job. But it cannot be denied that many male guests do try to attract the attention of the female entertainers. At a wedding I attended at which I was onstage with the entertainers until five o'clock in the morning, many guests took me for an entertainer and asked several times when this third lady was going to perform. Afterward, my "colleagues" told me that many men had "amraz"ed me. The female entertainer who took me with her was shocked by this expression and told the male musicians to shut up because I understood the *sîm*.

Food

There are many *sîm* words used in connection with eating, drinking, and smoking—for example, for tea, cigarettes, hashish, alcohol, food and meat. Entertainers also have a *sîm* verb for "to eat": *yirakhkhi* (*yâkul* in Egyptian Arabic). Without causing embarrassment for the host, entertainers can ask each other whether there is food and whether there is meat in it—and thus whether it is worth eating. The importance of food goes back to the tradition, still adhered to although on a lesser scale, of cooking a meal for all the guests of the wedding party. Entertainers were offered food before they started their performance. This has been replaced by plates with cold meat, cheese, carrots, and cucumbers or, if the party is held in a club, by a paper box with sweets and sandwiches. Quite often, the entertainers do not receive this new type of food.

Entertainers have various food-related beliefs. They sprinkle beer on the stage before the performance for good luck. Eating *lib*, or sunflower seeds, a common habit especially among Egyptian women, is believed to bring bad luck and is abstained from while onstage. A female entertainer who violated this rule was nicknamed Sayyida the *lib*-eater.

People

There are words in *sîm* for "man," "woman," "boy," "girl," "old man," "old woman," "bride and groom," etc. Entertainers could thus ask the person who took me with her, "Who is the woman whom you have brought?" (Egyptian Arabic: "*mîn issitt illi maᶜâki*"; *sîm*: "*mîn il-muzza illi fi ʾamrik*"). They have more than one word for "woman": *muzza*, *kudiyâna*, and *dinyâra*. *Muzza* is the most commonly used and widely known, even among nonperformers. *Kudiyâna* and *dinyâra*, according to Rowson, are also used in the *sîm* of homosexuals. In their *sîm* the *kudiyâna* is the passive sexual partner. This is opposed to *barghal*, which means "man" in the argot of entertainers and "active sexual partner" in that of homosexuals. A woman in the homosexuals' *sîm* is called *dinyâra* (1983: 19).

Other persons with a special name in *sîm* include people who play an important role in the profession, such as the *muṭayibâtî*, the person who arranges parties and pays the entertainers money in advance, and the *nabatshî*, the person who carries the entertainers' bags. *Khushnî* (plural: *khashânâ*)[4] is the word the older generation uses to denote the "intruders," the people without roots in the trade who have recently entered it. It is derived from the Standard Arabic *khishin*, "coarse" or "rough," and means that the newcomers are still ignorant of the subtleties and rules of the trade. In addition, there are secret words for "thief," "homosexual," "pimp," and "whore." *Sîm* for parts of the body, in combination with adjectives such as "beautiful," "ugly," "good," "bad," "drunken," and "crazy," gives entertainers ample opportunity to describe persons without being understood.

Warnings

The word *ammêh* is regularly used, and it was the first *sîm* word I learned. It means "Stop talking" and indicates that the entertainers do not trust or want to talk in front of a third person. It was used when Sayyid introduced me to a dancer. He explained my research aim, mentioning my interest in such subjects as Islamic fundamentalism, government permissions, and the like. The dancer immediately said "ammêh," suspecting that I might be from the government or tax department. Sayyid took her aside and soothed her doubts. According to Rowson, *ammêh* is also part of the *sîm* of thieves and homosexuals. A female entertainer told me a funny story. She went with her mother, a former entertainer, to a goldsmith. After bargaining for a while, they were still dissatisfied with the price, so one said to the other, "ammêh," meaning "Let's stop bargaining." On hearing this, the goldsmith threw them out of his shop, suspecting they were thieves.

Badha means "to leave." It can be said in the sense of "Let's finish" or "I want to leave." It can also mean "Take this man away from the stage." *Taknîsh* means "to steal" and is used in two kinds of situations. First, it is used when a female entertainer tries to hide tips in her costume. Sometimes tips are put in the brassiere or belt of the costume. An entertainer can try to shove the tip a bit deeper inside so that her colleagues, with whom she otherwise would have to share the money, will not notice it. It is like a game; a dancer told me that once she "stole" 300 pounds this way. Second, *badha* is the term used when one of the guests tries to steal the money; then it is no longer a game but theft. This can happen if one of the guests volunteers to collect the money for the performers. Especially if the party ends up fighting, the volunteer might use the confusion to pocket some of the tip money. *Shixtifish* means "to kidnap," and is an important term due to the increase in fighting, thefts, and kidnapping over the last ten or twenty years.

The main themes are thus money, the use of flirtation to get money, food, and occupational risks such as fighting, theft, and kidnapping. Although in theory many things could be said in *sîm*, in practice entertainers hardly ever communicate secretly. Most performers found it amusing to teach me the secret vocabulary. Yet their active stock of secret words was usually soon exhausted. If I mentioned words taught to me by other performers they recognized them, but the ones used often and that came to mind readily seemed to be limited. The importance of the *sîm* should thus not be overestimated.

A few words are used often and are part of the profession. I initially did not even know that they are not ordinary Egyptian Arabic. Some words—like "buttocks" and terms of abuse like "homosexual"—are preferably said in *sîm* in order to put things mildly. *Sîm*, however, is mostly used in specific circumstances during work to avoid embarrassment or unwanted problems with drunken guests. A dancer I accompanied to a wedding in Alexandria did not have time to eat before she left home. She told her colleagues in *sîm* that she was hungry and wanted to eat. Her colleagues told her where she could get some food. Directly addressing the host would have been insulting his hospitality. Away from work, entertainers rarely speak *sîm* in order to be incomprehensible, although they sometimes use it for fun. I went, for instance, with Bûḥa's sister Nagâḥ and her colleagues to a wedding party outside Cairo. One of the musicians had run out of cigarettes and jokingly asked Nagâḥ in *sîm* to beg me for a *tiftâfa*. He was very shocked and his colleagues amused when I turned around and offered him a cigarette. Occasionally, for the sake of politeness, entertainers use *sîm* in short secret conversations. Zûba and Ibtisâm, for instance, were once discussing whether a young girl they were taking care of for the afternoon should stay overnight. They spoke in *sîm* in order to avoid giving the girl the impression that she was not welcome. However, the argot is mainly a practical tool and confined to specific circumstances at work.

According to Bosworth, it is too simplistic to view argot as merely a defense mechanism that a group uses. He states that it is essentially meant for use within a group as an expression of the distinctiveness of the group. That is, small, clearly defined groups within larger ones use argot as a way of affirming their group solidarity (1976: 151). Within the Egyptian entertainment community, however, this is seemingly not the case.

Members of the older generation claim that they spoke *sîm* more often than those of the present generation. They also have the feeling that in the old days group solidarity was stronger than at present. Yet they mainly used *sîm* if outsiders were present, not among themselves. Although ties between entertainers were probably stronger before the intrusion of the *khashânâ*, in the past entertainers apparently did not express their distinctiveness by way of argot.

There is another group of *sîm* speakers—Egyptian homosexuals—whose use of the argot is more consistent with Bosworth's views. It is interesting to compare the entertainers' use of *sîm*—mainly as a defense mechanism or to avoid embarrassment—with that of homosexuals. The distinction is probably related to the different social status of the speakers. Homosexuals have the most flourishing argot of all *sîm*-speaking groups in Cairo. They use the secret language not only if a stranger is present, but also among themselves. Thus they both protect their group from being understood by outsiders and also affirm their identity as a special group. Due to their low status and marginality, they have a need to reinforce their group solidarity (Rowson 1983: 20). Prostitutes are another marginal group who might feel a need to protect themselves and to reinforce their group solidarity. However, after 1949, when prostitution was made a criminal offense, their *sîm* disappeared. Prostitutes used to work and live together on Clot Bey Street. After 1949, they were forced to work clandestinely and ceased to be a community, so their argot was lost.

Entertainers in the popular circuit are enough of a community to have a *sîm*. But, unlike homosexuals, they are not marginalized to the extent that they need to affirm their identity by using the *sîm* among themselves in the absence of outsiders. Due to the public nature of their trade, it is practical for them to speak *sîm* in order not to break the rules of politeness. Also, in case of danger, it can be important to use argot as a defense mechanism. However, entertainers are not such a fringe group that they feel a need to reinforce their group solidarity.

MOBILITY AND SPATIAL MARGINALIZATION

Members of most professions in Cairo used to live together, and to a large extent still live together, in the same neighborhoods. Most entertainers working at weddings and saint's day celebrations cluster around Muḥammad ʿAlî Street, although some—for instance, the Madbaḥ family—live in another working-class neighborhood. Recently, a number of entertainers, mostly from the younger generation, have moved to new neighborhoods. Muḥammad ʿAlî Street has increasingly become a mixed area comprised of artisans—mainly furniture makers—and entertainers. Yet all performers, regardless of where they live, keep in contact with Muḥammad ʿAlî Street and its employers. The male musicians usually sit in the coffeeshops during the day, while the female entertainers phone the agencies to hear if there is work.

Most entertainers working at weddings and saint's day celebrations thus share a locality. Yet, contrary to what might be expected based on the literature on dishonorable professions, their living areas probably were not and certainly are not located at the margins of the city. The nineteenth-century travelogues occasionally mention that the *ghawâzî* lived temporarily at the margins of villages and towns during their journeys. I have no information about the locality of early nineteenth-century urban entertainers. Muḥammad ʿAlî Street, which cut diagonally across the old city and connected the center via the palace to the citadel, was completed in the 1870s. The part between the palace and the center in which the *ʿawâlim* alley was situated seems to have been the spot for entertainers at least since the late nineteenth century (Buṭrus 1976: 123–126). In view of the fixed quarters for professions, entertainers might well have lived in the area before the completion of the street. In terms of locality, they are thus not marginal.

Mobility is an important characteristic of the profession. Most entertainers are employed for work in distant villages and towns and regularly leave the community to work somewhere else. From the very beginning of an entertainer's career, mobility usually plays a part. Many members of both the older and the younger generations who eventually settled on Muḥammad ʿAlî Street come from places outside Cairo. For example, Umm Muḥammad and Ibtisâm of the older generation and Baṭṭa and Yasmîn of the younger generation come from the countryside. Contrary to the claim of the older generation, who feel threatened by the newcomers from the countryside, around the same percentage—that is, approximately half of the recruits of the older and new generations—are from outside the capital. The influx of newcomers is thus not a recent phenomenon as the older generation maintains; a certain instability in the membership of the community played a part in the past as well. Due to the amount of travel they do, entertainers' sense of community is probably less than that of other social groups.

Some performers have personal reasons for working away from their place of birth. A female singer I met in Alexandria was born in Cairo. Although, according to her, working conditions were generally better in the capital, she preferred to work in Alexandria in order not to compromise her father's good name. The dancer with whom she performed was originally from Alexandria, but for most of her career she had worked on Muḥammad ʿAlî Street. When she was repudiated by her husband, a Muḥammad ʿAlî Street employer, she decided to return to Alexandria. In general, most female performers, even if their families do not object, do not work in their natal villages, towns, or neighborhoods.

Seasonal travel is a common pattern for many entertainers. In the past, provincial towns like Damanhûr and Mansûra used to attract many entertainers in the period after the harvest, which was the season for weddings. Presently, several entertainers travel to Alexandria in summer, and in the slack winter season try their luck in the south. European tourists visiting Luxor and Aswan are usually treated to Oriental shows in their hotels or pleasure boats. Since there are hardly any local performers, most are recruited from Cairo. Local weddings in the south are mainly celebrated with musicians and male singers. In Luxor there was still one *ghawâzî* family, but the young women in it were all about to stop performing because they were getting married.[5] In winter, due to tourism, there is more work in the south than in the capital. Last winter, Nagâḥ and her unemployed husband, for instance, tried to find work with a folk-dancing show in Luxor and Aswan. Ibtisâm left her children with Zûba because she contracted with a hotel in Aswan.

In the summer season, many performers go to Alexandria. Every night there are wedding parties in the many clubs and "casinos" along the beach. There are hardly any weddings in the streets and the organization of wedding parties is different from that in Cairo. In Alexandria, entertainers do not have fixed appointments to perform; instead, the rule of "first come, first served" is applied. This means that entertainers sometimes go to a party in the early afternoon in order to work as the first *nimra*, so that they can quickly run to the next party. In this way they can make three or four *nimar*. If they work late at the first wedding, they hardly have the time for a second or third job. How much they earn in an evening is thus dependent on their timing and strategy.

Besides seasonal trips, entertainers sometimes travel for several hours to perform one night at a distant wedding. Although Cairene entertainers mostly work in Cairo and its suburbs, they are occasionally asked to perform at greater distances. Especially performers from regional centers such as Ṭanṭâ and Mansûra travel widely. Mansûra has a street similar to Muḥammad ʿAlî Street in miniature with three booking agencies and a coffeehouse. Male and female entertainers gather and chat at the agencies before traveling to nearby or distant places such as Zaqaziq, Alexandria, and Port Said.

Work at saint's day celebrations is the entertainment requiring the most mobility. Bûḥa's family, for example, combine work at weddings with work at *mawâlid* in the Delta. Several others only work at saint's day celebrations. In particular, religious singers (*maddâḥîn* or *ṣayyîta*) mainly earn their income at *mawâlid*. Bûḥa stated that there is a great difference between "those working in a tent of cloth" (the religious singers) and "those working in a wooden theater" (the dancers, singers, and acrobats). Ḥagga Amîna and Ḥagga Amal, two female singers of religious songs, affirmed Bûḥa's distinction. I met Ḥagga Amîna in Ramadan in Cairo. She lives in a village near Mansûra. She always performs in long clothes and a headkerchief. She mainly works at saint's day celebrations, occasionally at private celebrations of a religious nature. She said she did not mind singing nonreligious songs provided the content was proper, but she considered it unthinkable to be onstage beside a dancer in a revealing costume.

Nightclub performers travel less, although they have begun traveling more since the adoption of the *nimar* system. They also occasionally contract for some months with hotels in the south or abroad, but their main source of work is in Cairo. As Karîma's working pattern revealed, nightclub performers hurry from nightclubs downtown to those on Pyramid Street and back. Some dancers have their own drivers for this purpose. In contrast to entertainers working at weddings and saint's day celebrations, they do not travel extensively, although they often make several short trips at night.

Thus, in general, entertainment is a mobile profession. This fact has numerous implications for the status of entertainers. On the part of authorities, moving groups are a nuisance because they are difficult to control. Throughout the nineteenth and twentieth centuries, there was accordingly an increasing tendency toward regularization of entertainment places and opening times. The government attempted to relocate the uncontrolled parties in the streets and restricted the saint's day celebrations. Currently, authorities also keep the influx of new dancers under control. Yet traveling, since it is a condition of the profession, cannot be totally prevented.

In the eyes of the public, mobile groups may be marginal in the literal sense; that is, during the time they are absent they are not part of the community. Yet, according to many Egyptians, mobility in itself is not necessarily a reason for avoidance and stigmatization or related to dishonor. Most Egyptians I spoke to equated mobility with fatigue and pitied mobile entertainers, particularly those working at saint's day celebrations. Mobility can, however, create opportunities to engage in immoral activities. This suspicion is mainly directed at female entertainers. Female singers and dancers were suspected of using the night as a cover for dishonorable meetings. A common reaction was "Maybe those women go home, maybe not, nobody knows."

Entertainers view travel as hardship and fatigue as well. Work at saint's day celebrations is especially seen as *marmaṭa*, a wretched life. They do not link mobility with dishonor but view it as a hardship of their profession. A female singer from Ṭanṭâ said: "Yesterday we were in Ismaʿiliyya, today in Ulʾâs. Every day we are somewhere else. When we are pregnant we give birth at some wedding or other and when death comes we die in whatever town we're in. Such is our trade." Travel, though, is in some cases perceived as an indication of status and fame. This mainly pertains to nightclub performers who successfully tour abroad.

In general, mobility is thus related to marginality in a literal sense—that is, for the time of their absence entertainers are marginal to the community—but not directly linked to disgrace. Two reservations should be made, though. First, although entertainment is a mobile profession, most performers return to their home every night for the greatest part of the year and are thus tied to their local communities. Second, for women it has an indirect relation to immorality. Although mobility per se is not the main cause of their low status, immoral behavior which is ascribed to them can more easily be carried out in work and travel at night.

SOCIAL AND ECONOMIC MARGINALITY

In general, entertainers do not belong to the lower rungs of society. A few famous artists are well-off, and especially those working in the better nightclubs can earn large sums of money. A few of the older generation, such as Umm Muḥammad and Sayyida, have become rather poor. Most entertainers, however, are part of the broad lower-middle class.

Lower civil servants are an interesting group for comparison, since their profession usually has higher esteem but pays less. Lower government employees strongly look down upon entertainers. They envy the higher earnings and spending of performers. Civil servants often have to live on 120 to 150 pounds a month, and think that a dancer can earn this in one evening. In their view, it is unfair that such a low trade brings in more money. Their ideas about the entertainers' wages are based on the amount they have had to put aside for their children's wedding parties. This, however, gives a too-rosy picture of the income of performers.

Musicians usually receive not more than 20 or 30 pounds for an evening. Female entertainers working at wedding processions have to be on their feet for a long time in order to earn 15 pounds. In addition, female entertainers usually stop working at a fairly young age, and dancers and the performers of the older generation have no pension. Moreover, all entertainers have to cope with the slack winter season. Performers are aware of people's ideas about the level of their profits and accordingly stress the hard working conditions and vicissitudes of fortune. They claim that they have to work many hours in difficult circumstances for an irregular and unpredictable wage, while the civil servant, who can comfortably sleep the whole day in an office, receives a fixed salary and a pension on top of it. In general, performers in their heyday are better off than civil servants but not to the extent that many people think.

There is a growing number of musicians who combine two jobs in order to secure their financial situation. Some combine work at weddings with work in an orchestra or, like my assistant Sayyid, in a dance company. They are thus civil servants in the field of art. Others work in the morning as government employees and in the evening as musicians in nightclubs or at weddings. In general, it can be concluded that economically, entertainers are not a marginal group.

The number of entertainers who had nonentertainment backgrounds and were married to people outside the branch also raises doubts about their marginality as a social group. There seems to be no unbridgeable gap between performers and other social groups. The image created by the literature on infamous occupations—that entertainers, although invited to central festive occasions, are avoided and sent away as soon as possible after the celebrations—seems questionable in the case of Egyptian entertainers working at weddings and saint's day celebrations.

In order to investigate whether entertainers are avoided by other Egyptians, I interviewed fifty people from different strata of Egyptian society.[6] I asked them each about the way they had celebrated their own wedding party and those of their children, as well as whether they would consider working as an entertainer or allow their children to work as performers. In addition, I asked them whether they would consider marrying a performer or would raise objections if their children were to do so. Their answers were not entirely negative, as would have been expected if entertainers were a marginal and despised social group. Two factors were generally important in the informants' answers: the class background of the speaker and the sex of the performer.

Upper- and upper-middle-class informants are generally quite liberal in their attitudes toward art and entertainment as far as it pertains to the performing arts circuit. Working as a performer in a theater or on television or marrying an entertainer of this level is not inconceivable. Entertainers working at weddings and saint's day celebrations, and to a lesser extent nightclub performers, are considered far removed from their life—they simply belong to a different class. "Muḥammad ʿAli Street performers and those of nightclubs are lower-class people, and entertainers working at saint's day celebrations are ignorant people," an engineer said. With regard to male entertainers, the elites usually look down upon them from a class perspective, not on moral grounds. Female performers are condemned because of their lower-class background and assumed immoral behavior. A university student claimed that the word *ghazîya* was the aristocratic term for a prostitute. An upper-middle-class girl related that she was pinched on the cheek by a belly dancer at her friend's wedding party. She was repulsed and ashamed to be touched by a dancer. "We only look at them; we do not talk with them," she said. Entertainers as a social group are thus viewed as belonging to a different *ṭabaʾa*, level of society, together with other lower-class trades. They are considered marginal by the upper echelon of society, but at least male entertainers are not rejected on moral grounds.

Middle- and lower-middle-class informants, including lower government employees, are most strict in their condemnation of entertainers. Although the higher circles of art find some favor in their sight, they generally suspect the way entertainers presumably live. Describing the profession as *ḥarâm* (taboo), disrespectable, immoral, shameful, dirty, bad is common among members of this class. They most clearly articulate religious opinions on entertainment. Some of them might accept their sons working as performers in a respectable place, because "whatever a man does, a man is a man, nothing is shameful for him." Working as a female entertainer is not acceptable in their eyes. With regard to marriage, a few of them would allow their daughters to marry entertainers, but sons could not marry female performers. A female civil servant explained the reason for this distinction. She said: "My daughter can marry a musician because he will work and 'open the house' [that is, provide for her]. But if my son marries a dancer, she will earn more than him. Even if she stops working, since she is used to having money, as soon as she feels that she has less to spend, she will return to dancing.

She is not capable of living like we do. If my husband doesn't bring in enough, we can live. But she is used to money pouring in easily." Most, however, prefer to stay away completely from entertainers. Like the upper class, they thus look down on entertainers. Yet, unlike the upper class, they have fewer differences in *ṭaba'ât*, levels of society, they can refer to, so they actively differentiate themselves on moral grounds. Their moral condemnation, however, is most severely directed against female entertainers.

Lower- and lower-middle-class people, comprising workers, artisans, and independent traders, are most closely related to the entertainment community. With regard to where they live, socioeconomic background, and lifestyle, they are similar to popular entertainers. They associate with performers at the frequent weddings in their neighborhoods and are in potential daily contact if they live in the same popular quarter. If entertainers are a marginal and despised group of people who are actually avoided, this rejection should be most clearly visible in the behavior of lower- and lower-middle-class people.[7]

Some lower- and lower-middle-class members draw distinctions between their own group and entertainers. They do not use vertical class distinctions, *ṭaba'ât*, but the horizontal notion of *bî'a*, the social environment. As a lower-class girl said: "Muḥammad ʿAli Street performers are raised in a certain environment. It is not that they are bad people or that they display low behavior, but their social environment allows things that are prohibited otherwise. They have their own habits and customs and allow their daughters and wives to work as dancers. In their social environment it is not shameful."

Yet the most common reaction to the entertainment profession is a shrug accompanied by the expression *"akl ʿêsh,"* "It is a livelihood." Most view it as a way of earning one's daily bread, like any other trade. They generally do not condemn the profession as long as it is practiced by men. Similar to the ideas of civil servants, the common attitude is that a man can do anything he likes, since nothing is shameful for him. "His deeds will not be counted against him [in heaven] as is the case with women," the above-quoted girl said. For women, although they recognize that it is *akl ʿêsh* as well, it is considered improper. Nonetheless, they are less strong in their rejection of female entertainers than civil servants are, because they are more acquainted with financial hardship and lack of options. "Even a dancer is a human being who has to work in order to earn her daily bread," a cleaning woman said.

With respect to work and marriage, many lower- and lower-middle-class informants have no strong objections concerning men; that is, their men could work as musicians and their daughters could marry performers. Some reject the notion of marriage with entertainers because of social strata. As a handyman said: "We are not of their level. They will never look for a marriage partner among us." With regard to female performers, the informants usually have objections. Although some believe marriage would be possible if an entertainer were "straight," others think it would only be possible if she "repented," that is, stops working. However, most men definitely prefer to marry outside the entertainers' branch. The opinion of a tailor is illustrative of the general attitude. He said: "As for a man, it is no problem. He is raised to be a musician like I am raised to work as a tailor. . . . Marrying a female performer is not possible unless she repents. And even if she shows remorse it is difficult because, as the saying goes, 'the piper dies but his finger still plays' ('yimût izzammâr wiṣbâᶜu yilᶜab')."

Although the entertainment profession is generally not held in high esteem, performers as a group are not marginal. Especially their social and economic counterparts, the lower class and lower-middle class, are mild in their judgments. Female entertainers, though, are generally rejected. This gender distinction is reflected in the views of the entertainers' community itself. I have already mentioned the feelings of ambiguity an entertainer feels if he allows his wife or daughter to work as a dancer, whereas he has no problem if his sons perform. A musician told me that his profession was respectable, with the exception of working behind a dancer and drinking.

Accordingly, it is no surprise that the strongest feelings of rejection are experienced by female entertainers. Baṭṭa, for example, had the feeling that people despise dancers and do not consider her a normal human being. "Son of a dancer" ("yabn il-raᵓâṣa or yabn il-ghazîya") is a serious term of abuse. The Madbaḥ family sometimes comes to blows with the neighbors when one of their sons is called "son of a dancer" by the neighbors' children. A female singer expressed her feelings as follows:

> The way people regard a female entertainer is not fair. They gossip about her because she talks and laughs with customers. But she does this as part of her profession. They consider it shameful, but if she doesn't do it, they don't want her. Whatever her own feelings may be, she has to please the guests. Even if something serious has just happened to her, as soon as she goes onstage she has to laugh and make jokes—and precisely for this reason she is condemned. A performer is like a candle; she sheds light for others but burns herself up.

CULTURAL MARGINALITY: *AWLÂD IL-BALAD*

The matter of cultural marginality—that is, whether entertainers are viewed as lacking in the habits and the qualities of "real Egyptians"—will be investigated by means of the concept of *awlâd il-balad*.[8] It is a central concept of Egyptian identity and characterizes the attributes of the "typical Egyptian." The notion of *awlâd il-balad* is, on the one hand, applied to a certain class of people; on the other hand, it represents general traits and noble characteristics which could be applied to all Egyptians. I make use of Messiri's interesting book *Ibn al-Balad: A Concept of Egyptian Identity* (1978a) and my own interviews with Egyptians of different social classes.[9] Messiri studied *awlâd il-balad* both from a historical perspective and according to the views of different classes. I asked several people how they define the concept, definitions that largely correspond to Messiri's analyses, and whether in their view entertainers exhibit these qualities of the "real Egyptian." First, I give a general account of the characteristics of the *awlâd il-balad*, which is an idealized picture of traits rather than an accurate account of a social group. Next, I discuss whether entertainers are seen as *awlâd il-balad*. Finally, I go into the perspectives of the performers themselves.

In particular after the 1952 revolution, with the end of foreign domination and the spread of national consciousness, the concept *awlâd il-balad* (singular: *ibn il-balad*) came to represent the true Egyptian. It is especially applied to Cairenes living in popular quarters. *Awlâd il-balad* usually belong to the lower-middle class and work as craftsmen and tradesmen or are employed in any kind of independent nongovernment job. Egyptian films displaying the *ibn il-balad* in a stereotypical fashion usually have a *miʿallim*,[10] an owner of a coffeeshop, or a butcher wearing a *gallabiyya*, a flowing gown, as its hero (Messiri 1978a: 46–49, 87). *Awlâd il-balad* are relatively wealthy and see themselves not only as earning a lot but especially as spending a lot.

Awlâd il-balad may be educated or illiterate, but they are perceived as highly knowledgeable about everyday life. They are *midardaḥîn*—that is, alert, intelligent, and educated in the ways of the world—and *fahlawiyya*, clever and shrewd. They are known for their gaiety, good humor, and tendency to live for the moment. They are usually perceived as tactful (Messiri 1978a: 2, 50, 88). My informants often used the expression "lisânu ḥilw," "His tongue is sweet." In addition, the *awlâd il-balad* are seen as hospitable, generous, helpful, and responsible. They express *shahâma*—that is, nobility, audacity, and a readiness to bear responsibility and to help without being asked or to settle a quarrel without knowing the persons involved. Finally, the *awlâd il-balad* are known for their *gadᶜâna*,[11] honorability and toughness, and for their masculinity and virility. They are assumed to have complete control over their homes and wives. The Egyptian wife is not allowed to leave the house without her husband's permission and her socially ideal roles are limited to mother and housekeeper.

The "daughters of the country," the *banât il-balad* (singular: *bint il-balad*), have similar characteristics and attributes.[12] They dress in the lower- and lower-middle-class style with a *milâya-laff*, a square of black cloth wrapped sari-like around the body, a multicolored headkerchief, high-heeled slippers, and, if possible, many golden bracelets. The *bint il-balad* combines coquetry and glamorous attire with a concern for reserve and modesty in dressing. Although ideally they are provided for by their husbands, many daughters of the country have to work. Some have traditional jobs such as bath attendants; others work in factories and tailor shops or as nurses, dressmakers, and—with sufficient education—government employees. The folk image of the *bint il-balad* is that of the *miᶜallima*, the chief, a female butcher or important merchant with a high status in the neighborhood (Messiri 1978b: 526–529).

Like the *ibn il-balad*, the *bint il-balad* is perceived as *fahlawiyya*, clever, unable to be fooled but likely to fool others. She views herself as alert, inquiring, and trained in the "school of life." She is talkative, good humored, and freely jokes about sex (Messiri 1978b: 525). She is hospitable and helpful and always ready to assist neighbors and relatives. *Banât il-balad* are very concerned with their reputation as honorable and chaste women. As one of my informants said, she is "midardaḥa bass sharîfa," "educated in the ways of the world but honorable." They will defend their reputation by any possible means and will even publicly beat a man in order to restore their good name. In addition, they are seen as *gidᶜân*, tough and courageous.

Entertainers share several characteristics of the *awlâd il-balad* as a social group; that is, they belong to the lower-middle class, live in popular neighborhoods, work in independent nongovernmental jobs, and are seen as big spenders. Yet to what extent are they considered to share the noble characteristics of the real Egyptians?

The upper-class people I interviewed were hesitant in their definition of the concept of *awlâd il-balad*. In their view, it has a slightly negative connotation. The sons and daughters of the country, although noble, honest, and helpful, lack refinement and sophistication. The *bint il-balad* is too tough and manly in her behavior to be totally acceptable to the upper and middle classes. Yet most of them abstract the qualities from the class it is associated with and stress traits rather than social background. They thus reply that the good character and noble behavior of a real *ibn il-balad* can be found in any person. They define these attributes as personal characteristics and, asked whether entertainers are *awlâd il-balad,* they accordingly reply that they cannot tell without knowing the individuals.

Civil servants usually perceive themselves as *awlâd il-balad.* Entertainers are in their eyes primarily *awlâd il-kâr*, sons of the trade, rather than *awlâd il-balad.* They consider belonging to the entertainment trade an obstacle to having the qualities of charity and helpfulness; that is, in their estimation the lure of money spoils performers. Especially the entertainers of nightclubs are thought to be interested only in earning money. Male performers from Muḥammad ʿAlî Street, however, are sometimes viewed by civil servants as *awlâd il-balad*, in good part because these performers daily deal with and work for this group of people. Dancers, however, are generally excluded from the status of daughters of the country. A government employee explained: "A *bint il-balad* protects her reputation, defends herself—she has a sweet tongue and is clever. I can say of a dancer from Muḥammad ʿAlî Street that she is a *bint il-balad* in the sense that she is quick-witted, alert, and clever, she talks with everyone in the right way. In words she is a *bint il-balad*, but not with regard to her behavior . . . a *bint il-balad* would never show her body."

The lower and lower-middle class are the groups of people that most strongly associate and identify themselves with this concept. A *bint il-balad* gave the following opinion of Muḥammad ʿAlî Street and nightclub performers:

> A real daughter of the country helps her neighbors, guards her home and family, and will never betray her husband. An *ibn il-balad* has complete authority over his home and wife; everything goes according to his orders and wishes. Muḥammad ʿAlî Street performers can certainly be regarded as *awlâd il-balad.* They may accept that their wives or sisters dance, but in their behavior toward neighbors they are very brotherly. And a dancer, if she dances at night that doesn't mean she is out of her husband's control or betraying him. . . . Performers in nightclubs on Pyramid Street do not fraternize with each other like those on Muḥammad ʿAlî Street. They are jealous and their purpose is to get money at the expense of humanity and solidarity.

Members of the lower and lower-middle classes agree with civil servants that in certain respects it is difficult to see a dancer as a *bint il-balad* because she shows her body instead of keeping her dignity by covering herself. Yet, since "not all fingers are alike," a few dancers are said to be really *gidᶜân*, honest and incorruptible.

Entertainers generally identify themselves with the *awlâd il-balad*. Only one dancer considered herself *afrangi*, westernized and modern, and dissociated herself from the traditional *banât il-balad*. Most entertainers, however, try to integrate and to be viewed as normal citizens and therefore identify with the *awlâd il-balad*. Bûḥa and Nagâḥ saw themselves as real *banât il-balad*. Nagâḥ said she always dresses in the *milâya-laff* except when she goes to work, and Bûḥa joined in, saying: "If I visit an *afrangi* neighborhood I get embarrassed easily. I don't know how to eat with a knife and fork and want to use my hands. We are educated and everything, but our voices are loud." They see themselves as typical *awlâd il-balad* not only because they live in a working-class neighborhood and dress, speak, and eat like the sons and daughters of the country, but also because they display noble character traits. They are hospitable and helpful, as are "real Egyptians." They are *fahlawiyya*, clever, and *midardaḥîn*, educated in the ways of the world, and have extensive training in talking to different levels of people in the right tone. They are *gidᶜân*, tough and courageous, and the female performers have the ability to act manly in order to secure their rights and reputation.

Ibtisâm identifies with the image of the *bint il-balad* to the extent that she had a dance show called "bint il-balad." Also the shop she tried to open on the ground floor (of which only the sign on the outside wall remained) is named "bint il-balad." Mona, a dancer in her early thirties, invited Sayyid and me to a lunch which was prepared in the *awlâd il-balad* style, that is, with three times as much as we could eat. She said she only liked to work at the weddings of *awlâd il-balad* like themselves, not only because they are nice and receive people well, but especially because they better understand the nature of her profession. "They understand that this is my work and nothing else," she said. Mona is right that the lower and lower-middle classes are the most mild in their evaluation of the trade. Although they generally reject it because of the roles women in it assume, some of them seem to understand the trade in the way entertainers do. A taxi driver, defining himself as an *ibn il-balad*, remarked: "They just want to earn a living. Tip givers think they can go home with female performers after work. But the performers are not like that. They lead the customers by the nose, take their money, and go home. If someone asks a dancer to go with him, she says OK to avoid problems. But at the end of the evening she just goes to her own home. Those on Pyramid Street are worse; they want money. Female performers on Muḥammad ʿAlî Street simply want to eat."

In order to analyze whether entertainers are marginalized, it is thus important to distinguish the views of the different classes. The largest group of society, the lower and lower-middle classes, generally accept entertainers. They do not stigmatize and actively avoid or reject them. Only if the upper-middle-class view is taken as the decisive one could it be concluded that entertainment is a low trade, and only if civil servants' views and religious opinion are accepted as conclusive could entertainment be seen as an immoral profession. With regard to female performers, however, things are different. Although the lower and lower-middle classes are milder in their evaluations, female entertainers are generally rejected. Yet before drawing a final conclusion and explaining why the profession is considered to be more disgraceful for women, it is important to analyze differences within the trade. Neither all male nor all female performers are put in the same category.

SIX

HONOR AND SHAME

In this chapter, I focus on the entertainment activity itself; making music, singing, and dancing by both sexes in different types of settings will be central. After gaining insight into what activity makes entertainment shameful for whom in which context, an answer to the main question of whether the tainted reputation of female entertainers is due to the dishonor of the profession or to the prevailing gender ideology can be formulated.

In the first section, I give an overview of the theoretical discussions on honor and shame, and criticize the approach viewing honor and shame as a binary opposition. As mentioned in Chapter 1, I define concepts, including honor and shame, as "experience-near," in other words, as evident from everyday life and discourse. The second section consequently examines people's ideas on the different forms and contexts of entertainment for male and female performers and investigates whether they use the concepts of honor and shame in their evaluations. In the last section, the perspective of entertainers themselves will be central. In contrast to public opinion, which mainly centers on shame, the entertainers' discourse focuses on honor.

THE HONOR AND SHAME SYNDROME

In the first collection of articles on honor and shame in Mediterranean societies (Peristiany 1965), Pitt-Rivers defines honor as "the value of a person in his own eyes but also in the eyes of his society. It is his estimation of his own worth, his *claim* to pride, but it is also the acknowledgement of that claim" (1965: 21). He distinguishes two meanings of honor and shame. First, as the basis of reputation they are synonymous: to be shameless is dishonorable. Honor and shame defined as the presence or absence of personal virtues pertain to both men and women. Yet whereas certain virtues such as honesty and loyalty are common to both sexes, others are ascribed to only one of them. For instance, a woman is dishonorable if she loses her sexual purity, while sexual adventures on the part of a man do not taint his honor and in fact may add to it. Second, honor and shame can also be defined as unrelated: "Shame, no longer equivalent to honour, as shyness, blushing and timidity is thought to be proper to women, even though it no longer constitutes virtue, while honour, no longer equivalent to shame, becomes an exclusively male attribute as the concern for precedence and the willingness to offend another man" (Pitt-Rivers 1965: 42).

Of the two concepts, it is honor that most captivated the imagination of anthropologists. And of the two possible meanings of honor—usually referred to as honor = virtue versus honor = precedence—it is the male attribute of rivalry that received the greatest attention. Shame almost disappeared from the stage except as the reverse and less interesting side of honor and the domain of women. Blok (1980, 1981b), for instance, analyzing the horn symbol, a disgraceful attribute of the deceived husband, claims that women have no honor (1980: 219; 1981b: 438). According to him, honor and shame are a complementary opposition which stands in a homologous relation to other binary oppositions such as men–women, strong–weak, good–evil, rams–billy goats, etc. (1981b: 430; see also Bourdieu 1965 for an analysis in binary fashion.)

With regard to Egypt, the early studies also centered on honor = precedence. Abou Zeid (1965), studying Bedouin society, initially mentions the different meanings of honor and shame in their individual and communal connotations. Whereas individual shameful acts are called *ʿêb*, communal shame which affects the wrongdoer and her or his kin is denoted as *ʿâr*. Yet honor, *sharaf*, is his main focus. And although he acknowledges that honor has an individual meaning connected to personal virtues, he is mainly concerned with its communal sense—that is, honor depending on the pursuit of superiority and distinction. Female honor (*ʿird*) pertains only to chastity, prudence, and continence. Since the Bedouin society is paternalistic, it is, according to Abou Zeid, only natural that the honor of the group is primarily determined by the achievements of men rather than women. Whereas male and communal honor (*sharaf*) can be augmented, female honor (*ʿird*) can only be lost by misconduct. Women's main contribution to the honor of the lineage is by their passive role of preserving chastity and purity (Abou Zeid 1965: 253, 256).

The approach outlined above has been criticized for numerous reasons (Herzfeld 1980; Gilmore 1987). Several authors suggest refocusing the attention from the concern for the pecking order among men to the more general concept of honor as a personal virtue. According to Gilmore, the classical honor of precedence is not a serious concern for most Andalusians. The everyday concerns of men and women center around trustworthiness and reliability in the company of their peers. According to him, honor could thus better be replaced by the concept of honesty (1987: 94). Herzfeld argues that in Greece honor might be usefully displaced by the descriptively simpler and less ambiguous concept of hospitality (1987: 75). Besides, the approach of honor as virtue leaves more room for the less powerful to share in activities acknowledged by their social group as honorable. Herzfeld describes, for instance, the case of a poor woman who provides her unexpected guests with bread, a few olives, and some water. Although a humble offer, it was acknowledged by all to be the best she could manage and was therefore considered hospitable and honorable (1980: 342). Lever also criticizes the honor/shame dichotomy, stating that most writers tend to concentrate on the values of middle-aged married men with economic power (1986: 83).

Abu Lughod makes similar points in her book on Egyptian Bedouins, *Veiled Sentiments* (1987). She states that most analyses take the perspective of those at the top of the hierarchy who are able to realize social ideals. According to Abu Lughod, a number of values are important in Bedouin society. In addition to honor, *sharaf,* meaning generosity, honesty, sincerity, loyalty to friends, and keeping one's word, there is the complex of values associated with independence which is even more important: "Being free (*ḥurr*) implies several qualities, including the strength to stand alone and freedom from domination. This freedom with regard to other people is won through tough assertiveness, fearlessness, and pride, whereas with regard to needs and passions, it is won through self-control" (1987: 87). These values are shared by all Bedouins—male and female, young and old. Yet only few Bedouins are able to realize the ideals—namely, older men. Most women and young men are not completely able to live up to the code of honor due to their situation of dependency. They can realize the social ideals when they are in contact with equals, but not in association with superiors. They consequently avoid contact with more powerful men in order not to be put in a situation of inequality. If it nevertheless happens, they voluntarily adopt an attitude of *ḥasham*, modesty, shame, and shyness.

In contrast to other authors, Abu Lughod does not relate female modesty solely to sexual conduct. In accordance with local parlance, she argues that *ḥasham* is better understood as "both feelings of shame in the company of the more powerful and the acts of deference that arise from these feelings" (1987: 107). Women and young men voluntarily and freely exhibit deference so as to underline their independence and freedom. *Ḥasham* is not opposed to honor but part of it. It is "a dignified way of being weak and dependent in a society that values strength and autonomy" (1987: 117). Honor is thus not a male concern only. All members aspire to realize the social ideals but not all are equally able to do so.

Another line of criticism questions whether honor is even important in everyday life. Brandes suggests that in some areas, such as the Arabic Mediterranean and Greece, people focus on honor, while other groups focus on shame (1987: 123). Several authors working in Spain hold that the term "honor" is virtually obsolete, while "shame" is frequently used in natural conversation throughout rural and urban areas (Lever 1986: 85; Brandes 1987: 128). Even concerning the Arabic Mediterranean, Wikan (1984) argues that, at least in Cairo, shame is the primary concern in everyday life. *ʿÊb* (shame) is the word which is constantly heard among the poor in the back streets of Cairo. People use it "unselfconsciously, as it were colloquially." Shame is thus an experience-near concept. Honor, on the other hand, is an experience-distant concept, one, that is, "which specialists of one sort or another, . . . an ethnographer, or . . . an ideologist employ" (Geertz 1983: 57–58).[1] Wikan suggests that in Egypt, and probably in many areas of the Mediterranean, honor is bound up with male ideology and is not on a par with shame (1984: 638). As will become clear, people's discourse with regard to female entertainment in Egypt also centers on shame, *ʿêb*. The observation of Wikan that shame is of overriding importance in people's daily discourse is not merely a terminological argument. As Wikan notes, *ʿêb* refers to actions, not to people. Honor is thought of as an attribute of the whole person (1984: 637). A person who displays shameful conduct has not totally fallen into disgrace; only part of his or her behavior is criticized. As also Brandes observes in Spain shame is attributed to concrete actions and events that have occurred in the immediate past. It is transitory and only affects one's reputation over the long run (1987: 122). The fact that shame is a thing of the moment should be borne in mind in order to understand that the lower-middle class does not totally reject female entertainers. For instance, the fact that many popular female entertainers have married men outside the profession, especially after they stopped working, reflects the transitory state of their shame.

Two other points should be made. First, the study of Abu Lughod not only shows the unequal ability of women and young men to realize the ideals of independence, strength, and freedom, it also underlines the importance of being sensitive to the different ways such people use to express their sentiments. The less powerful express their divergent views on the honor code—their dissatisfaction with it and other feelings which cannot be expressed in public discourse—in a veiled way through the use of poetry. Second, Wikan stresses the importance of taking the nature of the public into account. She calls for identification of those who are regarded by different categories of persons as their "significant others" and thus constitute their "society." If honor and shame pertain to the value of people not only in their own eyes but also in the eyes of their society, it should be carefully studied who is judging them as honorable or shameful. For women in Sohar (Oman), Wikan argues that in the eyes of a woman's male associates, her husband and kinsmen, honor might be dependent on her sexual integrity, but among her female associates other qualities, such as hospitality and loyalty, are the values by which she is measured (1984: 645). The same argument can be made with regard to socioeconomic or class background. In Greece, for instance, a family's honor is not necessarily diminished if its female members perform agricultural labor "when public opinion recognizes the necessity of it" (Herzfeld 1980: 342). A lower-class audience might see the necessity of having female family members work and consequently judge it as respectable, while middle-class people might call it shameful. The most significant groups to deny or ascribe honor to Egyptian entertainers, as noted in the previous chapter, are the lower and lower-middle classes. They are the entertainers' "significant others" and constitute their society.

It is thus important to analyze carefully how concepts are defined by the people under study. Or, as Pina-Cabral proposes: "We have to learn to do without universalistic categories [and] rely more directly on the indigenous categories and think . . . in terms of these. This means that we need historically informed and regionally specific processes of contextualization" (1989: 403). By using the approach of contextualization, we can see that some societies primarily focus on honor whereas others center on shame. Even within one country there can be regional differences, as the studies of Abu Lughod and Wikan show. While the Egyptian Bedouins' discourse concentrates on honor, the Cairene poor are concerned with shame. It should also be noticed that within one social group there may be various definitions of honor and shame or diverse ways of expressing values, notably deriving from distinctions in power and wealth and from gender differences.

Finally, the approach of contextualization makes clear that the assumption of binary classification is not tenable in all contexts. It is not simply that honor is not to shame as men are to women. Both studies on Egypt reveal that the two concepts are not in a relation of structural opposition at all. Abu Lughod shows that shame is *part* of the honor code of the weak. Wikan argues that these concepts are derived from dissimilar types of discourses—that is, from experience-near, indigenous categories versus ideological, experience-distant classifications—and that they are therefore not structurally related or opposed. As argued in Chapter 1, in my view, experience-distant concepts can be useful if they are demonstrably founded on experience-near concepts, whether distilled from words, sayings, proverbs, jokes, images, or behavior. Yet to state that people classify in terms of binary oppositions such as honor versus shame is to assume the very thing that should be the object of study.

The approach of contextualization thus calls for careful specification of how concepts such as honor and shame are defined and by whom. Honor and shame, and other concepts as well, are social constructs that can have different meanings according to the time, place, context, class, and gender of the judge and the judged. The next section investigates how different groups of people evaluate the diverse types and contexts of performances and which concepts are involved in their judgment.

ENTERTAINMENT AND SHAME

The first reaction of the people I interviewed on various types and contexts of entertainment ranged from very negative to mildly positive. The strongest, particularly religious, terms of condemnation they used are taboo (*ḥarâm*), diabolic, sinful, blameworthy (*makrûh*), and shameful (*ʿawra*).[2] According to a *sheikh*, a religious leader, all forms of female entertainment are *ḥarâm*, and all female entertainers will go to hell. Even those who talk about it will burn! Other strong moral terms are "corrupt," "indecent," "immodest," "immoral," "deviant," "outrageous," and "seductive." Yet the most common reaction is "*ʿêb!*," "Shame!" A tailor talking about female entertainers—singers and particularly dancers—said: "Those jobs are shameful and detestable. I don't like it . . . but I do like to watch it. Once in a lifetime we invite them; it is *ḥarâm*, but the fault is theirs." However, reactions were also expressed at times in morally neutral terms—for example, "They are poor and pitiable people" and "It is a livelihood." Several people even acknowledged the positive aspects of singers and dancers at weddings and said that they enliven the party and bring a happy and merry atmosphere. With regard to the arts performed in theaters, most informants agreed that it is valuable and beyond dispute. As an upper-class boy summarized: "Art and entertainment are a two-edged sword; they can be great or they can be awful."

In order to investigate people's ideas on entertainment in general, and on the different forms and contexts of performances in particular, I used a set of cards. I made thirty cards on which the names of various types of workers were written. These ranged from workers in white-collar professions, such as civil servants and officers, to blue-collar workers, such as garbage collectors and cleaning women, to those in traditional trades, such as matchmakers and mourners. Half of the cards pertained to workers in different forms and contexts of entertainment and art. I asked fifty people to arrange the cards, according to their view, from good to bad professions, starting with the best one at the top.[3] In general, cards with white-collar professionals were put at the top, followed by cards with workers in the professional performing arts circuit. Next came cards with blue-collar workers, and finally cards with those in the traditional trades, performers at weddings and saint's day celebrations, and nightclub entertainers. However, if the view of the different classes is taken into account, the picture changes slightly. The upper and upper-middle classes usually did not distinguish between the jobs in the last two categories, considering them all mediocre or low trades. The lower and lower-middle classes generally differentiated the blue-collar jobs from entertainers working at weddings and saint's day celebrations. They were generally milder in their evaluation, and fewer professions, particularly for men, were viewed as bad. With regard to art and entertainment, most people ordered the cards according to three criteria: the context of the performance, the form of the entertainment, and the sex of the artist.

In judging the three possible contexts of a performance—the art circuit of theaters, the nightclub circuit, and the circuit of weddings and saint's day celebrations—most people agreed that, especially for women, working in a nightclub is the worst. In particular, lower-class and lower-middle-class people who had never entered a nightclub had a negative opinion of them. Their ideas were mainly based on the old image of *fatḥ*, the time that singers and dancers sat and drank with customers. Although *fatḥ* has been abolished, the image is kept alive by way of old films featuring nightclub scenes and belly dancers which are regularly broadcast on television. Only some upper-class people who occasionally visit nightclubs preferred nightclub performers to entertainers of Muḥammad ʿAlî Street, because their artistic level is higher. Yet in the view of most informants, nightclub entertainers are improper because they are

FIGURE 9

A Muḥammad ʿAlî Street singer.

hidden in disreputable places, whereas Muḥammad ʿAlî Street performers are visible and "work in front of the people." One of my informants explained that men cannot visit nightclubs with their families, which is the touchstone for respectability. Her husband joined in, saying that respectable families go to Muḥammad ʿAlî Street to contract with singers

FIGURE 10

The candelabra dance performed in a folk-dance show at a hotel.

and dancers for their weddings, not to Pyramid Street, the street where the nightclubs are located.

There are many grounds for the stronger suspicion of nightclubs. Some things that happen in nightclubs—mainly pertaining to money, alcohol, and sex—are not just shameful but entirely *ḥarâm*, taboo. Nightclub performers are perceived as extremely greedy. "They want apartments, big cars, and jewels, whereas those on Muḥammad ʿAli Street are poor," a housewife explained. The conduct not only of enter-

FIGURE 11

A theater performance of whirling dervishes.

tainers is criticized, but also that of their customers. A taxi driver, who regularly drives Saudi tourists to Pyramid Street and watches the shows with them, remarked: "The customers show how much money they have and the women show their flesh, that's all." According to several people, customers who show off by hanging necklaces of money around a dancer or throwing hundreds of pounds over the head of an admired singer have no respect for money. "If they lavish pounds that easily, the money must have come from forbidden practices; otherwise they would not spend money like water," one informant said.

Not only the sums of money which are thrown away are a thorn in

FIGURE 12

A folk singer with male dancers from Upper Egypt.

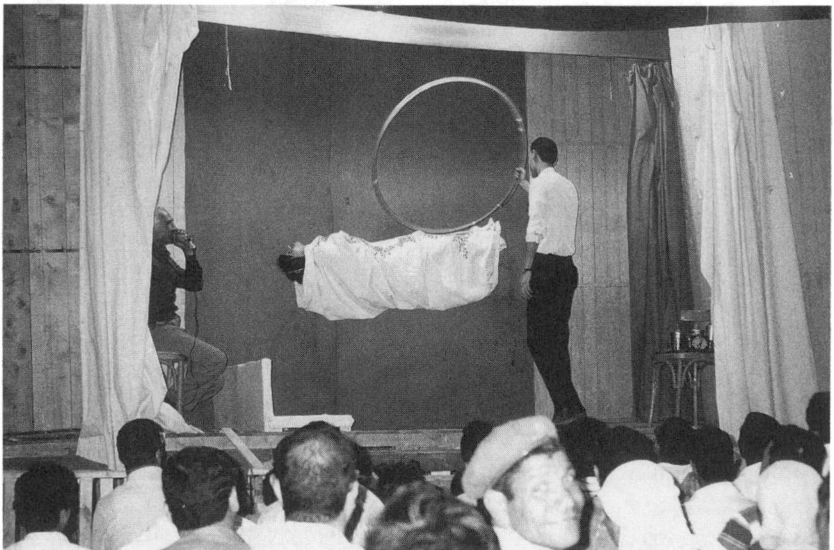

FIGURE 13

The act of the flying lady performed at a saint's day celebration.

FIGURE 14

Young women working at a wedding procession.

the side of the less well-off, but also the way tips are earned is frowned upon. Nightclub performers are depicted as doing everything in order to increase their tips; it is a "sheer rip-off" and has nothing to do with art in the eyes of most Egyptians. The performers are regarded as flatterers and hypocrites. They flatter, compliment, and extensively thank the tip giver in order to stimulate competition among customers. This holds true at weddings as well. Yet at weddings the compliments and congratulations are part of the celebration and not sheer hypocrisy. More important, the tips are part of a reciprocal process and are not solely induced by flattering entertainers—the tip giver gives the amount equivalent to the sum the host has given at his wedding. Moreover, in the past and increasingly at present, the tips are gathered by the host and not by the entertainers.

Alcohol is another factor people mention to characterize the low and immoral practices in nightclubs. It stimulates the generosity of the customers and thus adds to the clubs' rip-off image. Although *fatḥ* has been abolished, in the minds of most people there is still a strong connection between nightclubs and drinking. And even though the guests at weddings in the street also drink beer and smoke hashish, it is considered less typical and less necessary for enjoyment than alcohol in nightclubs. People who visit nightclubs are seen as mainly interested in getting drunk and excited, while guests at weddings first and foremost come to congratulate and pay their respects to the members of the wedding. Entertainers are thus considered flatterers by profession, but nightclub performers are more severely attacked for hypocrisy and dishonesty.

The way female performers earn tips, however, becomes very dishonorable. They not only flatter customers by nice words and compliments, but excite them through their revealing costumes and alluring dresses. Nightclub dancers, in particular, are viewed as bewitching the customers with their enticing bodies. Most people believe that singers and dancers working at weddings and saint's day celebrations, since they work with their husbands and relatives, go home after a performance. They strongly doubt that nightclub dancers do so. The huge tips nightclub performers receive are usually thought of as advance payment for sexual services after the performance. Another suspicion strongly directed at female nightclub performers is that they sleep not only with generous customers but also with the owners and managers of the clubs, in order to be guaranteed work. In the eyes of many Egyptians, female nightclub performers are thus mere prostitutes.

Whereas people characterize nightclubs as scenes of excitement, dishonesty, and drunkenness, they see weddings primarily as expressions of happiness connected to family occasions. Because of this, people view the same behavior of performers differently in the two contexts. A female entertainer who shakes hands, talks, and dances with the men of the couple's family at a wedding is congratulating and complimenting the families, whereas the same conduct on the part of a nightclub dancer is perceived as making a rendezvous. At weddings, for instance, a dancer occasionally performs in front of the couple and puts their hands on her belly and breasts while she rolls her belly and moves her breasts. I expected this to be considered outrageous behavior. Yet several people explained that it was innocent merriment and fun (*farfasha*).[4] A nightclub dancer who exhibited the same behavior, lacking the context of a happy occasion and working in an atmosphere of sexual excitement, would be considered prostituting herself to earn money. At weddings, people have good reasons for celebrating, while going to nightclubs is suspect. The distinction in the respectability of the two circuits also reflects on the entertainers. It is more respectable to make people happy than to excite drunken customers. Whereas singers and dancers working at weddings increase people's happiness about a marriage, nightclub performers stimulate "bad intentions and desires" on the part of customers.

There are two other contexts which I must mention: the art circuit of theaters, conservatories, radio, and television; and the religious context of saint's day celebrations. Theaters are generally considered respectable, and the nightclubs of five-star hotels, which are closely related to the higher levels of fine arts, are prestigious as well. However, particularly actresses[5] and female folk dancers are still regarded with ambivalence, despite the respectable context they work in. There are various opinions about saint's day celebrations. Upper- and middle-class people have only a vague notion about what *mawâlid* are and usually lump them with weddings in the streets because both belong to the lower classes. Lower-class and lower-middle-class people, who have a clearer understanding of saint's day celebrations, sometimes put the card for saint's day entertainers under that of wedding performers, because in their view the artistic level of saint's day performers is lower. Besides, *mawâlid* should be religious occasions with *zikrs* and other religious celebrations. Singing, particularly the praise songs, are seen as compatible with the devout atmosphere. Dancers, however, are considered out of place and strongly condemned.

The second line along which people arranged the cards was according to the form of entertainment. In general, music was considered the most respectable art form, followed by singing, acting, folk dancing, and, finally, belly dancing. Music was considered respectable for women because female musicians usually work in an orchestra or a music ensemble. Female musicians performing at weddings have vanished, and they rarely work in nightclubs. Their present working conditions are thus respectable. Besides, they usually completed an education in music and are thus "learned women." Moreover, in theological discussions on art and entertainment, music is the least under attack.

Singing, which takes place in various contexts, is much more dubious. It is generally acceptable for men to sing, although if done in nightclubs it also taints their reputations. For female singers, it heavily depends on where they perform and on the content of their songs. Singing for radio and television is respectable, but singing at weddings and in nightclubs, although better than dancing, is questionable. Female singers are generally perceived as more respectable than dancers, because they are more properly dressed and because they do not move. Yet, even female singers are first assessed with an eye to their appearance and only secondarily for their voice. As a young woman remarked: "A female singer at a wedding is also not good. Men at the party are interested in how she moves and what she wears, not in how she sings. For male singers it is no problem—they don't move."

In strict religious opinion, female singers are *ḥarâm*. The saying of the Prophet, "ṣawt al-mar'a ʿawra," "The voice of women is a shameful thing," is often used to discredit female singers.[6] Listening to the voice of women can evoke tempting images. For that reason a *sheikh* I spoke to even claimed that listening to the voice of a woman on the telephone is unlawful. If female singers are concealed, as used to be the case in the past, they could still seduce the male audience. Presently, they are visible and therefore considered even more seductive, because excitement aroused by looking is considered more powerful than excitement aroused by listening.

Because it is thought that excitement is more strongly aroused by the eye rather than the ear, female dancers are considered more shameful than female musicians or female singers (see Chapter 1). Dancers' gravest transgression of the norms is the fact that they move. According to some informants, a singer is less shameful because she is not moving, though others say she is shameful because she also moves.[7] The central point is the perception of the extent to which the female entertainer moves. When I asked a *sheikh* whether female folk dancers are less *ḥarâm*, he resolutely replied: "No, they also move."

Yet not all people reason according to strict religious principles. Although all dancers move, for most people how they move and how they are dressed are the deciding factors. Folk dancers are therefore considered more proper because their movements are trained and their bodies are by and large concealed. As a woman from the south explained: "In Europe, men and women dance in the same way. If my husband and I watch a folk dancer, our view is the same, but if we watch a belly dancer then he will look at her body, whether it is beautiful, whether it is white." She regarded belly dancing as an expression of femininity and female sexuality.

There is another important view of dancing in general and of the *baladî* dance—that is, the nonstylized belly dance—in particular, as an expression of rejoicing and happiness. "Dancing is happiness and at weddings people dance out of rejoicing. Even people who never dance, the happiness in their hearts makes them stand up and dance the *baladî* dance. It's a sudden joy they can't resist," a man explained. A housewife related her ambivalent feelings after responding to a sudden feeling of happiness at her brother's wedding: "I love dancing, but I only dance at the weddings of people who are very dear to me, like my brother or my son. I danced at the wedding of my brother in a club. The feeling of happiness inside me made me forget myself. Afterward, I didn't feel comfortable—it's not proper to dance when strangers are present. . . . I don't go to a wedding with the intention of dancing—on the contrary—but with the wedding procession and everything you are so happy inside that you have to express the feeling." According to a tolerant *sheikh*, the mother of the bride is allowed to express her irrepressible feelings of happiness in dancing. Girls and women who dance at weddings, however, should wear respectable clothes and move within proper limits.

Professional dancers performing at weddings, although they interpret and bring out people's happiness, transgress these limits. However, they are regarded as necessary to enliven the party. I witnessed several times how, for instance, Ibtisâm brought a merry atmosphere to a dull group around the bride and groom by making the mothers and sisters of the couple dance. Yet wearing a revealing costume and dancing with male guests easily changes the nature of the happiness into sensual pleasure. This sensuality is even more pronounced with belly dancers in nightclubs—they merely "excite and seduce." Although the *baladî* dance is essentially an expression of happiness, if it is done professionally for money with revealing clothes and in a sultry atmosphere, it takes on the meaning familiar in the West, that of eroticism and sexuality.

The third line along which people arranged the cards was according to the sex of the performer. Ordinarily in the eyes of lower- and lower-middle-class people it is not shameful for men to work as singers or musicians at weddings. "Nothing is shameful for men" is the expression commonly used to voice this distinction. It is not totally correct, though. For men there is also a difference according to the context of a performance. In the higher circles of fine art, the gender difference is generally least important in people's evaluation. Men have more esteem, but women are respected as well. It is especially in the circuit of weddings that the gender distinction is significant. Working at weddings brings no moral stigma to men—it is a trade, although not a highly esteemed one—but for women it is shameful. Yet working in nightclubs is not very proper for men as well as for women. The vices attributed to nightclubs partly apply to male performers as well—that is, the greed for money and the use of alcohol. Female performers are blamed, though, for the gravest sins: sexual excitement and prostitution.

Similar distinctions along gender lines can be perceived with regard to the form of entertainment. Instrumental music is relatively gender-neutral, but in singing it makes a crucial difference whether the singer is male or female. Men are evaluated on their voices and skills, but female singers are primarily assessed for their physical attributes and only secondarily for their talents as singers.[8] This standard is even more pronounced in the case of dancers. There are no male belly dancers anymore—only male folk dancers in theaters and in wedding processions exist. They are not highly esteemed, yet this is not on account of their immorality but because they do "women's work." In general, as the above-quoted woman stated, male performers do not move. And even if they do, they are not seen as having exciting bodies. I once asked a *sheikh* why male dancing is not *ḥarâm*. The answer was easy: "A man's body is not shameful [*ʿawra*]," and regardless of how it moves and shakes, "it cannot excite."

THE ENTERTAINERS' CODE OF HONOR

It is not surprising that entertainers refute public opinion by stressing their honor, respectability, morals, and good manners. They actively defend themselves against the accusations of shameful behavior and low morality. They are conscious of their status and concerned with their dignity and self-respect. They usually point out that entertainment is a trade like any other, and in general a respectable one. Yet often they are on the defensive. Female entertainers frequently justify themselves by emphasizing that they bear responsibility for relatives and children. As Ibtisâm said: "If I did not dance, then maybe my children would have to dance." It is no shame to work for the sake of the children's education and well-being. In addition, they present themselves as strong, fearless persons, "as tough as men," who are not to be taken for easy-going weak women.[9] Another general legitimation for the entertainment profession is that it makes people happy. A former *usṭâ* said: "How can our profession be shameful? We make people happy! Someone is going to marry. Why should this happen in silence? People want to enjoy themselves. God provides everyone with a livelihood; everyone works for a decent piaster. God created us to make people happy." For this reason she did not consider the profession to be *ḥarâm*.

Most female performers, however, are aware that, strictly speaking, their activities are sinful, and they are concerned about the afterlife. "*Rabbina yitôb ʿalêna*," "May God forgive us," is often heard from those working, while those who have stopped performing often sigh, *"tôbt lillâh,"* "I've repented." The neighbor of the Madbaḥ family, for instance, related that at the time she was working she often exclaimed: *"rabbina yitôb ʿalayya, ya rabb,"* "May God forgive me, O Lord." But since it was her "bread and salt" she had to keep on working. "Five years ago, I repented," she continued. "Praise be to God!" The Madbaḥ family joined in with a hearty "Praise be to God!" Dancer Mona was troubled by her sins. She decided that dancing invalidated her prayers and stopped this religious duty. After repentance she intends to resume praying. Others related that they prayed before performing and purified themselves after work. They expressed the hope that God in his omniscience will judge people by their inner selves and will forgive their outer activities. A singer from Muḥammad ʿAlî Street said: "For Muslims it is forbidden to reveal your body, but we do not know who will go to heaven or to hell. Maybe a dancer does a good deed which gives her absolution." Some made the pilgrimage to Mecca and were absolved of their sins. A singer from Mansûra was not so lucky. She intended to stop working and made the pilgrimage, but unfortunately she was forced to start singing again and thus invalidated the remission of her sins.

Most female performers thus resign themselves to their fate of doing things contrary to Islam because entertainment is their only livelihood. Yet the Islamic fundamentalists find little favor in their eyes. "It is easy for them to talk—they have better jobs. May God make things easy for them, but I am one of those who have to earn money from dancing," Ibtisâm said. Bûḥa bitterly exclaimed: "Fundamentalists say that we do things against our religion, but we eat from our work. I raise my children from it. . . . Let them provide us with another job, with enough to pay for the school and all the other expenses for my children. I struggle for them."

Facing God, they can only hope for his mercy, but when facing people they can defend their claim to honor. Although it is difficult to deny their religious transgressions, they can and do strongly defend themselves against accusations of shameful behavior. The older generation in particular held that the profession may be *ḥarâm*, but is not *ʿêb*, shameful. In addition to their general legitimation of being responsible, tough women who make people happy, the different groups of female entertainers used various strategies to whitewash their tainted reputation.

According to the Muḥammad ʿAlî Street performers, in the past their trade was respectable and entertainers were respected. In particular the *ʿawâlim* who only sang and danced in front of women were honorable, and no one could accuse them of indecency. But the entertainers who performed for men also used to be bound by rules of proper conduct. The older generation of Muḥammad ʿAlî Street performers shared a code of honor. Since in the past they formed a community of cooperating families, there was strict social control. As a result of their sense of community, their reputation was considered to be tarnished by misconduct on the part of any one of them. *Usṭâ* Zeinab from the Madbaḥ family clearly stated that if one of her performers misbehaved, her reputation was also tainted: "The girl I bring with me must be respectable, because if she is humiliated I am humiliated as well. As the saying goes, 'The slave has the standard of his master.' " If a performer misbehaved, she could be refused work.

Some rules of honor applied to all performers. Accepting food at a party, for instance, was disgraceful for all performers. The mother of the bride or groom usually prepared food for all the guests and offered a plate of it to the entertainers before the performance. Although it was a sign of respect from the side of the hosting family, most performers said it was shameful to eat at a party and claimed that they refused the offered food. Umm Sayyid once explained that there used to be much respect for performers and that they were always offered food. Zûba interrupted her and said: "Not all performers accept the food. We, if we could eat salt at home we would not eat the meat at the wedding, impossible. We are not such types." Zûba continued by explaining that otherwise people might think that entertainers are hungry and poor, an impression they like to avoid. I attended a wedding near Manṣûra and observed that most performers accepted the food.[10] Only one singer refused because, as she later explained, it is shameful to eat at the party: "I have a home to eat in." She only accepted a cup of tea. Eating and drinking during work was also not proper except for a cup of tea or, for men, a cigarette. Female performers were scolded if they smoked and were fined if they drank beer on stage.

Most rules defined proper relations between female performers and men, both male colleagues and customers. Although there was a relatively free association between male and female performers, work relationships differed from the atmosphere of the home. A nonrelated entertainer was not allowed to enter the house. Whenever there was work, a messenger boy was sent to the performer with advance money. He was not received inside but waited at the door. At work, male colleagues had to guard and protect the women on their way to work and when they went home. A singer from the community related that "Uncle Ḥenkish," Sayyid's father, always called a taxi for her and made sure that the driver took her safely home. He did not allow "his daughter" to talk with people after the performance because this was shameful. She had to return home immediately. The parties were said to be without drunkenness and quarrels, "people were sitting like roses," and there was no danger of theft and kidnapping. If there was trouble, the women were protected by their colleagues. Zûba, for instance, related how she once went to a party with Sayyid's father. While she was dancing onstage, a customer asked her to come with him. Sayyid's father became enraged and shouted at the man: "Do you think I'm a pimp? You son of a dog, get off the stage."

The *usṭâwât*, the leaders, also kept a close eye on the women's conduct toward customers. They guarded the women, and whenever they behaved improperly they were fined or beaten. A former performer told me a story about the punishment she received from her *usṭâ*: "I remember once I was singing in Alexandria. A man got on the stage and wanted to dance with me. The *usṭâ* told him to leave the stage, but he refused. I was told to sit in my chair and to keep my self-respect. She cursed me and beat me up in front of the people because I had accepted his invitation to dance." The women were allowed to laugh and talk with the musicians but not with strangers. *Usṭâ* Zeinab described a respectable performer as follows:

> She does not accept a cigarette or beer. She works and sits in her chair afterward. She respects herself and does not talk with customers or ask them, "Give me a water pipe," or "Give me hash." That causes trouble. If a girl is impolite and does not respect herself on the stage, then I'll beat her. If she is doing dirty things, I'll send her away. If there is a tough guy, and I accept a cigarette, beer and then hash, and we talk together, the whole evening I dance for him . . . that becomes an affair. . . . It is better to stop bad things at the beginning.

It was thus not respectable to talk, laugh, or dance with customers. Receiving tips was, of course, part of the performer's job, but it was bound by rules of honor as well. Allowing men to put money in the costume was dishonorable. It should be placed in the hand. *Tashnîb*, begging or going round collecting money with a tambourine, was also considered disgraceful. The type of costume female performers wore was another factor which could increase or decrease their claim to honor. Most of the older generation stated that they did not wear costumes but a dress that did not reveal their bellies and thighs. Finally, the profession has certain age limits for women and it is considered shameful to work if well on in years. The age at which a woman should stop depends on her attractiveness and is slightly older for singers. But as all female performers are eventually evaluated on their appearance, they should stop if their beauty fades, lest they become an *aragûz*, an object of mockery.

Members of the older generation safeguarded their reputation, at least within their own community, by adhering to the code of honor. These rules were not very different from those of the general public, although their working conditions made it necessary to liberalize them. According to their code of honor, it was not immoral to perform publicly for men as long as no personal relations were established with them. Dancing was not bad if it was done in a proper way and in a modest dress. Earning money from the trade was not bad—it was a necessity—but it had to be collected in a respectable way. The older generation claims that, in comparison with the past, the level of their art has been lowered and the code of honor lost. Since the market is overflowing with *khashânâ*, "intruders," the beauty and respect of the old days are gone. "The present girls dance as if they have stomach cramps," Zûba snorted. "We used to be honored to say that we were dancers," another former performer said, "but today dancers accept business cards from customers, they get drunk and go home with the men, *ḥarâm*!" According to Sayyida Madbaḥ, the expression *yabn il-ra'âṣa*, son of a dancer, used to be a joke, but it has become a strong term of abuse. "Muḥammad ʿAlî Street has become a brothel," Bûḥa voiced.

The code of honor has apparently changed. Although the older generation surely represents the past as being better than it was, the accounts about rules, social control, fines, and beatings are highly consistent. Also, some younger entertainers admit that the trade has deteriorated and have doubts about their own work. When the older generation describes the "intruders" as "rotten apples that should be removed before they contaminate the others," this might be understood as a conflict of generations. However, the loss of respectability can be considered less questionable because the present generation mentions it as well. Bûḥa's co-wife Baṭṭa, for instance, has worked in theaters in Syria and Jordan. When she came back she started working at weddings. She related:

> At the time I came here, I was not able to work at weddings. I was used to the audience of the theater. They are quiet and respectable. But here it is noisy and . . . not on a refined level. In the theater, I had the idea that I was dancing in a good and beautiful way and that I did not have to make certain movements like I do here, just to be asked again. The weddings force me to make certain movements . . . and to dance with men. . . . I remember the first time I was working with Samia. She danced before me and every time I saw a vulgar movement in her dance I sweated with embarrassment. . . . But I got used to it.

Her housemate Zizi explained that at saint's day celebrations they are their own masters and can do what they like. If there are no police officers around they voluntarily wear more revealing costumes than usual. I asked her why they like to wear such costumes. She replied: "We are women like any others. They only buy tickets if they can see our legs." A performer from Alexandria said that flirting with men, accepting their business cards, and allowing money to be put in the costume were normal business practices: "Such is our job."

Most performers, however, acknowledge the indecent practices of the trade but clearly dissociate themselves from them. There is a tendency among most female performers to claim dignity and respect for themselves by way of blackening someone else's reputation. Just as the older generation claims respectability by blaming the "intruders," members of the younger generation blame each other for the bad reputation of the trade. ʿAida, the dancer I saw at my first wedding, accused Zizi of continuously lifting her skirt. She felt embarrassed and once grabbed her. According to ʿAida, Zizi did not have enough concern for her reputation and that of others. Singers often blame dancers for their low morality and revealing costumes and consider themselves more respectable. "As long as I am singing and wearing a dress with half-length sleeves, I am not doing a shameful thing," a singer said. Folk dancers accuse belly dancers of spoiling the reputation of dancing. ʿAbîr, a folk dancer from Minyâ, said: "Folk dance has respectable movements and decent clothing. Belly dancers are shameful. Certain movements are whorish and their dresses are vulgar. Dancing and shaking is already shameful in Egypt, but in a revealing costume it becomes very bad. You could at least remove one bad thing by dressing properly like we do." Finally, Muḥammad ʿAlî Street performers accuse nightclub entertainers of tarnishing the profession and the latter blame the entertainers of Muḥammad ʿAlî Street for the cheap entertainment and their low morality.

Corresponding to the growing individualization of the trade, the adherence to norms of proper conduct is individualized. The present generation is concerned increasingly with personal self-respect and less with that of the group as a whole. Mona, a Muḥammad ʿAlî Street dancer, said: "If another dancer wears a revealing costume, it is not my business. She has her style and I have mine. I cannot advise her, because she will think I am jealous. So I keep out of it. Others can drink or smoke a water pipe. I don't care. I have my work. If someone offers me a drink and I tell him that I don't drink, he respects me more. At the next party when he sees me again, I am different from the others for him." In accordance with the concept of shame, *ʿêb*—that is, *ʿêb* pertains to shameful acts and not the person as a whole—a singer from Ṭanṭâ said: "Entertainment is not shameful. It only becomes shameful if someone does a shameful thing. The view of the people and their gossip are not important to me. People are never pleased. If you wear torn clothes they gossip, and if you wear clean clothes they ask where you got them from. The most important thing is that I am convinced that my work is not shameful."

The attitude of nightclub entertainers toward honor and shame differs from that of the older performers working at weddings and saint's day celebrations. Common professional ethics have never existed among them. From the start, they had a personal approach and often say: "There are women who do this or that, but I don't do such things." Nightclub performers, like the younger generation on Muḥammad ʿAlî Street, thus mainly have an individualized notion of honor and shame. They often blacken the reputation of their colleagues. Especially the talented performers strongly object to those working in cheap clubs and accuse them of prostitution. The working conditions of female entertainers working in five-star clubs, and particularly of those performing in nightclubs of five-star hotels, are less compromising. They usually claim respectability on account of their artistic level. Those at the cheaper clubs, however, say that in order to keep one's honor one must show strength of will and self-respect. They are exposed to many temptations and it depends on the strength of their will whether they give in or not. It depends on the female entertainer whether she allows the tips to be put in her costume or not, whether she accepts tissues with addresses or not, and whether she dances on the tables of Saudis or not. Yet they are under pressure to put up with impolite customers. Whereas the talented women at five-star clubs can refuse money if men try to put it in their costumes, those at the cheaper nightclubs can easily be fired if they show such willpower.

For those at the bottom of the "hierarchy of shame"—dancers, particularly those in the cheaper nightclubs—it is even more difficult to project an image of respectability as a performer. They consequently develop two different personalities, one for their home life and the other for their work. Magda, for instance, said: "In this profession you are exposed to greediness, covetousness, and temptation. You need a strong will to resist. Sometimes people challenge me and say, how can you work in a nightclub? I tell them that I'm like a clown: when I'm on the stage I can do anything, but as soon as I leave the stage I change completely. During work I do anything I please, I accept beer and whiskey . . . but at home I don't even smoke." Karîma as well claims to have "two personalities or even more." She admits to flirting with men and making "impolite movements" which give men the impression that they can sleep with her. Nevertheless, she has her own professional ethics: "The dancer tries to make men happy. For instance, if I see a customer who is angry or bored, then I try to give him the smile he needs. Some dancers only smile at men with money—I smile at all. Once there was a man who apologized because he did not have money. I told him that it did not matter and I danced for him as for all the others. The next day he specially returned to bring me a tip and to thank me. I earn my money in a respectable way . . . , you don't need to take the wrong path." The performers of the cheaper clubs thus implicitly acknowledge their indecent working conditions. Yet, since they have split personalities and manage to keep even the compromised part clean as a result of their willpower, they view themselves as respectable individuals within a shameful trade.

With regard to the central question, it is evident that although entertainment is not generally viewed as dishonorable, it is a dishonorable profession for women. Men are excused by the widely used expression, "whatever a man does, nothing is shameful for him." This does not mean that the trade is very honorable for men, but rather indicates that male entertainment activities are evaluated less in moral terms. Female entertainers, however, are mainly viewed in terms of respectability and shame. Returning to the various "infamous" occupations as distinguished by Blok, the relevant category with regard to performers is the one pertaining to people "who publicly exhibit their bodies for profit" (1985: 34). It has become clear that in terms of the Egyptian context this definition needs specification, since there the crucial aspect of dishonor appeared to be the exhibition of the female body. Whereas the female body is apparently thought of as easily exciting men, the male body is an ordinary instrument used to earn a livelihood. Whereas the male body is neutral, the female body is shameful. Male entertainers thus earn profit by way of exhibiting skills, while female entertainers exhibit their exciting bodies, by means of which they earn a shameful living. Why the female body is viewed as exciting and shameful will be elaborated upon in the next chapter.

SEVEN

GENDER

In the first section of this chapter, I discuss the concept of gender and the notion of the cultural construction of femininity, masculinity, and sexuality (Ortner and Whitehead 1981; Caplan 1987). Gender will be used as a heuristic notion, and it will be assumed that in order to find out what femininity and masculinity mean they should be investigated within a specific context. The notion of the seemingly natural body will also be dealt with as a cultural construction. In the second section, the diverse ways in which femaleness and maleness are defined and the notion of the body will be examined in the Egyptian context. In the last section, I explore the ways in which female entertainers contradict the dominant ideas on femininity. I subsequently answer the question raised in Chapter 1 as to whether female entertainers are viewed as disturbers of the moral order and whether they are feared for their rebellious nature.

SEX AND GENDER

A recurrent theme in feminist anthropology is the sexual asymmetry encountered in most if not all societies (Rosaldo 1980). Although the studies focusing on women's roles and activities show that women are sometimes powerful, it often has to be concluded that they play a subordinate role in certain respects, whether in the economic, social, political, or symbolic field. Universal male dominance has been explained, for instance, by the nature/culture model and by the domestic/public distinction. In "Is Female to Male as Nature is to Culture?" (1974), Ortner argues that women's secondary status is due to the fact that their physiology and reproductive functions are closely associated with something every culture devalues—that is, nature. The domestic versus public model, although focusing on women's activities rather than on symbolic associations, is based on a similar argument. Rosaldo explains women's universal subordination by the structural opposition between the "domestic" orientation of women—that is, their role as mothers and rearers of children—and the "extra-domestic" or public ties that are primarily available to men (1974: 17–18). Since the public domain generally subsumes the domestic sphere, women's activities are considered less important than men's.

The domestic/public distinction, like that of nature/culture, is thus ultimately based on women's reproductive functions. Both universalistic analyses thus approach the pitfalls feminist anthropologists seek to avoid; that is, they still perceive women as a biological category. The point here is not to criticize these models in detail (see, e.g., MacCormack 1980; Brown and Jordanova 1981; Moore 1988), but to indicate the link between such universal approaches and biological explanations. Universal approaches toward the asymmetry between the sexes assume that women in all times and places share certain characteristics which make them subordinate. Whereas the growing numbers of ethnographic accounts of women demonstrate the differences among women and the great variability in female power and social activities, the universal approaches assume the sameness and unity of women as a category. This raises the question as to what these unifying characteristics could be, given the cross-cultural variations, other than women's biological features. Universalistic explanations still stick to essentialist notions of womanhood.

The understanding of the inherently problematic nature of "the category of women" and of universalistic approaches resulted in a shift of focus from the sameness and unity of women to differences among them and from universal models to specific analyses. There was the realization that we cannot be assumed to know what the category of women and the notions of femininity and masculinity mean. If they are regarded not as natural entities or biological givens but as cultural constructions, their meanings should be investigated within specific contexts. This train of thought has led to diverse analyses in different fields of women's studies. I follow the track of gender as a way of escaping the biological determinism of women.

The concept of gender was introduced in feminist anthropology in 1975 by Rubin. She argues: "Gender is a socially imposed division of the sexes. . . . Men and women are, of course, different. But they are not as different as day and night, earth and sky, yin and yang, life and death. In fact, from the standpoint of nature, men and women are closer to each other than either is to anything else—for instance, mountains, kangaroos, or coconut palms. The idea that men and women are more different from one another than either is from anything else must come from somewhere other than nature" (1975: 179). Rubin developed the "sex/gender system" which she defines as "the set of arrangements by which a society transforms biological sexuality into products of human activity, and in which these transformed sexual needs are satisfied" (1975: 159). She thus provides an analytic concept to differentiate the biological category of sex from the socially and culturally constructed notion of gender.

Ethnographic studies in the field of feminist anthropology demonstrate the variabilities in the sex/gender system and the diverse notions of femininity and masculinity in different cultural systems. The degree to which cultures have elaborated notions of femininity and masculinity in itself varies. The concept of manhood might be highly developed, whereas that of womanhood might be relatively unsystematized (Ortner and Whitehead 1981: 6). Besides, it makes a crucial difference whether the category of women in a particular culture is defined in relation to the female role of mother, sister, or wife. Ortner and Whitehead speculate that in cultural systems in which the female role of wife is emphasized, more ideological prominence is given to the sexual aspects of women. In such cultural systems, women are mainly perceived as sexual partners rather than as mothers or sisters (1981: 23).

At the theoretical level, the various gender studies have led to elaboration of the concept of gender. Both Harding and Moore distinguish three related aspects or levels of gender. Gender should be analyzed first at a symbolic level, second as a gender structure or social role, and finally at an individual level. Women are not passive objects or victims of symbolic constructions and structural constraints; they should also be analyzed as social actors (Harding 1986: 18; Moore 1988: 12–42).[1] Although these analytic distinctions are important, it is notable that the sex/gender system is replaced by a gender system. It is understandable in view of the biological explanations of the past that the social and cultural concepts of gender receive the greatest attention, yet I think it is important to analyze sex, sexuality, the body, and anatomy in relation to gender as well. Several studies I discuss below indicate that the biological category of sex is not a natural given either. Like the concept of gender, it is socially and culturally constructed.

The biological factor within different cultural definitions of gender is variable. Some cultures, such as the Western societies, claim that male-female differences are almost entirely based on biology (Aalten: 1991), whereas other cultural systems place little emphasis on biological differences (Ortner and Whitehead 1981: 1). In some cultures, for instance, the defining features of gender are not only anatomy but also behavior and social role (Whitehead 1981: 86). It is therefore possible that some persons are anatomically neither fully female nor male and that they are perceived as an intermediate or third gender category. It is also possible that some individuals are anatomically male but socially and culturally female due to the social role they fulfill.

The *berdaches* of native North America, for instance, are anatomically male but they assumed aspects of the status of women.[2] These aspects pertain first to specific areas of productive activities, such as weaving, and second to clothing and mannerisms. The *berdache* is thus a man with regard to anatomy but a woman with regard to work and external appearance. Since the defining features of gender, anatomy, and social activity are given equivalent weight, the *berdaches* are mixed creatures. They are "part-man part-woman" or, phrased in the negative, "not-man not-woman" (Whitehead 1981: 88). The *berdache* is perceived as neither a man nor as a woman, but as a different gender category.

The *hijras* of India are another example of an institutionalized third-gender role. In *Neither Man nor Woman* (1990), Nanda describes the religious community of the *hijras*. The *hijras* are men who dress and act like women. They have specialized professions, such as singing and dancing at homes when a male child is born, at weddings, and at temple festivals. They also engage in homosexual prostitution. Some *hijras* are born intersexual; others undergo an operation in which their genitals are removed. *Hijras* are thus not men by virtue of anatomy and appearance, but they are also not women, although they are "like" women. They are not women in that, for instance, they do not menstruate or give birth. Also, they oppose the Hindu ideals for females of demure conduct and restraint by their public dancing and coarse and abusive speech (1990: 17–18). *Hijras*, as neither men nor women, form an institutionalized third gender category.

As a last example, I would like to mention the institutionalized transsexual role of the *xanith*[3] in Oman (Wikan 1977, 1978). The *xanith* are anatomically male but socially and culturally classified as women. With respect to, for instance, clothing and work, they take an intermediate position between men and women. They usually wear the male ankle-length tunic but with the tight waist of the women's dress. They do their own domestic work, which is women's work, and are employed as domestic servants, yet by this employment they support themselves as a man should. In situations where segregation by gender is observed, however, the *xanith* go with the women (1977: 307–308). The process by which a *xanith* can return to a male identity gives insight in the defining features of gender identity in Oman. The critical criterion is marriage, or, more precisely, the ability to take the male—that is, active—role in intercourse.[4] By way of potency they prove to be men. Wikan therefore concludes: "It is the sexual *act*, not the sexual organs, which is fundamentally constitutive of gender. A man who acts as a woman sexually, *is* a woman, socially. And there is no confusion possible in this culture between the male and female role in intercourse. The man 'enters' (*yidâxil*), the woman receives, the man is active, the woman is passive" (1977: 309). Behavior, particularly sexual behavior, and not anatomy, is thus the basis for the Omani conceptualization of gender identity.

These examples question the seemingly natural category of sex, that is, the biological categories of male and female, their anatomy and bodies. To start with the notion of the body, it makes a crucial difference for the way the body is perceived whether gender is based on anatomy, sexual acts, or productive activity. Further, as Ortner and Whitehead (1981) suggest, the emphasis placed on a particular female role by a society—be it the role of wife, sister, or mother—influenced the way women's bodies in that society are perceived. In cultural systems emphasizing women in their role of wives and stressing the sexual aspects of women, their bodies are probably conceptualized as "sexual bodies." In societies where women are defined in their capacity as mothers, the "nurturing body" might be central, whereas if stress is laid on productive activities as the defining feature for gender, the conceptualization might be that of the "productive body." These remarks are of course subject to study. Probably different discourses on women will exist side by side and will find their counterparts in various notions of the body. I thus argue that just as femininity and masculinity are cultural constructions, so are the concepts of the male and female bodies.

With regard to the body as anatomy, the biological body, it is clear that its weight in the gender construct is variable. Although gender is often defined in terms of anatomy, or anatomy constitutes one of the criteria for gender ascription, this is not always the case. The example of the *berdaches* demonstrates that productive activity can be given equivalent weight, whereas in the case of the Omani *xanith*, sexual activity rather than anatomy is the crucial factor. The example of the *hijras* also shows that the category of gender and sex is changeable. Nanda observes:

> We now accept almost as a truism that gender is a cultural construction, the content of which varies from society to society. . . . But even as cross-cultural research has begun to raise questions about the content of gender

> categories and the mutual exclusivity of masculine and feminine, the view of *sex* (the biological categories of male and female) as dichotomous and unchanging over the individual's lifetime has been so authoritative that this view is still extended to many aspects of gender. . . . As we have seen in India, the *hijras* are evidence that the Indian—or at least Hindu—cultural system not only conceives of more than two genders, but also incorporates the idea, both in myth and reality, that both sex and gender can be changed within an individual's lifetime. (1990: 128–129)

WEAK WOMEN AND FEMMES FATALES

The perfect woman is the woman with a perfect body, at least according to Sheikh Nefzawi. The author of the sixteenth-century treatise on love, *The Perfumed Garden* (1963), describes the praiseworthy woman:

> [She] must have a perfect waist, and must be plump and lusty. Her hair will be black, her forehead wide, she will have eyebrows of Ethiopian blackness, large eyes, with the whites in them very limpid. With cheek of perfect oval, she will have an elegant nose and a graceful mouth; lips and tongue vermilion; her breath will be of pleasant odour, her throat long, her neck strong, her bust and her belly large; her breasts must be full and firm, her belly in good proportion, and her navel well-developed and marked; the lower part of the belly is to be large, the vulva projecting and fleshy, from the point where the hairs grow, to the buttocks; the conduit must be narrow and moist, soft to the touch, and emitting a strong heat and no bad smell; she must have the thighs and buttocks hard, the hips large and full, a waist of fine shape, hands and feet of striking elegance, plump arms, and well-developed shoulders. (1963: 98)

Yet in order to be perfect and desirable, this beauty must be silent:

> She speaks and laughs rarely, and never without reason. She never leaves the house, even to see neighbours of her acquaintance. She has no women friends, gives her confidence to nobody, and her husband is her sole reliance. She takes nothing from anyone, excepting from her husband and her parents. . . . She does not try to entice people. If her husband shows his intention of performing the conjugal rite, she is agreeable to his desires and occasionally even provokes them. . . . She does not surrender herself to anybody but her husband, even if abstinence would kill her. (1963: 98–99)

In *Woman in the Muslim Unconscious*, by Fatna Sabbah (1984), the question of why silence, immobility, and obedience are key criteria of female beauty is taken as a starting point for deciphering Muslim discourses on the female body. The view of orthodox scholars, which demands women's seclusion, silence, obedience, and subjugation, is well known in the West. The extensive writings on the power of female beauty and sexuality, and the view that abstinence can kill women, however, reveal other dimensions of the Muslim view on women.

The discourse on sex and gender in the Muslim world is not an easy thing to describe. It should be borne in mind that there is not just one discourse, and that the multiple discourses do not define actual behavior. In addition, discourses are neither stable over time nor undisputed. In this section, I compare two discourses on gender and sexuality, first the orthodox discourse (Sabbah 1984), comparable to what Mernissi calls the explicit theory of female sexuality (1975), and next the implicit theory and its extension into the erotic discourse.

The orthodox discourse centers on the relation between God and the male believer. Men are created to serve God. God possesses everything and the believer has access to material and immaterial goods only through the worship of God. Women and children are material riches that God has created for the male believer. God created them to serve men, and only through attending to the needs of male believers do women and children indirectly serve God (Sabbah 1984: 74–75). According to Sabbah: "The contribution of the strong, powerful one can only be economic. The offering of the weak, inferior, economically deprived one can only be affective" (1984: 88).

In the relation between the sexes, economic support is likewise exchanged for affection and submission. Men are providers for women, and the Quran states that male superiority is justified by the fact that men provide women with *nafaqa*, the cost of living. In exchange for support, women should be obedient and serve their providers. They should keep their virginity until marriage, since their bodies are the possession of their future providers. After marriage, loyalty, chastity, and complete dedication to their husbands are the prerequisite for securing maintenance. Women cannot act on their own accord without the permission of their masters. Total submission, attendance to all their husband's needs, and providing children are given in exchange for material support.

In the field of sexuality, the desires of the male believers are central as well. Male desire is conceived as strong and capricious. Yet it must be gratified in the legal context of marriage lest *zinâ'*, illicit intercourse, take place. Polygyny and repudiation are institutions that can be interpreted as providing gratification of the male desire without committing *zinâ*ʾ. Polygyny provides the strong male desire with up to four wives at a time, whereas repudiation prevents a man from losing his sexual appetite through boredom by providing new objects (Mernissi 1975: 17).

Women are seen as weak and as easily overpowered by men. They therefore need protection against the strong desires of men. In the orthodox discourse, women are not perceived as lacking in passion—although theirs is less intense than men's passion—but they are not capable of resisting men. And as Delaney rightly observes, female sexuality is perceived as indiscriminate. It is generally believed that if a woman and man are together alone for more than twenty minutes, they have had intercourse. According to Delaney, it is not just that the woman is overpowered by the man's or her own desire, but that she is considered to have no power of discretion or resistance.[5] Women should be guarded and protected, since they are so vulnerable and open to persuasion (1987: 41). Hence women should be secluded and kept away from unrelated men.

Women should thus satisfy the sexual needs of their providers. Classical Islam defines the wife's obligation to provide sex as being of greater importance than her obligation to reproduce and mother.[6] Wives cannot refuse to perform the conjugal duty (Naamane-Guessous 1990: 194).[7] They should fulfill this duty so as to prevent men from committing illicit intercourse. Yet this also protects them, for it keeps their husbands from marrying a second wife. Lacking legal power, women have recourse only to their "feminine power" to ensnare and control men. *Qaid*, "the power to deceive and defeat men, not by force, but by cunning and intrigue" (Mernissi 1975: 5)—a form of "destructive intelligence" (Sabbah 1984: 32)—is perceived as a general character trait of women. Besides cunning and magic, women have only their bodies to entice men. Tempting the husband and satisfying his desires are ways to secure maintenance. The focal issue is not to satisfy one's own desire, but to arouse and gratify the man's appetite. On the wedding night, Moroccan mothers thus advise their daughters to be always attractive and desirable for their husbands (Naamane-Guessous 1990: 195). Only women who know how to please their masters are capable of assuring their attention and support. Keeping within the limits of prudence and chastity, women are thus faced with a subtle game of being obedient yet desirable, virtuous yet sensual, and ignorant yet available (1990: 217).

The powerlessness of women can potentially be inverted if they can manage to ensnare men through cunning and seduction. Orthodox scholars acknowledge this danger, and since men are primarily created to worship God, they warn against female seduction and particularly against attachment to women. The eleventh-century Muslim scholar al-Ghazâlî warns: "Among the dangers of marriage [is] the danger inherent in permitted pleasure, the temptation to give oneself up totally to playful bandying with women, to take too much pleasure in their company, to wallow in enjoyment of them. Marriage risks plunging the body and spirit of the believer into day-long and night-long preoccupations which are intrinsically sexual and which thus prevent man from thinking about the Hereafter and preparing for it" (cited in Sabbah 1984: 50). Women are created as objects for the believer's sensual pleasures, yet they should not become objects of emotional involvement. God requires the believer's total love and all of his capacity for emotional attachment: "Emotional attachment divides man's heart, and Allah hath not created man with two hearts within his body" (Quran Surah III: 4). God is acknowledged to be a jealous God, particularly of anything which interferes with the believer's devotion to him (Sabbah 1984: 63–64). Love between husband and wife is thus dangerous to the believer's religious devotion. The conjugal unit should consequently be weakened. According to Mernissi, polygyny and repudiation can be interpreted as legal devices to this end. Both prevent emotional involvement between a couple. Sabbah likewise argues that God is hostile toward the wife as a potential source of pleasure and emotional investment. Therefore she is reduced to the status of object or material riches (1984: 103).

The belief that women should be reduced to objects lest they lure men away from God reveals that women are perceived as potentially powerful. Mernissi, investigating the implicit theory of female sexuality, argues that women are feared for their disruptive potential. *Fitna*,[8] chaos provoked by sexual disorder that is initiated by women, is feared (Mernissi 1975: 4). Seen from this perspective, several institutions usually interpreted as instruments of male power, such as seclusion and sexual segregation, can be explained as devices to protect men. Men must be protected against the powerful female sexuality. Women's ability to provoke *fitna* is thus mainly invested in their bodies and in the nature of their sexuality.

According to the implicit theory of female sexuality, men are not alone in having passion and desire that are strong and in need of gratification. Al-Ghazâlî emphasizes the similarity between the sexual nature of males and females.[9] Both have an active sexual nature, and women's desires should be satisfied as well as men's. Al-Ghazâlî therefore recommends foreplay, quoting the words of the Prophet: "'No one among you throw himself on his wife like beasts do. There should be, prior to coitus, a messenger between you and her.' People asked him, 'What sort of messenger?' The Prophet answered, 'Kisses and words'" (cited in Mernissi 1975: 10). If women are not sexually satisfied they create *fitna* by enticing men other than their husbands. Hence: "The virtue of the woman is a man's duty. And the man should increase or decrease sexual intercourse with the woman according to her needs so as to secure her virtue" (al-Ghazâlî, cited in Mernissi 1975: 10).

The need to satisfy the female desire and the difficulties men have in fulfilling this duty is the topic of the erotic discourse. The erotic discourse is an extension of the implicit theory and deals with female desire as mirrored in men's thought. It is an attempt by religious scholars to counsel the believer regarding righteous conduct toward sexual desire. The orthodox discourse mainly focuses on the strength of male desire, the implicit theory considers the active sexuality of both sexes, and the erotic discourse is chiefly centered on the aggressive nature of female passion. While male passion is perceived as intense and capricious in the orthodox view, it is viewed as weak and impotent in the erotic discourse. Female passion is active in the implicit theory, but it becomes aggressive, insatiable, and threatening in the erotic discourse.

"The woman loves the man only for the sake of coition" and "Women's religion is in their vulvas," the reader of *The Perfumed Garden* is told (Nefzawi 1963: 79, 120). Sheikh Nefzawi counsels the believer in detail on how to satisfy the female desire: "You will excite her by kissing her cheeks, sucking her lips and nibbling at her breasts. You will lavish kisses on her navel and thighs, and titillate the lower parts. Bite at her arms, and neglect no part of her body; cling close to her bosom, and show her your love and submission" (1963: 125). He describes twenty-five positions of cohabitation and pays special attention to the act of coition among persons of different length and size. Yet female passion is so strong and insatiable that the believer is left insecure about his potency. Women's desire greatly surpasses that of men and is sheerly impossible to gratify. "Some people have said that the sexual appetite of woman is greater than that of man. Others have said while woman is never sated nor exhausted by copulation, man, on the contrary, is very quickly sated and exhausted, and his desire to copulate ebbs if he indulges in it immoderately. If one copulates, it seems night and day, for years and years with a woman, she never reaches the point of saturation. Her thirst for copulation is never assuaged" (Ibn Kamal Pasha, cited in Sabbah 1984: 27). Whereas cohabitation energizes women, it weakens men. Men consequently need special diets and magic in order to regain their potency. Meat, honey, and eggs are among the strengthening foods Nefzawi advises for the man who would "passionately give himself up to the enjoyment of coition, without undergoing too great fatigue" (1963: 160).

In the erotic discourse there is thus a reversal of roles. Whereas in the orthodox discourse men are hunters and their intense and capricious desires need a constant renewal of supply, in the erotic discourse women's passion is insatiable. Women resort to cunning, *qaid*, in order to achieve sexual gratification. Nefzawi ends many stories in which women's insatiable quest for intercourse leads to fornication, with the lesson "Learn from this the deceitfulness of women, and what they are capable of." In the erotic literature women are thus aggressive, active, and strong, whereas men are passive, weak, and cuckolded. While women are feared for their power to distract the believer from the hereafter in the orthodox discourse, in the erotic discourse women are rebellious and frightening. Virginity and fidelity are impossible demands for the "omnisexual woman" (Sabbah 1984: 32). Women cannot be satisfied with one husband, let alone with sharing one man with three co-wives. They are by definition rebellious against the moral order and are a constant source of *fitna*, chaos.

Although there are differences between these constructions of gender and sexuality, it is striking that they converge in their definition of women as primarily bodies, particularly sexual bodies.[10] Whether a woman passively tries to keep her legal husband's attention through being desirable or actively seduces other men, in both cases her sexual dimension is central. In both discourses the female body is reduced to the sexual aspect and women are seen primarily as sexual beings. According to Leila Ahmed (1992), who traces the varieties of discourses and how they have changed in the history of Middle Eastern Arabic women, it was in the Abbasid era (±750–±1260) that the word "woman" became almost synonymous with "slave" and "object for sexual use." Marketing of women as commodities and objects for sexual use was an everyday reality in Abbasid society. It is no wonder that Muslim scholars of that period, such as al-Ghazâlî, mainly define women as sexual beings. This period was, however, constitutive for the formulation of Islamic law and thus has had a profound impact up to today.

Sabbah argues that "Muslim culture has a built-in ideological blindness to the economic dimension of women, who are ordinarily perceived, conceived and defined as exclusively sexual objects. The female body has traditionally been the object of an enormous erotic investment, which has clouded (if not totally hidden) woman's economic dimensions" (1984: 16–17). In addition, the relations between the sexes are generally eroticized. As a result of this, working outside the home by women is often experienced as erotic aggression (1984: 16–17).

The images of the weak woman and the femme fatale—as well as those of the strong man and the weak man—coexist. They are derived from theoretical discourses by male scholars and it still has to be examined whether these ideas are "experience-near" for Egyptian men and women.[11] I particularly investigate these models in daily life with regard to female singers and dancers. Are they conceived as dangerous and as rebellious against the moral order?

FEMALE ENTERTAINERS AND *FITNA*

The explanations people give for veiling and seclusion indicate that the two discourses on women exist in daily life. Women should cover their bodies, with the exception of the hands and face. They should use non-transparent material without adornment, and the clothing must be loose in order not to reveal the form of their bodies. Women usually explain the need for veiling as a device to protect themselves against men as well as a device to protect men against women.[12] Women should be protected against harassment by men and should not be exposed to male desire. Yet they are also aware of their seductive potential and equally explain veiling as a way of preventing the temptation of men. Veiling prevents them from being victims of male desire and from provoking men, who cannot control themselves in the presence of unveiled women. In both cases the female body is perceived as sexual and lust-enticing. In keeping with this rationale, the dress prescriptions for older women, who are perceived as less attractive and thus no longer able to provoke *fitna*, are less strict. Seclusion likewise functions as a double device. If women work outside the home, they should try to be unattractive in order to go unnoticed by men who would prey on them and in order not to seduce weak men who cannot restrain their passion (Naamane-Guessous 1990: 97).

The double device thus refers to the images of both the weak woman and the femme fatale. Yet it does not assume that women are aggressive and omnisexual. Female sexuality is powerful and makes men lose control, but women are not perceived as actively seducing men in order to gratify their own sexual appetite. Women are seductive but not hunting for personal sexual gratification. The crucial thing is that women are by definition sexual beings; their bodies by nature are enticing and seductive. This gives them power, but their sexual nature is not necessarily directed at their own pleasure.[13]

Women in particular stress their vulnerability rather than their aggressive sexuality. They occasionally accuse other women of being "only after sex" and angry if a night passes when the husband does not "bathe" them (Atiya 1982: 13). Yet mostly they are burdened by harassment in the street or by the husband's desire for sexual intercourse. They usually restrict themselves to the more passive strategy of inciting the desire of the legal husbands. Women are proud of being desired by their husbands.[14] As one woman related in *Khul-Khaal*: "And some women, because they pride themselves greatly on how often their husbands sleep with them, walk around in the morning with their heads wrapped in a towel to show that they have bathed and washed their hair, which we must do after intercourse" (Atiya 1982: 112). Allusions to sex, banter about "sports," and hanging up the towel used for hair drying where others will see it are common among married women, at least among women of the lower-middle class (see also Messiri on the *bint il-balad*). Yet the active and aggressive seductress, tempting all men due to her insatiable sexual needs, is not a common image among women. They do not regard a woman as an insatiable femme fatale searching for sex. In general, they recognize the weakness of men in the face of a beautiful woman, and they use this knowledge with regard to their husbands. Seduction is directed at security, however, rather than sexual gratification. It is a way of keeping the husband's attention and support. Being desirable is an important asset in the game of power with one's husband. Yet, with regard to strange men, women feel in need of protection—that is, they feel they are more threatened by the men than they are threatening to the men. In their view, women are not rebellious against the moral order. On the contrary, they are the keepers of morality. The image of rebellious omnisexual women is thus experience-distant, at least for women.[15]

Although the rebellious femme fatale is experience-distant with regard to women as a category, it may be an experience-near image when applied to female entertainers. Female singers and dancers might be an outstanding symbol of *fitna*, since they work with their seductive bodies to earn money. They do not keep the rules as prescribed by the orthodox discourse. They are not invisible, secluded, and devoting all their attention to the needs of the husband, the children, and the home. Although most of them, particularly those of the circuit of weddings and saint's day celebrations, are "socially covered," since they are married, they are not literally covered (Delaney 1987: 41). On the contrary, they uncover themselves, wear revealing clothes, and exhibit their attractiveness as women to gain a living.

The ways gender is understood and the different notions of the male and female body explain why female entertainers are considered shameful and bad while their male colleagues are not blamed for similar activities. In the previous chapter, it was concluded that male entertainers are not dishonorable since their bodies are neutral, while female performers are bad because their bodies are *ʿawra*, shameful. The female body is shameful because it is by definition eroticizing and enticing, whereas the male body has several dimensions and is not by nature seductive. The male body, although sexual in the presence of a female body, has other dimensions—for instance, in the economic or political field. These constructions of gender and the body explain why the body of male performers is a "productive body" whereas that of female performers is by definition a "sexual body." Female entertainers' main instrument for making money consists of their *ʿawra*, their sexual bodies and voices. Female entertainers thus use the female power to seduce to secure a living. They profit from the cultural construction of the female body as seductive but pay for it in terms of status and respect.

Female entertainers thus make use of what is feared by Muslim scholars: the feminine power to ensnare men and to create *fitna*. They are accordingly bad and immoral women. But are they also considered insatiable and dangerous, as might be expected from the erotic discourse? Do people fear female entertainers? To determine whether the image of the dangerous and aggressive seductress in search for sexual gratification is experience-near, it is necessary to go beyond religious texts to whether people actually express fear in their sayings and behavior.

In the interviews I conducted with Egyptians from different socioeconomic backgrounds, I found that female entertainers are indeed considered harmful in certain respects. A few men and religious leaders mentioned the bad example female singers and dancers set for young girls who attend weddings. As an employee explained: "If a young girl watches a dancer who seduces men and sees that all men eagerly watch her, she will act like her. She will imitate her."[16] This refers to the idea, on the one hand, that women have a lack of discernment, and on the other that women strive to hold the attention of men. For that reason a *sheikh* maintained that women are not allowed to watch a "vulgar dancer."

Another danger ascribed to performers in general, and particularly to female entertainers, is their ability to ruin people financially. Both male and female entertainers entice money out of the pockets of customers, but female performers have the power to bewitch the customer—they make him lose his mind and throw his money over their heads. This particularly holds true in nightclubs. In the 1930s, there was a famous case of an employee of the *waqf*[17] ministry who embezzled enormous sums of money to please his favorite dancer (*Rûz al-Yûsif* 8-6-1935). In the same period, a son of a pasha stole money from his grandparents to maintain a dancer (*Rûz al-Yûsif* 22-6-1936).

The gravest danger, however, is that of tempting men. The general belief is that even the toughest man, if he sees a scantily dressed woman moving in front of him, must succumb to her. This could result in his giving money and presents to her, so that income is taken from another woman's household. The temptress could eventually seduce the man and take the husband of another woman. It was striking that this accusation was never specifically directed at female entertainers. Any woman is potentially capable of seducing other men. Female singers and dancers, although immoral and bad, were not referred to as a specific group of "husband takers."

Although especially nightclubs are known as corrupt places where "moral crimes" are committed, the most common comment was that whatever female performers do, "the sin is theirs." In general, people do not fear the influence of these "bad women." Except for wedding celebrations, performers are mostly removed from the public's social life. Most people took the view that although female singers and dancers are shameful, they themselves do not commit sin when they invite them to their weddings and watch them perform. "If a dancer takes the wrong path, she only harms herself," a housewife commented. Their behavior occasionally endangers the morality or wallet of an individual, but female entertainers are not an outstanding symbol of *fitna* and disaster. They harm occasional individuals but do not endanger the entire moral order.

Neither are they perceived as rebellious. Although female entertainers transgress the prescriptions for decent women, they are considered to act as they do because of circumstances rather than from rebellion. It is commonly felt that if they have the chance they would change their way of living. Popular entertainers are viewed as pitiable people who would prefer a decent living, while nightclub performers are regarded as greedy—for tips rather than for sex. It is generally recognized that these bad women engage in their profession to earn money, not because of an insatiable sexual appetite. Just as the erotic discourse, with its stress on voracious female desire which is counter to the moral order, is experience-distant in daily-life discourse, the erotic discourse is absent in people's views on female singers and dancers. As for other women, seduction is an instrument for securing income rather than a way of satisfying their sexual desires.

In experience-near discourse, their indecency is thus generally not perceived as dangerous. Female entertainers are in many respects women like other women; that is, they have the power to seduce and bewitch. They differ from "decent women" mainly because they actually employ their potential. Instead of using their feminine power in the legal context of marriage, they tempt male customers in public. They publicly exhibit their bodies to all men for profit. The fact that "sex" is exchanged for "material" does not make them radically different from other women, either. Yet outside of the context of marriage it becomes "prostitution."

The idea, mostly found among the lower and lower-middle classes, that female entertainers would prefer a "decent" living rather than one in which they seduce men, is similar to the view that female entertainers themselves have of their profession. The harm female performers occasionally do to individuals is recognized by them. The fact that they make men spend money that should be used for the household is admitted by a few of them. A former performer, who has now repented and made a pilgrimage to Mecca, looked back and commented: "The profession is *ḥarâm*. Someone can visit a wedding with twenty-five piasters in his pocket with which he could feed his children. If he sees someone dancing beautifully in front of him and hears the names of all the other men mentioned, he wants his mentioned as well and must give money. So he will give the twenty-five piasters to the dancer and his children will have nothing to eat." Also the fear religious leaders expressed that women might imitate female entertainers and take up their profession is not without grounds, since a few of them started their careers themselves when they saw the glitter and glamour of female performers.

They are aware of their power to bewitch and seduce. As Baṭṭa said: "A man, regardless how tough he is, even if he is praying on his prayer mat, does not have the power to resist a dancer moving in a revealing costume." This power, however, is a double-edged sword for female performers. It is clearly an instrument for earning money. Women can use their beauty and attractiveness to earn money, a strategy which does not work for male entertainers. The nightclub performer Yasmîn commented: "The customer wants to see a woman, not a man. . . . If he drinks and gets drunk and sees a dancer or a female singer in a nice dress . . . she will bewitch him. But if a man is performing, this will not affect him to the same extent." Men must use their voices and talent. It is difficult for women to be evaluated for their talents instead of their bodies. A serious female singer, who insisted on being estimated for her voice rather than her appearance, related that she had unconsciously made it a habit to close her eyes during singing. Once at a wedding, a man shouted at her, "Are we so ugly that you close your eyes all the time?" Then she realized that she closed her eyes to avoid the lustful gaze of the audience. Beauty and being desirable thus mean money. Yet it can also mean trouble. Female singers and dancers sometimes feel very vulnerable and threatened by men at a party. And the growing incidence of robbery and kidnapping gives them reason to fear.

Some female performers make a direct link between revealing costumes and troubles at a wedding. *Usṭâ* Zeinab from the Madbaḥ family commented: "The belly-dancing costume should be prohibited. It causes problems because it is too revealing. If men see this part of the body naked, here open, there a small piece of material—and, please forgive the expression, they sleep on their backs and have their legs open [she describes the act in which a dancer, while on her knees, bends over backward]—even the toughest man, if he sees this . . . he is human after all." Yet, most dancers feel forced to wear these costumes at the request of the employer for fear they will be replaced by a more obedient woman. Ibtisâm was relieved when the vice squad ordered that costumes should cover the belly and that splits should not start above the knees. In the view of female entertainers, men are thus weak regarding female beauty and seduction, and at the same time threatening and aggressive. They regard women as powerful and tempting, but as weak when it comes to physical violence.

Seduction is thus an important weapon for earning money, yet it is in the dancers' own interest to manipulate this instrument subtly. They must be feminine, but if they go too far and are too revealing and indecent, they will lose their reputation in the community of entertainers and create trouble for themselves and the group. Sayyid once remarked of a woman who was shaking her behind at the spectators in a vulgar way that he would not take her to a wedding for fear of fighting and kidnapping. How female entertainers cope with this need to be feminine and seductive, yet decent and invulnerable, will be dealt with in the next chapter.

EIGHT

FEMALE ENTERTAINERS: FEMININE AND MASCULINE

In this chapter, I examine the self-presentation of female entertainers as respectable wives, mothers, and working women. I concentrate mainly on the female singers and dancers of Muḥammad ʿAlî Street.[1] In the first section, I deal with their roles as wives and mothers. Many, particularly of the older generation, were wife and mother at a young age, and their strongest claim to honor is based on these roles. The younger generation continues to work for home and children. They consider being a good housewife and mother the most important and respectable tasks for women. Working outside the home is of secondary importance and is done in the service of their home and children. They thus strongly identify with the construction of femininity as mainly wives and mothers.

Yet their work behavior does not accord with prevailing ideas on femininity and respectability. To begin with, female entertainers work outside the home, which is de facto disrespectable for women, since it is perceived as erotic aggression. Also, female entertainers work with their shameful bodies and display all kinds of "unfeminine" behavior such as smoking, drinking, and verbal and occasionally physical abuse. How do they cope with the contradiction of being respectable female entertainers working in the male public space? How do they deal with the most problematic aspect of their profession, their bodies? Why do they behave in "unfeminine" ways?

Before drawing the final conclusions, it is important to consider female entertainers in the broader setting of working women from the lower-middle class. In the last section, I therefore return to the image of the *banât il-balad,* the "daughters of the country," discussed in Chapter 5. Although on account of their profession and the use of their seductive powers female entertainers are more strongly condemned than other working women, they share the same problems and solutions in dealing with contradictory demands. They face similar difficulties in upholding their reputation while working in the male public space. A female entertainer must be feminine yet invulnerable, female yet "one who can be trusted among a hundred men" (Messiri 1978b: 534).

HOUSEWIVES AND MOTHERS

Ibtisâm is a clear example of a performer who struggles for her children. As a mother at the age of fifteen and giving birth to five children, her life is marked by motherhood. After her first marriage, she was left the choice of keeping the children or the house. She chose the children. During her second marriage, it appeared that her husband was married and already had two children. She wanted a divorce not only because he was already married, but also because she could not accept money which should have been spent on his first wife and their children. Besides, the first wife told others that the husband did not spend money on his own children but on "the children of a dancer," a remark Ibtisâm found humiliating. Moreover, since he did not support his first wife, in the long run, she and the child she was carrying would probably have met the same fate. Ibtisâm therefore asked the father of her first two children for maintenance. He refused unless the children were placed under his guardianship. They went to court and Ibtisâm signed a contract stating that she handed over the children. She only intended to teach him a lesson—to show him that bringing up children involves a lot of expenses. She expected him to be bored by the responsibility and to return the children soon. But things did not turn out as she planned; when she asked to see her children he refused. She begged his family and wife to be allowed to see the children and tried by all means to get them back, but it was to no avail. Only when he left for France and did not send money was she able to get her children back.

Ibtisâm strongly identifies with her role as mother. Her stories are interspersed with references to motherhood and the well-being of the children. "I have to dance. If I did not dance then maybe my children would have to dance." "I have five children. None of them is yet married. How could I live and take care of them? What else can I do than dance?" Even the reason she gave for wearing a costume that covers her belly is related to motherhood rather than personal respectability. She said: "If you wear an open costume, the police make a report. I don't want someone to come to my house and tell the children: 'Your mother is at the police station because her belly was uncovered.' My children must not hear such things." She regards herself as a working mother with no other option than dancing. She has kept her children out of the profession. She taught them "what is right and what is wrong." She was happy when one of her daughters started wearing the Islamic veil. Before I met Ibtisâm personally, other performers on Muḥammad ʿAlî Street proudly told me of "a dancer whose daughter is veiled." Despite her "sinful" profession, she kept her children on the "right" path.

Bûḥa similarly works in order to keep her children out of the profession. She said:

> I suffered and experienced calamities, but I bore it all because of my children. . . . I wanted to give them an education better than anyone else's. I let my oldest son enter a foreign university with foreign languages. I had to pay in dollars. I wanted him to have a high education. When Ṣalâḥ wanted to take my money and have the children play the drum or flute, I refused. I said: "No, I am tired of it. I don't want them to work. I want them to have high positions so that when I stop working or when I die, I'll be honored by them." . . . I could have owned a few houses if I had let them work and not spent on them like I did. But I wanted them to have a better life. I struggled for them. . . . If someone says "son of a dancer" to my children, I commit a crime. I gave three children a high education!

A performer from Alexandria, Niʿma, also witnessed disasters at work and in her personal life, but she bore it all because of her son. She started as a performer after the death of her son's father. She became a good singer and dancer and was in demand. She married a performer to have protection, but the marriage failed. Her third husband let her work at saint's day celebrations, which she felt to be under her level. Also, he lived off her money. Since Niʿma had insisted on including the right to divorce in her marriage contract, she could separate from him. He disagreed and once, in a fit of rage, he threw strong acid in her face. Her face bears the marks of this accident and one of her eyes is damaged and closed. She wanted to stop working so as not to be confronted with painful remarks about her face. But when she was offered work she had to accept in order to earn money for her son. Her solo career is finished and she now works in a group with three other performers. Occasionally she meets with remarks about her eye: "Especially young men at weddings rag me about my eye. I tell them: 'If you knew why I work—that I have someone of your age to take care of—you wouldn't pester me like this.' Sometimes I cry while I'm dancing. . . . But my son is my life and I work for him."

Dancer Magda, who started in nightclubs but later worked at weddings, also set the education of her two children as her primary goal in life. Her daughter's marriage was similarly important for her feeling of having achieved something. She related:

> If my daughter gets a good job with her university degree, I'll feel like I've achieved something. I want her to be at a level where she will always remember me, not at a level where she'll work and give me money. No, she's got to achieve something despite the hard conditions we've lived in. She's engaged now to an officer. When he came here for the first time, he said: "I expected to enter the house of a dancer, but I feel like I'm entering the house of a relative." I asked him: "What do you want?" He said: "I want to become engaged to Saḥar." I said: "Bring your father and mother and we'll talk." They came and I showed them a belly-dancing costume. I told them that the belly-dancing costume is Saḥar's father and mother. I said: "I am a dancer, not something else. I am a father and a mother to my children." They swore they didn't mind my profession. I told them to write it down on paper. Saḥar's fiancé wrote down the condition so that someday he can't say: "I divorce her because her mother is a dancer."

I visited her several times after this first interview. A few months later, she proudly showed me Saḥar's university degree. She had stuck it on a framed picture of herself in a belly-dancing costume and happily said, "I did it by my dancing." A year later her other wish, the marriage of her daughter, was fulfilled. She arranged a wedding with many *nimar*, mostly colleagues who performed free of charge, and the party lasted until the early hours.

Because most women work for the expenses of their children, they only intend to work for a limited period. Bûḥa's sister, Nagâḥ, hopes to leave the trade soon. At present, her husband is unemployed, her oldest son is in the army, and the youngest is still at school. But as soon as the youngest finishes school, she wants to stop. Mona, a dancer in her early thirties, also plans to work for a fixed period of time. Once the school expenses of the children are less, she will stay at home. She refuses to work in nightclubs, although she has had several offers and knows that she could earn more money at clubs than at weddings. She is afraid that she would get used to the higher income and raise her material aspirations. She would then have to keep on working until she obtained a better house and other material goods. She prefers to work at weddings once or twice a week to earn enough for "the extras" and to leave the trade as soon as possible. "I'm happy when I've been to a good wedding party given by nice people and have earned good money, so I can buy some sweets for the kids. And if they need something the next day, I can buy it for them because I still have some money left over."

Most female performers are not only mothers but also wives. Most are, or have been, married—some several times. Marriage is important to them, just as it is the most important goal for other Egyptian women. Marriage for an entertainer means, among other things, protection of her reputation. A former performer, who started working after her divorce, married a colleague because, as she said: "This trade is a son of a bitch; the woman who has no man . . . that one desires her, that one wants her. I did not want to remarry, but you need a man in this trade." This protection mainly refers to the name of the female performer as a respectable married person. The husband of ʿAida, the Muḥammad ʿAlî Street dancer I saw at the first wedding, confidently said: "A real man at home is a real man outside the home. People know I'm a good person, so Umm Maḥmûd [his wife, ʿAida] must be good too. A woman is known by her man. They can't say anything bad about Umm Maḥmûd because her husband is a real man. They can about Ṣalâḥ [Bûḥa's and Baṭṭa's husband]." Because most male performers have ambivalent feelings about wives who also work in the trade, their wives have to be careful not to make the husbands suspicious about their fidelity. Samîra Madbaḥ related that her husband Ibrahîm occasionally follows her to check on her behavior and whereabouts. Once a wedding party ended early as a result of fights, and when Ibrahîm arrived Samîra was gone. He anxiously inquired about her to the musicians and was assured that she had just gone home. He hurried back and found her at home. If the husband is known as a "real tough man" who "controls his house" and jealously guards his wife, she has no opportunity to betray him. The reputation of female entertainers is thus partly derived from the masculinity of the husband.

The expectancy of material security is another important reason that leads female entertainers to marry. Most of them who have married aspired to become housewives and were promised to be kept at home. Due to financial circumstances, they continued or started working and wait for the time that they can afford to leave the trade. Like all women, they expect their husbands to provide for them. They work "to help him" with "the extra expenses" or with "the education of the children." Yet the husband must pay for the basic cost of living. A former performer was shocked at Sayyid's suggestion that she more or less kept her former husband. "No, he was a real man and provided for me," she responded.

Although reality may be different, female performers adhere to the standard that the husband is responsible for the basic cost of living while they are responsible for household expenses and the children. If necessary, they work for "the extras." They blame the husband and ask for a divorce if he takes their money for the basics. ʿAbîr, a folk dancer from Minyâ who now works in Luxor as a result of fundamentalist agitation in her native town, is still unmarried. She wants to marry and expects her future husband to make her a housewife: "If I marry, I want to stop dancing. I am like that. No Egyptian can accept that his wife dances for other men. 'If you want to dance, you dance for me inside the house.' There are men with soft blood and kind hearts. I'll never marry such a man. I must marry a man who is hot-blooded, who is jealous. 'You shake in front of other men, go to hell. I'll divorce you!' That's the kind of man I want. Otherwise my life won't change. But if I stop dancing for him, my life will be different."

Most performers consider their tasks as mothers and wives more important than their work as performers. They see themselves as mothers and wives first and only secondarily as working women. "The house comes first" or "My children come first," they often say. "First of all I'm a wife and mother, and only second to that am I an artist. But I would prefer to be only a housewife," they repeatedly said.

Notwithstanding their wishes, they are mother, housewife, and performer—they must combine the three roles. Especially in the summer season, when there are many weddings, their days are busy and they hardly find time to rest. They often return home at about seven o'clock in the morning and have to wake up a few hours later to shop, clean, and cook. At five or six o'clock in the afternoon, they start preparing for their evening job. The neighbor of the Madbaḥ family recounted that in the early morning, when she returned home from work, she did the shopping. She cleaned, cooked, and did the laundry, and only then could she sleep. She woke up in the late afternoon and went to work again. "I sometimes slept only two hours after I finished the household chores. I lost weight from lack of sleep and sometimes I felt dizzy while working. But I had to take care of the children and the house. It wasn't possible to get someone to come in to do my washing. She would have just taken the money I earned, and besides, you can't trust other people—she could have stolen everything. Now I'm only a mother and a housewife, praise be to God!" On account of her hard life, dancer ʿAida exclaimed: "I wish God had made me a man, Almighty God!"

Most performers have some help, though. They rarely have paid help, but often a relative lives with them or nearby. Ibtisâm's daughters do most of the cooking and cleaning if she has too much work. In addition, two of her children are taken care of by Zûba. Bûḥa's oldest son and his wife live with her, and the daughter-in-law usually cooks and cleans. Baṭṭa leaves her youngest with Ṣalâḥ's mother, who lives nearby, and occasionally drops the oldest at Bûḥa's place. The Madbaḥ family lives together in one house, so the children can easily be taken care of by one of the sisters or by their sister-in-law, Samîra. Mona's mother-in-law lives with them and cares for the children if Mona works. Magda has a maid, a retarded orphan, whose parents worked for Magda when she performed extensively in nightclubs. Magda takes care of the girl, who helps Magda with household chores.

Their days are thus filled with domestic duties and sleeping. Especially in summer, there is not much time left for socializing. When I visited them, I rarely found visitors at their homes other than relatives or male colleagues who came to arrange work. The fact that female performers do not frequent each other's houses is partly due to lack of time. It seems, however, that they also do not like other performers to visit their homes. I regularly heard: "We do not like each other." Jealousy and gossip about the dishonorable behavior of female colleagues contribute to the lack of friendship among female performers. As already mentioned, there is a tendency among most performers to claim dignity and respect for themselves by blackening another's reputation. Friendship generally seems to be a fragile tie among them.[2] Moreover, many performers, particularly those who live away from Muḥammad ʿAlî Street, prefer to keep the atmosphere of the home separate from the workplace. Ibtisâm, who is considering leaving the trade to sew costumes for a living, pointed out the drawback of such a livelihood: it would mean that dancers would enter her house. "I don't want any of them to enter my house, and I don't want to go to their houses," she said. Magda, who lives away from Muḥammad ʿAlî Street, also said that she doesn't want performers to visit her house. "I respect my home and children. . . . People in high positions live next to us. They say of us: 'She has lived here twenty years already. She's an artist, but we never hear anything bad about her or her children. She's not like other artists who have constant visitors—all sorts of people.'" The atmosphere of the home must be kept pure and the children far removed from the trade.

Female entertainers thus consider being a good housewife and mother their most important and respectable tasks as women. Earning money is done to carry out their main female duties. They strongly identify with the construction of femininity as mainly wives and mothers. They claim respectability on account of their suffering and self-sacrifice for their children and home. Bûḥa ended her story as follows:

> I struggled for my children. I slept on a reed mat, without food. I carried my husband's drum on my head. We walked ten kilometers a day across fields, summer and winter, until the earth filled our ears. . . . Why do I hate my family? Why do I hate my mother? Because she took me from school and made me work. If she had struggled like I did, I could have finished school and I would not have married [this person]. I would have carried the dirt of her shoes on my head [I would have done anything for her]. You see how I struggled and suffered?

FEMININITY AND MASCULINITY AT WORK

Although for reasons of respectability female entertainers dissociate themselves from their trade, work is more to them than just trouble and affliction. Despite negative remarks about colleagues, made in the atmosphere of the home, at work they are friendly and have fun together. And despite negative comments on their hard working conditions and the quarrels and fights at weddings—which I indeed often witnessed—they also like their profession. They like singing and dancing and the contact with colleagues. A good wedding, without quarrels and fights, means more than just money, although money is the main reason to work.

The liking that entertainers have for their trade was shown in numerous ways. The Madbaḥ family chose their careers as performers because they liked the profession. Bûḥa was very bored on the winter evening I first went to visit her. She had not worked for a month and needed money and a change. Niʿma as well, despite the hurtful remarks about her injured eye, prefers working and the companionship of her colleagues to being at home. Magda also likes her work. Her family tried all means to get her out of the profession, but she refused. Her daughter was about to marry and leave the house around the time I met Magda. What was she supposed to do at home the whole day? "I'll be bored and feel suffocated," she said. A few times she showed me around some clubs when she had no work herself. She did it to help me, but she also liked to be among her colleagues. Besides, her work brought a degree of freedom to smoke, to drink, and to associate freely with people. She phrased the distinction between her behavior at home and that at work as being "respectable at home" and "free at work." As noted before, she claimed that she does not even smoke at home (which is not true), whereas at work she can do anything she likes. "I do anything that comes to my mind. . . . I can accept beer or whiskey if I am invited to have a glass. . . ." When I accompanied her to a wedding in Sohâg, in the south, she conjured up a brown medicine bottle. She asked me with a wink whether I would liked to taste her medicine. And so we drank brandy together until it was time to prepare for the wedding.

At work female entertainers behave differently than at home. They associate freely with male colleagues and customers and exchange light-hearted remarks with them. Many smoke cigarettes, and some accept beer or whiskey while onstage in front of an audience. Bûḥa is inseparable from her water pipe and also smokes in public during work. A few female entertainers occasionally take a puff of hashish from the water pipe of a male colleague. Ibtisâm, who often dances with a water pipe on her head, once worked at a wedding in the hashish quarter. For that occasion, the water pipe was filled with hashish and she now and then took the water pipe from her head to have a puff. Although some of the performers also smoke and occasionally drink at home, for most these are work-related activities.

In general, smoking and drinking among Egyptian women are very uncommon. Although they can smoke and drink at home if their husbands allow them, women rarely do so in public. It is not just bad or immoral behavior, it is unfeminine. The water pipe, alcohol, and hashish are stimulants for men. Dancer Mona explicitly related her abstention from smoking and drinking to femininity. She said: "It is not suitable for women. Femininity means that a woman does not drink beer or alcohol, and does not smoke a water pipe. These things belong to men." Few women openly smoke and drink. Many female performers, however, display this type of "male" conduct. What is their own rationale for behaving in an "unfeminine" way?

They probably simply like the taste of cigarettes and alcohol. However, smoking and drinking are also conditions of their work. Sometimes they are forced to accept beer or cigarettes from drunken men in order to avoid problems. They must be careful in accepting or refusing cigarettes and beer and must be experienced in dealing with drunkards. *Usṭâ* Zeinab from the Madbaḥ family explained how she handles customers: "When I am working at a wedding, I look at all the people and know what they want. This one offers me a cigarette and I tell him: 'I don't smoke.' 'But I saw you smoking.' I tell him: 'I do not like to change my brand, dear.' 'Here, a glass of beer,' another says. 'No, I don't drink.' When I receive my money and I want to drink, I take a bottle and drink

FIGURE 15

A former usṭâ *at home.*

FIGURE 16

A nightclub dancer at home.

at home, not at the wedding. Imagine me getting drunk at a wedding! That'd be a mess." The strategy of Zeinab's neighbor is to accept cigarettes and beer and to simulate smoking and drinking in order to avoid problems. Samîra Madbaḥ denied accepting beer or cigarettes but admitted that the present generation is forced to accept these in order to please drunken customers. The explosive atmosphere of drunken, competing men trying to attract the attention of female performers sometimes puts the entertainers in a position where their wisest course is to accept a cigarette or beer.

Yet I think that smoking and drinking on the part of quite a few female entertainers should be understood in the light of a broader complex of

FIGURE 17

A Muḥammad ʿAlî Street dancer before work.

"masculine" behavior.[3] The fact that they work in a public place puts female entertainers in a male world. Earning a livelihood or being the breadwinner of the family is not the common pattern for Egyptian women. Also, weddings require tough manly behavior of female performers. On the one hand they must be quick-witted, gay, free, nice, feminine, and responsive. On the other hand, they must be alert, able to

FIGURE 18

A Muḥammad ʿAlî Street singer and dancer smoking a water pipe.

foresee problems, strong, tough, and manly. Dancer ʿAida related an incident with a drunkard who gulped down a bottle of cheap spirits and started dancing with two knives on the stage. After injuring a dancer he said, "I'm sorry, I'm drunk." She described the present state at weddings: "Everything is nice until suddenly some young men start a ruckus. Hop, hop, the chairs fly through the air, the lights go out, and the wedding is spoiled. They don't smoke hash anymore, that is too expensive. They drink cheap spirits instead. They buy a bottle and empty it at one gulp. They want to be drunk and create problems." Female entertainers must be able to deal with aggression and drunken men. They must face situations involving violence, theft, and kidnapping. If the employer does not give them their money or if a male customer bothers them, they must be—and usually are—able to defend their rights and to protect themselves. The nature of their work at weddings thus makes tough, masculine behavior a prerequisite. Baṭṭa related that she used her femininity to avoid problems with drunkards: "I am so sweet and nice to all people that even the biggest bully becomes embarrassed and won't hurt me. On the contrary, he will protect me." Others, however often resort to tough male behavior.

Most are quite adept at defending themselves by cursing. A dancer described herself as having a rude tongue which she had effectively used the evening before I interviewed her. Another dancer had publicly called her a prostitute, after which they started fighting, first with abusive language and later with fists. "Son of a bitch," "ass," "bastard," "your mother's cunt," are common curse words. The female entertainers occasionally resort to physical violence as well. They are sometimes in dangerous situations, so that they have to use physical violence in self-defense. In particular the past generation of leaders, the *usṭâwât*, were seen as *gidʿân*, noble, tough, and courageous, a word usually applied to men. If it was necessary, they resorted to violence to protect the female performers and themselves. *Usṭâ* Zeinab, for instance, related: "I was honest, courageous, and tough [*gadʿa*], I was haughty and respectable. I did not like to talk or to make jokes with people. I would immediately beat up anybody who talked to me. I carried a knife with me. Once I used it in self-defense—only once. After that, whenever people saw me, they said, 'Hello, bruiser' [*ahlan ya fitiwwa*]."[4]

It is not always danger that prompts female entertainers to describe themselves as tough, strong, ready and able women. These traits help them to maintain an image of respectability: "If a woman is not strong in this trade, she's lost," Magda said. The women sometimes use terms of abuse or violence against men who compromise their reputation. Sayyida Madbaḥ related a story about a man she beat up because he tried to assault her.

> Once there was a man who cheated me. He said he was the head of the opera. His name was Aḥmad. He came to me and said: "I want you at a wedding, but the owner of the party has brought a group himself."[5] I said: "OK." I prepared my bag with costumes and we went to the place. We went into a building and he took my bag and took me to a room and said: "I love you and I want to do this and that with you." So, what could I do—he had a knife. Then he brought in another man and said: "This man killed Imtisâl Fawzî.[6] I told him: "OK, I'll give you what you want, you can send the other man away—but first I'd like to have lunch." He said:

> "OK." While he was out buying food, I immediately disappeared [blows on the back of her hand, the characteristic gesture for running away] and took a horse cab. I told my father and mother about what happened. Next day, I wore slippers with high heels. I took my parents and three or four other men from the neighborhood and we went to his quarter. We went to a coffeehouse. I told the owner that I wanted Aḥmad and told him the story. He said: "OK, I'll bring you Aḥmad and let you beat him up." So he called him. . . . He came and I told him: "It's me, Sayyida!" I took off my slippers and began hitting him in public. I gave him a good beating. The owner of the coffeehouse and the people with me all helped me beat him up.

By publicly hitting him, she exposed his ruthless acts. More important, she restored her respectability by beating him up. She proved willing to protect her reputation by all means available. The owner of the coffeehouse and the other men who accompanied her considered it her right to beat him and even helped her to restore her good name. Another performer of the older generation told a similar story. She traveled with her father's *teatro* in Upper Egypt. A young man chased her and tried to flirt with her. As she had "big hands," she immediately began beating on him. Unfortunately the young man was the mayor's son. She had to apologize for beating him up or the *teatro* would have remained without an audience by the mayor's order.

Female entertainers must be, and are, strong, tough, and ready to defend themselves. People lose respect for weak women because they are considered unable to resist men. Weak personalities are expected to engage in affairs with male colleagues and customers. Only women with a sharp tongue and the ability to beat up an assailant are viewed as capable of protecting themselves without going astray. This conduct protects them from being perceived as too easy-going. Female entertainers generally consider themselves as tough as men.

Female entertainers generally do not consider their trade more difficult for women than for men. Some said that the job is more difficult for women because they have to stand on their feet the whole evening, whereas the male musicians can sit on chairs. Others observed that men have to work hard, whereas female performers only occasionally make a *nimra*, get to sit on a chair, and earn more money than the male musicians. Although these remarks contradict each other, female entertainers do not consider themselves too weak to face violence and drunken men. I expected them to feel more threatened by fighting, but they simply responded: "If someone throws a bottle at entertainers, a male musician can be hit as well." Since they are as tough and strong as men, they are not more bothered than their male colleagues. They admit that they are confronted with customers who try to flirt and bother them, which makes working more difficult for them. On the other hand, this same fact makes earning money easier. As zither player Samîḥa il-ʾUrashî said: "The trade is more difficult for a woman, especially if she wants to stay clean, because all the men want her. But if she is successful, her work gets easier. A woman moves by her beauty. She has many assets which can make her successful." Female entertainers thus "move" by their femininity, but they must also be masculine to protect their reputation and face dangerous situations.

They are thus confronted with very conflicting demands. They must be nice, pleasing, and feminine yet at the same time tough, strong, and masculine. Female entertainers are not the only women who work in fields in which they must defend themselves in a strong, masculine way. Baṭṭa's housemate, Zizi, was almost kidnapped by a gang of young men. She fled into a nearby house. It happened that only women were present inside. When the men tried to enter the house, she became scared, afraid that a few women would not be able to protect her. But to her surprise all of them seized big knives and ran onto the street and chased the men. Later Zizi heard that these women were hashish merchants. "And those types are stronger and tougher than men," she concluded. Hashish merchants and female entertainers are extreme examples of a larger group of independent women working in the male space.

DAUGHTERS OF THE COUNTRY

Since I propose to use a contextualizing approach, it is important to place female entertainers in the broader setting of lower-middle-class urban working women. If the behavior and self-presentation of female performers are compared to those of the *banât il-balad*, the daughters of the country, it becomes clear that female singers and dancers are not so strange or exotic. Their actions accord with the model of the *bint il-balad*. Although the public does not regard female entertainers as *banât il-balad* because of their shameful profession, in their behavior and views female entertainers are very close to the daughters of the country.

The *banât il-balad* belong to the lower middle class and live in the working-class quarters of Cairo. Many work outside the home, some in traditional jobs such as bath attendant, others in factories or tailor shops.

A few are employed as servants. Many work in shops or have their own small businesses and, depending on education, a few work as government employees. Some have an active role in their husband's work at home—for instance, in the food trades.

The *banât il-balad* mainly think of themselves as housewives and mothers. Although many work outside the home, they would prefer to be only housewives. Their duties as wives are to "prepare his bath, dress him, cook for him, clean and take care of the home, and please him" (Messiri 1978b: 539). They pay great attention to their appearance and sex appeal. The choice of the husband is mainly in accordance with the common saying, "He who desires you, not the one whom you desire" (Messiri 1978b: 534).

If they work, the *banât il-balad* consider their income a supplement to their husband's. They can use it as they wish and have no obligation toward the household expenses. The support of the family is the full responsibility of the husband—it is essential to his manhood. A "real man" fulfills his obligation to the family and meets all the needs of the home (Messiri 1978b: 537). The *banât il-balad* expect the husband to demand that they stop working. If he wants to assert his identity as a man, he should not need the financial help of his wife.

Besides supporting the family, the husband must control his home. He must be tough as a lion, otherwise his wife will not respect him. A *bint il-balad* said: "As long as the husband is soft, the woman will do what she wants. Unless he is like a 'lion,' the woman will neither fear nor respect him. If the woman gets spoiled it is due to the man; if she stays pure it is also due to him" (Messiri 1978b: 538). A real man is supposed to be jealous and to beat his wife. Wives do not mind the husband's beating because it is an expression of jealousy that "springs from love." Since beating is also an expression of their husband's masculinity and toughness, it is not shameful to be beaten (Messiri 1978b: 538). The husband must also be virile. The stress on virility springs not only from the importance of intercourse to the *banât il-balad* but also from the status derived from being an "object of sexual attention" (Messiri 1978b: 538).

Many themes already discussed reappear in this description of the *banât il-balad*. They conceive of themselves mainly as wives and mothers. Support is exchanged for affection in marriage, and attractiveness is an important asset for a woman seeking a man to maintain her. Like the female entertainers, the *banât il-balad* prefer to be housewives and expect their husbands to provide for them. Although most have to work, they consider their income a supplement. The type of virile, tough husband they want is similar to the ideal that ʿAbîr, the folk dancer from Minyâ, described. The description of the *banât il-balad* and female entertainers as mainly wives and mothers is in close correspondence with the general construction of femininity as outlined in Chapter 7. As working women, the conduct of the *banât il-balad* also clearly resembles that of female entertainers in important respects. Both categories of women behave in contradistinction to the prevailing ideas on femininity.

Among the *awlâd il-balad*, there is a free association between women and men, in the neighborhood as well as at work. Women are not secluded from men. This makes the *banât il-balad* vulnerable to gossip that can harm their reputation. They therefore have to defend their good name by all possible means. A twenty-year-old *bint il-balad* related:

> A certain cowardly hashish merchant persisted in flirting with me several times. He even followed me to the movies and sent me tea with the waiter in the movie. The fact that I rejected his advances prodded him into saying dirty things about me in the quarter, like "loose woman" and "daughter of a whore." One day I became furious and followed him to the *baladi* coffeehouse, snatched off his glasses, and beat him with my shoe. He tried to insult me again, but I answered back with a flood of insults. He even took a chair and tried to hit me with it, but I ducked and he fell and I fell on him and beat him. On that day I shocked the market; everybody heard about this incident, particularly since this man was known and feared as a tough guy. Since that day he has lost the respect of others. Had I not done what I did, he would have kept on saying I am a loose woman. (Messiri 1978b: 535).

Another young *bint il-balad*, who expressed her fear of being molested by men in the street, was told by the men present: "Do you really fear men in the street? I am sure that if any man dares to bother you, you would immediately take off your shoe and beat him" (Messiri 1978b: 534).

Working women who daily interact with men must have strong, fearless, and tough personalities. Their work requires foresight, intelligence, and experience in dealing with all kinds of people. They must be men among men. It is said that "one *bint il-balad* equals twenty men in trading" (Messiri 1978b: 532). In particular the *mi*ᶜ*allima*, the female leader, comparable to the *usṭâ* in the entertainment trade, has a strong character. The term *mi*ᶜ*allima* mainly refers to important market women or female merchants in the quarter, such as butchers, hashish merchants, and coffeehouse keepers. Messiri described the *mi*ᶜ*allima* as follows:

> They are usually reputed to have powerful status in the hitta [quarter].[7] They direct large and successful enterprises. Traditionally the muᶜallima[8]

> has in her shop a large special chair or sofa on which she sits and smokes a water pipe. She is coquettish, gives much care to her appearance, and adorns herself with expensive jewelry. Her dress, however, is a man's *galabiya* (long flowing gown) which is complemented by a mannish air and a look of seriousness and toughness. She participates in quarrels like a man and disciplines anyone she dislikes with a beating. The muᶜallima is considered a local leader within the hitta. (1978b: 527)

Some women become the "strongmen" (*fitiwwât*) of the neighborhood. Especially in the first half of this century, *fitiwwât* formed a traditional element of popular quarters. They were the local leaders of the quarters and protected the neighborhood against outsiders. Usually this task was carried out by strong young men. Yet occasionally women were leaders. One of them, ᶜAzîza al-Faḥla, was described as "a giant lady who possessed extraordinary strength. Around her arms were tons of gold bracelets. A blow from her hand was enough to knock any man to the ground. A blow from her head would split a stone. She was married to a man called al-Faḥl al-Kabîr. He used to support his wife in any quarrel but this was rare because ᶜAzîza was always capable of gaining victory by herself" (El-Miligi in Messiri 1978a: 64–65).

Some *banât il-balad* are thus extremely tough, strong, and masculine. Yet they are also feminine, care for their appearance, and are coquettish. One of my informants defined a typical *bint il-balad* as "nice, feminine, and coquettish, yet tough and not indecent or weak." Most people, explaining the characteristics of the *banât il-balad*, referred to her toughness and masculinity. During my interviews with people from popular quarters, I occasionally saw a *miᶜallima* smoking a water pipe or cigarette in front of her shop. A man said: "The *bint il-balad*'s only fault is that she interferes in the affairs of men. She acts like a man and does business like a man."

Being feminine and masculine at the same time is thus not typical for female performers. Neither is cursing or beating. However, protecting their reputation by publicly hitting someone and using abusive language is done by both *banât il-balad* and female entertainers. The young *bint il-balad*'s story about beating the hashish merchant is similar to Sayyida's account. The *miᶜallima* is comparable to the *usṭâ*, who is also often depicted as a strong, fat woman wearing many gold bracelets and smoking a water pipe. Bûḥa's preference for the water pipe is thus not unique. Also the title "*fitiwwa*" Zeinab gained after using a knife in self-defense is not unprecedented.

Female performers' tough and "unfeminine" behavior is thus not so strange as it might appear at first glance. They act according to the existing model of the *bint il-balad*. Their conduct differs slightly from that of the *banât il-balad*, but it is a matter of degree rather than content.[9] First, female entertainers are more frequently confronted with dangerous situations; they must deal with drunken men and persistent flirts, situations in which they have to behave in a masculine way in order to defend the integrity of their bodies. Second, they have to remove stronger suspicion with regard to their respectability. Female entertainers, particularly dancers, are more vulnerable to accusations of immorality and prostitution. The fact that they publicly exhibit their bodies for profit makes them dishonorable. Consequently, they have to make stronger claims to honor and respect than other women working in the male space. Female entertainers therefore strongly act according to the masculine characteristics of the *banât il-balad*.

To remove the suspicion of female weakness and looseness, they present themselves not only as masculine and tough but also refer to themselves as "a man among men." A female musician explained:

> I am a man among men, not a woman whom they [male colleagues] have to treat in a different way. If a woman has a strong personality, she knows how to survive in this work. If she is weak, she doesn't. If she has a shaky personality or if she is weak, she will stray from the narrow path. But if she is straight and does not engage in relationships with men, no one can talk. You observed my behavior with men. It is man to man. It is not indecent. I try not to be feminine and soft. I am serious and straight like a man.

The expression "I am a man" has several meanings. The entertainers are men because they work in the male public space. They often say, "Inside the home I am a woman, outside I am a man." Outside they are men because they earn a living. They engage in activities that express the essence of manhood: labor. A female singer of religious songs called herself "the son of her father" because she provides for him. The expression "I am a man," however, also implies a denial of their femininity. Or, to put it more precisely, the entertainers deny the femininity of their bodies. Since the female body is primarily perceived as sexual, this negation means a denial of their sexual dimension. Ibtisâm remarked: "I used to drink beer and smoke hash, but we were all polite, we were like men together. It wasn't like women and men together—it's like we were all men." If they are men, how can they be suspected of having affairs with other men—that is, clients or colleagues? They try to disclaim the source of their dishonor by redefining themselves as men. The negation of their femininity is thus ultimately related to their efforts to be perceived as respectable women. The expression "I am a man" finally means "I am a respectable working woman."

By defining themselves as masculine in the public sphere, female entertainers are trying to neutralize and redefine the femininity of their bodies. They are trying to negotiate the meaning of their body and to reduce its sexual dimension. They view themselves as workers and their bodies as a productive force. It is not sexual and shameful but a means to earn a living. For them, their bodies are neutral productive instruments, like the male body. By presenting themselves as men among men they protect their reputation as respectable women. They thus uphold their respectability as women by using the male gender in public. According to female entertainers, singing and dancing are a livelihood and, for women as well as for men, a trade like any other.

NINE

CONCLUSIONS

I would like to conclude and summarize the main points by looking into the approach I have used throughout the book. The conclusions I have drawn are, of course, largely dependent on the perspective I have chosen. My approach can be characterized by four related key terms: contextualization, experience-near concepts, the perspective of the "significant others," and, finally, the views of the people under study. Returning to the first part of the main question—that is, is entertainment generally a dishonorable profession?—it must be concluded that, at least in Egypt, it is not.

First, I studied the entertainment trade in a historical and local context. In the historical chapters, it became clear that the status of the trade is not static. It has risen and fallen in the course of the last two centuries. From a refined art in the late eighteenth century, entertainment became closely related to prostitution in the course of the nineteenth century. Gradually some branches of the trade regained prestige during the twentieth century. Nightclubs have a higher status now that they are regulated and have been cleaned of *fatḥ*, whereas the uncontrolled weddings of the lower-middle class and saint's day celebrations have declined.

In the second half of this century, entertainment ceased being a unified trade with a coherent status system for all performers. The process of professionalization broke the former unity of the performing arts. A growing number of art schools and academies provided entertainers with certificates and licenses. They monopolized the respected state-controlled cinema, TV, radio, and theaters. The performing arts circuit became the standard against which the nonrecognized forms of art and entertainment are measured. As a result, the circuit of weddings and saint's day celebrations lost esteem.

Due to the process of professionalization, the different forms of entertainment have become separate activities as well. Since the mid-nineteenth century, many performers sang, danced, acted, made music, told jokes, and sometimes performed acrobatics as well. At present, these performing arts are different branches of entertainment. Acting, music, and singing have gained prestige through academies and conservatories. Dancing—that is, the local belly dancing—has lost esteem and has been overshadowed by such dance forms that require formal training, such as folk dancing and ballet.

The contexts I have focused on—mainly the circuit of weddings and saint's day celebrations, and the nightclub circuit for comparison—should be differentiated. They are dissimilar contexts and have different meanings for Egyptians, which influences the status of the performers working in them. Whereas weddings are joyful celebrations and can be defined as the context of happiness, nightclubs are considered the domain of greediness, excitement, and sexuality. Whereas female performers enliven people's happiness about a marriage, nightclub singers and dancers stimulate "lasciviousness and bad intentions" on the part of customers. Nightclub performers are therefore generally less esteemed than entertainers from Muḥammad ʿAlî Street.

The contextualization approach thus provides insight into the variability within the trade. The form and context of entertainment have become increasingly decisive for the status of the performer. Entertainment can no longer be considered one trade. In order to investigate the status of the profession, the various forms and contexts of performances must be differentiated.

Second, taking the opinions of the "significant others" of the people under study as central—an extension of contextualization, since the informants are studied in their own context—brings also refinement to the proposition of entertainment as a dishonorable profession and entertainers as marginal people. By distinguishing the views of the different classes of Egyptian society, the dishonor and marginality of entertainers are differentiated. The largest group of society, the lower and lower-middle classes, are the entertainers' "significant others." Because entertainers live in the same neighborhoods with them, work and intermarry with them, there is a degree of integration between them. Most lower- and lower-middle-class people accept male entertainers as ordinary citizens and do not stigmatize, avoid, or reject them. They generally consider entertainment a livelihood and, depending on the context, regard it with high or low esteem. Since men should provide for their families, entertainment is perceived as a productive or economic activity. Although not all people consider entertainment a trade like any other, every trade has its own *bîʾa*, social environment, and many lower- and lower-middle-class people regard entertainment as a trade not worse than their own.

In the view of performers working at weddings and saint's day celebrations, entertainment is a trade like any other. They are integrated and share the lifestyle and views of their "significant others." The men also share the ambivalence of needing their wives to augment their income by working yet wishing they were housewives. They aspire to be perceived as normal citizens and strongly identify with the concept of the real Egyptian. They are *awlâd il-balad*, like their "significant others."

Yet, as has been argued, women are marginalized to a greater extent than men in the entertainment field. Although to hold that female entertainers are outcasts and totally marginalized would be to overstate the case, they experience insults and rejection in their daily life. Many men reject the trade and would never marry a female performer. Yet within the community of entertainers and their "significant others," there is a certain tolerance of women working in the trade, in particular if extra money is needed for the children and the home. The situation is disliked but tolerated. Most female performers from the circuit of weddings and saint's day celebrations are not women without men, which could be a clear sign of marginalization. They are thus not socially marginalized to any great extent. They are not, however, considered to exhibit all the qualities of really good Egyptian women. They are not perfect *banât il-balad*. On account of their livelihood they are culturally marginal. Female entertainers on the nightclub circuit are more strongly marginalized. Their "significant others," middle-class people, reject the trade. Female nightclub performers are accordingly often women without men.

By looking at the perspective of the various classes toward entertainers, we can see who considers them marginal. Only if the view of the upper and upper-middle classes are taken as decisive can it be concluded that all entertainers are low or marginal. For female performers, however, a different picture emerges. Although lower- and lower-middle-class people are milder in their evaluations of popular female singers and dancers, all classes consider the trade disrespectable for women.

This conclusion is supported by looking into the experience-near concepts people use in evaluating entertainers and at the everyday behavior people exhibit toward entertainers. Experience-distant concepts are useful if they are demonstrably founded on experience-near notions, whether distilled from words, sayings, proverbs, jokes, images, or behavior. Just as the opinion that entertainers are marginal is not demonstrable in the sayings and behavior of entertainers' "significant others," so the proposition that entertainers are generally considered dishonorable also proves to be unwarranted. In religious discourse, listening to and practicing most forms of music, singing, and dancing are frowned upon and regarded as distracting believers' attention from devotion to God. In daily life discourse, however, entertainment is perceived as innocent enjoyment. In particular, male entertainers are not evaluated in moral terms. For men, "nothing is shameful" and their deeds are not counted against them in heaven, as is the case with women. According to the sayings and daily life behavior of lower- and lower-middle-class people, entertainment is not a problematic trade. Although male nightclub performers are perceived in an unfavorable light because of their greediness and drunkenness, since they are men they are forgiven because it is recognized that they must make a living.

Women, however, are frowned upon in both the religious discourse and in the sayings and behavior of ordinary people. Female nightclub entertainers are often perceived as prostitutes. Although female performers from Muḥammad ʿAlî Street are viewed in a more favorable light than nightclub singers and dancers, for all of them the trade generally is perceived as bad and shameful. The term of abuse "son of a dancer"—in which either the general term for dancer (*ra'aṣa*) or the more specific word for dancer from the circuit of weddings (*ʿalma*) or from the countryside (*ghazîya*) is used—indicates that all female dancers are considered bad. Although dancing is perceived as worse than singing, all women are mainly perceived as women, who should not publicly exhibit themselves. That is, female performers are evaluated primarily as women and only secondarily as performers, and because they are women who exhibit their bodies, they are shameful. Women, in contrast to men, are primarily evaluated in terms of shame and respect.

If entertainers' own views are taken into account, this picture is strengthened. They generally view the trade as an honorable one, yet both male and female performers ascribed any indecencies to female colleagues. For men entertainment is a trade like any other. The older generation of female performers from Muḥammad ʿAlî Street claims respect on account of their code of honor but accuses the younger generation of singers and dancers of immorality. The younger generation accuses the nightclub singers and dancers, as well as the newcomers in the circuit of weddings and saint's day celebrations of spoiling the image of the trade. Female nightclub singers and dancers blame entertainers of Muḥammad ʿAlî Street for their cheap art.

According to many people, female entertainers are thus bad and shameful. The view that they are dangerous, however, proved to be experience-distant. Although this view exists in Muslim religious discourse, it is nonexistent in people's sayings and behavior. According to religious texts, all women are powerful and disruptive. Their power to distract the believer, to seduce him and make him lose his mind, is dangerous for the moral order. In the behavior and sayings of most people, however, no specific fear is expressed of female entertainers. Most people take the view that female singers and dancers are shameful but that they themselves are guiltless when they invite performers to their weddings and enjoy the entertainment. "The fault is theirs," they usually say. Female performers are *ḥarâm* and shameful, *ᶜêb*, but not dangerous. Female entertainers themselves are aware that, religiously speaking, they commit sins. They acknowledge that the profession is *ḥarâm* for women. Yet they do not regard their work as shameful. It is their livelihood, and they work hard for their children and their home. They themselves are respectable, good people who earn a decent piaster.

Only if religious opinion is taken as decisive can it be concluded that entertainment ipso facto is a dishonorable profession. Only if religious texts are taken as decisive can the trade by its nature be considered immoral. Yet in both experience-near and experience-distant discourses, in religious texts and ordinary people's actual behavior, there is congruency regarding the immorality of female entertainers. Although entertainment itself is not an immoral profession, it is a dishonorable profession for women.

The approach I have used has thus refined the distinction of entertainment as a dishonorable profession. Taking the lower- and lower-middle-class view rather than that of the upper and upper-middle class as decisive, taking experience-near rather than experience-distant discourse as central, and taking behavior rather than texts as focal, the conclusion can be drawn that entertainment is not a dishonorable profession. Yet at the same time I concluded that for women entertainment is a dishonorable profession. In order to understand this conclusion, gender as a social and cultural construction has to be taken into account.

Why is the trade for a man a neutral living, whereas for a woman it is a dishonorable profession? Why are entertainment activities provided by males perceived as productive activities, while those supplied by females are evaluated in moral terms? This is related to the prevailing construction of gender and particularly to the construction of the male and female bodies. The crux of the gender issue is that women are generally viewed as sexual beings. Their bodies are enticing, regardless of what they do. Women who work in the male public space are all suspect—

working among men is generally perceived as erotic aggression. Whatever women do, they are first and foremost perceived as sexual bodies. They and their bodies seem to have only one dimension. The male body, although sexual in the presence of a female body, has several dimensions; for instance, it can function in the economic or political field. For that reason, the body of a male performer is perceived as a productive body. According to the *sheikh* quoted in Chapter 6, even if the male body shakes and dances, it is not primarily perceived as enticing. Although this total denial of the erotic dimension of the male body seems exaggerated, it is striking that the erotic dimension of the male body is not its most prominent aspect. Women, in contrast, even if they do not move or dance but simply walk or work in the male space, are perceived as sexual beings. Even if they use their bodies as productive instruments, they are perceived as sexual bodies. The bodies of female entertainers are accordingly sexual when they are at work.

These constructions of gender and the body pertain to all Egyptian women. In many ways female entertainers are thus perceived as women like other women—that is, as sexual beings who can bewitch and seduce. They mainly differ from "decent" women because they use their bodies to make a living instead of hiding them as much as possible. They publicly employ the power of their bodies. Instead of using their feminine powers in the legal context of marriage, they tempt male customers in public. The fact that they exchange "sex" for "material" does not make them radically different from other women either. Yet outside the context of marriage it becomes prostitution. They thus employ the sexuality of their bodies for a living, which makes them shameless and shameful. They profit on a material level from the cultural constructions of gender and the body, but pay for it in terms of status and respect.

Female entertainers are ambivalent in their attitude toward their bodies. Their femininity and sexuality help provide them with a living, yet they also cause troubles, assaults, and the loss of respect. Female performers accordingly try to neutralize and negate their femininity. They assume aspects of male behavior. They can be coarse, tough, and rude, occasionally beating someone up and cursing. They behave in such an "unfeminine" way in order to protect the integrity of their bodies as well as to counterbalance the image of the loose, weak woman. They present themselves as men among men in order to be perceived as respectable. They try to modify the feminine image of their body and to reduce its sexual dimension. They want their bodies to be perceived as neutral instruments. For them, their bodies are productive just like male bodies.

Throughout the book the notion of the body has proved to be central.

There has not yet been much study on social and cultural constructions of the body. Most studies tend to see it as a natural given which needs no elaboration. In particular, the study of entertainment, in which the body is focal, provides an opportunity to demonstrate the way in which the body is interpreted. Entertainment was initially defined as "publicly exhibiting the body for profit" (Blok 1985: 34). This definition, however, is without a historical or local context and, most importantly, the body is not gendered. It has become clear, however, that the notions of the body are variable. In the Egyptian context, the crucial aspect of dishonor of the entertainment trade is the public exhibition of the female body. Whereas the male body is neutral, multidimensional, and productive, the female body is sexual, seductive, shameful, and one-dimensional. However, this ideological construction of the female body as sexual is not undisputed. It is challenged by female entertainers, albeit unsuccessfully in the eyes of the public. They perceive their bodies as productive and try to modify the meanings attached to them. The body is thus not an undisputed natural given, but an interesting field for further anthropological and feminist research.

METHODOLOGICAL NOTES

From September 1988 to April 1989 and from August 1989 to February 1990 I conducted fieldwork among female singers and dancers in Egypt. Since I wanted to know the view of Egyptian society on entertainers, I talked with 50 Egyptians of different socioeconomic backgrounds: 23 lower- and lower-middle-class people, comprised of workers, artisans, and independent traders; 14 members of the lower-middle and middle class, including lower government employees; and 13 upper-middle-class and upper-class people. I asked them each about the way they had celebrated their own wedding party and those of their children, as well as whether they would consider working as entertainers or would allow their children to work as performers. In addition, I asked them whether they would consider marrying a performer or if they would raise objections if their children wanted to do so.

I also used a set of cards in order to investigate people's ideas on the different forms and contexts of performances for male and female performers. I gave the cards to 42 people, including 12 female entertainers, during the first fieldwork period and to 28 people, including 8 female performers, during my second stay. In the first period, I used 32 cards. During my second stay, I changed some of the cards and used 30 cards. Some terms I had used appeared not to be value-free; for instance, I was told that the word for nightclub was *kabarêh*, which, as I found out, was a very negative term. I replaced it with the locality of the nightclubs, to wit, Pyramid Street. Some cards, such as male and female author, gravedigger, female tourist guide, and female secretary, did not add information and were dropped. Particularly after the first fieldwork period, it became clear that people ordered the cards according to the form, context, and gender of the performer. I therefore divided the cards more evenly among these criteria. I added male folk dancer, male singer in Pyramid Street, and female singer at saint's day celebrations.

In the second period, I used cards with the following professions: White collar professions: officer (*zâbit*), male and female civil servant (*muwazzaf* and *muwazzafa*). Blue collar professions: charwoman (*shaghghâla*) and garbage collector (*zabbâl*). Between these two: the informants' own profession (*mihnitak/mihnitik*), nurse (*mumarriḍa*), female shop assistant (*bayyâᶜa*), and housewife (*sitt il-bêt*). Traditional jobs: female mourner (*naddâba*), moneylender (*murâbî*),[1] female matchmaker (*khaṭba*), and female drum-player at the *zâr*, a spirit possession ceremony (*tabbâla fizzâr*).[2] Concerning art and entertainment, the following cards were used: actor and actress (*mumassil* and *mumassila*), male and female musician (*ᶜâzif* and *ᶜâzifa*), female singer on radio and TV (*muṭribit izâᶜa wtilifizyôn*), male and female singer at weddings (*muṭrib* and *muṭribit afrâḥ*), male and female singer in nightclubs on Pyramid Street (*muṭrib* and *muṭribit shâriᶜ ḥaram*), male and female folk dancer (*râqis* and *râqiṣa funûn shaᶜbiyya*), female dancer at weddings (*râᶜaṣit afrâḥ*), and female singer and dancer at saint's day celebrations (*muṭriba* and *ghazîya fi mûlid*). Finally, I included the male assistant to the dancer (*ṣabî il-ᶜalma*)[3] and the prostitute (*mûmis*) in the set of cards.

I asked people to arrange the cards, according to their views, from good to bad trades and to explain the order they had made. Not all the informants were able to read or to express their evaluation in numbers. Some people lumped together many cards and made broad categories, others made finer distinctions. In order to facilitate comparison, I made the categories *very good*, *good*, *reasonable*, *mediocre*, *bad*, and *very bad*. These categories were based on people's spontaneous remarks, like "bad," "reasonable," "beautiful," "so-so," or exclamations of dismay. As explained in Chapter 6, the higher classes evaluated most male professions as high or low, rather than as good or bad. The cards were mainly used as a general impression and to trigger discussions about people's opinions on performers. Together with the general discussions concerning themselves or their children working as a performer and marrying a performer, they gave a clear impression of their views on the diverse forms and context of male and female performances.

The general pattern in the first and second period are equivalent, concerning both the groups as a whole and the distinctions according to class. That is, the white collar professions are put at the top, followed by the professional performing arts circuit, the blue-collar jobs, and, finally, the traditional trades, performing arts at weddings and saint's day celebrations, and nightclub entertainment. Distinguishing between the different classes, the picture slightly changes: The upper and upper-middle class mix the blue-collar, the traditional, and the entertainment trades and consider them all low or mediocre. The lower and lower-middle class differentiate the blue-collar from the entertainment jobs. They are generally milder in their evaluation, and fewer professions, particularly for men, are considered bad. Although I used the material of both periods for analysis, I only present some examples from the second period because those cards were more specific and accurate. The general order of the second period compared with that given by female entertainers is presented first, followed by the refinement by class.

Comparison of public opinion and female entertainers, second period

public (20)
very good

1. officer
2. housewife
3. own profession
4. nurse
5. m. civil servant
6. f. civil servant

good

7. m. musician
8. actor
9. f. musician

reasonable

10. f. singer TV
11. f. shop assistant
12. actress
13. f. folk dancer
14. garbage collector
15. m. folk dancer

f. entertainers (8)
very good

1. officer
2. nurse
3. actor
4. f. singer TV
5. actress
6. m. musician

good

7. f. musician
   housewife
8. m. civil servant
   f. civil servant
9. own profession
10. m. singer nightclub

reasonable

11. f. folk dancer
12. f. singer nightclub
13. m. singer weddings
    f. shop assistant
14. m. folk dancer

16. charwoman

mediocre

17. f. matchmaker
18. m. singer weddings
19. f. singer *mûlid*

bad

20. m. singer nightclub
21. f. singer weddings
22. f. singer nightclub
23. f. dancer weddings
24. f. dancer *mûlid*
25. f. drum-player *zâr*

very bad

26. f. dancer nightclub
27. m. assistant of dancer
28. f. mourner
29. prostitute
30. moneylender

15. f. singer weddings
16. f. dancer nightclub
17. f. dancer weddings

mediocre

18. charwoman
19. f. singer *mûlid*
20. f. matchmaker
21. f. dancer *mûlid*

bad

22. garbage collector
23. f. drum-player *zâr*
24. m. assistant of dancer

very bad

25. f. mourner
26. prostitute
27. moneylender

Comparison of different classes, second period

higher-middle class (5)

very good

1. own profession
2. actor

(lower) middle class[4] (6)

very good

1. housewife
2. own profession

lower (middle) class[5] (8)

very good

1. housewife
2. officer

good

3. nurse
4. m. musician
   f. musician

reasonable

5. officer
6. m. civil servant
   f. civil servant
7. f. singer TV
   housewife
8. actress

mediocre

9. f. folk dancer
10. f. shop assistant
11. m. singer
    nightclub
12. f. matchmaker
13. garbage collector
    f. singer *mûlid*

bad

14. m. singer
    weddings
    m. folk dancer
15. f. singer nightclub
    f. singer weddings
16. charwoman
17. f. dancer *mûlid*
18. f. dancer
    weddings

3. officer
4. m. civil servant
5. f. civil servant

good

6. f. singer TV
7. nurse

reasonable

8. f. folk dancer
   m. musician
   f. musician
9. f. shop assistant
10. actor
    actress

mediocre

11. m. folk dancer
12. garbage collector
13. charwoman
14. f. singer *mûlid*
15. m. singer
    weddings
16. f. matchmaker

bad

17. f. singer weddings
18. m. singer
    nightclub
19. f. dancer *mûlid*
20. f. dancer weddings

3. nurse
4. m. civil servant
   f. civil servant
5. own profession

good

6. actor
7. f. shop assistant
8. m. musician

reasonable

9. f. singer TV
10. f. musician
    garbage collector
11. actress
12. f. folk dancer
13. m. folk dancer
14. charwoman

mediocre

15. f. matchmaker
16. m. singer
    weddings
17. f. singer *mûlid*
18. m. singer
    nightclub
19. f. drum-player *zâr*
20. f. singer weddings

bad

21. f. singer nightclub
22. f. dancer
    weddings

very bad	**very bad**	**very bad**
19. f. dancer nightclub	21. f. singer nightclub	23. f. dancer *mûlid* f. dancer nightclub
20. prostitute	22. f. drum-player *zâr*	24. m. assistant of dancer
21. m. assistant of dancer f. drum-player *zâr*	23. f. dancer nightclub	25. f. mourner
22. f. mourner	24. m. assistant of dancer	26. moneylender
23. moneylender	25. f. mourner	27. prostitute
	25. moneylender	
	26. prostitute	

NOTES

1. INTRODUCTION

1. For Gypsy entertainers in Pakistan see Berland (1982); for Bulgaria, Silverman (1986); and for Egypt, Sobhi Hanna (1982).

2. Arabic words used in the text are included in the Glossary.

3. Contrary to commonly held ideas in the West, Islam has a positive view of sexuality, viewing it as necessary for women and men provided that it is expressed in the legal framework of marriage. See also Chapter 7.

4. See also discussion on honor and shame in Chapter 6.

5. The orthodox caliphs reigned from 632 to 661 A.D.; see further *Encyclopaedia of Islam* 1965: 1072–1075 (*Ghinâ'*).

6. For this debate, known as *al-samâ^c* (listening to music), see Robson 1938; al-Ghazâlî 1901, 1902; Chelebi 1957; Farmer [1929] 1973; al-Faruqi 1979, 1985.

7. The singing slave girls (*qainât*) at the court of, for example, al-Mutawakkil (847–861) are described by Stigelbauer (1975).

8. The fact that I left out the performing arts circuit influenced my choice to concentrate on female singers and dancers and to exclude musicians (I spoke to only two female musicians). Although there used to be female musicians in the circuit of weddings and saint's day celebrations, as will be described in the historical chapters, they have vanished. At present, female musicians are mainly employed in orchestras, seldom in nightclubs or at weddings. Performers at five-star nightclubs, particularly nightclubs in five-star hotels, are closely related to the performing arts circuit. However, most of my informants from the nightclub circuit, although some worked in five-star nightclubs, were not among the top performers.

9. I spoke with 18 former female performers (6 extensively or repeatedly) and 20 working female entertainers (12 extensively) from the circuit of weddings and saint's day celebrations. In addition, I talked with 10 men related to the trade (dressmaker, composers, musicians, impresarios). With regard to the nightclub circuit, I spoke to 2 former and 12 working female singers and dancers (6 exten-

sively) and to 5 men (managers, head of a trade union, head of department for licenses and censorship).

2. FEMALE ENTERTAINMENT IN NINETEENTH-CENTURY EGYPT

1. It is remarkable that J. Tucker in *Women in Nineteenth-Century Egypt* (1986), for which she used all kinds of Arabic sources and archives, also turns to travelers' accounts for her chapter on female entertainers. The few available Arabic sources (ʿArafa [1947], Buṭrus [1976], Gabârtî [1983], Ṭahṭâwî [1988]) are used as well.

2. For instance, the Western sense of superiority, the "essentializing" and fixing of the "Orient," separating "them" from "us" and putting them at a distance (in the past), the "orientalizing" of the "Orient," and the above-mentioned stress on the exotic, erotic, and bizarre. See Said (1979), Alloula (1986), Kabbani (1986), Peters (1982), and Rodinson (1974).

3. The saint's day celebrations of Ṭanṭâ and Dessûq are still the celebrations most frequented in the Delta.

4. About fifty artists and scholars accompanied the military occupation of the French during the Napoleonic expedition (1798–1801) in order to describe every detail of Egypt. This resulted in the twenty-six volume *Description de l'Égypte*.

5. I describe the wedding party in some detail in order to compare it with the present-day celebration in the next chapter.

6. Burckhardt mentions Monday and Thursday (1972: 136); Lane, Friday or Monday evening (1978: 165–166, see also his note correcting Burckhardt p. 562).

7. The word *ghawâzî* comes from the verb "to invade," so probably they were not native Egyptians. They seem to be of Arabic descent. Gypsies in Arabic are called *ghagar*. The exact relationship between the *ghagar* and the *ghawâzî* is unclear. Buonaventura states that the original *ghawâzî* were Gypsies (1989: 39), Lane that they descended from a different branch of the Gypsy family (1978: 375). Burckhardt, however, mentions no relationship at all between the two (1972: 178–179).

8. Present-day entertainers working at weddings and saint's day celebrations also have a *sîm*, but I did not find any similarity between them (see Chapter 5).

9. This resembles the current practice in nightclubs, where banknotes are sometimes tucked in the dancer's costume.

10. Nowadays, the word *shobash* is rarely used though widely understood. The word for tips, *nuʾṭa*, is still used at present-day weddings of the lower-middle class. In general, many aspects of the tipping and arrangements concerning remuneration were strikingly similar to present practices. See Chapter 3.

11. The important role of *nuʾûṭ* is expressed in the proverb "Singing without remuneration [*nuʾûṭ*] is like a dead body without perfumes [*ḥunûṭ*]." The last word means embalming oils, a mixture of camphor and rose water, with which the face of a dead person was sprinkled (Burckhardt 1972: 155).

12. In the eighteenth century, there were administrative differences between public dancers and prostitutes. Prostitutes fell under the jurisdiction of the *wâlî*, a government official who kept a list of them and collected monthly taxes. He could get extra money by threatening to register a woman discovered in a compromising situation as a prostitute unless she paid a considerable bribe (see next section). Although public dancers were not formally under his control, he could register those suspected of prostitution, who would thus become subject to his rule (Tucker 1986: 151; Lane 1978: 124).

13. Tucker mentions a monthly tax (1986: 151), Sonnini a weekly tax of six medin every Friday (1798 vol. 3: 322). According to Burckhardt, the *ghawâzî* paid an annual capitation tax in 1817 (1972: 177). This contradicts the information from Baer, who writes that the general capitation tax was introduced by Muḥammad ʿAlî in 1820, but that entertainers were among the few to be taxed separately (1964: 85–86).

14. Although certain professions belonged to guilds with social and religious significance, entertainers merely constituted units for the purpose of taxation. During the eighteenth and nineteenth centuries, the social traditions of most guilds degenerated; administrative and fiscal functions became their main raison d'être. All trades and services were thus organized. There were even guilds for prostitutes, beggars, thieves, and other "immoral or criminal" persons (Baer 1964: 5–9).

15. According to an 1801 list, entertainers were subdivided into the following guilds: singers, female singers, minstrels, people with monkeys, male dancers, and two guilds of female dancers. It could be that the existence of two guilds of female dancers affirms the above-mentioned distinction between the common dancers for the lower and lower-middle classes (called *raqqisîn*) on the one hand, and the *ghawâzî* on the other (just called dancers without the Arabic word being given) (Raymond 1957: 158–161).

16. According to Buonaventura, it was also favorable to the French for the purpose of taxation (1983: 41).

17. According to Auriant, four hundred public dancers and prostitutes were arrested and drowned in order to frighten others so they would not enter the barracks (1948: 13).

18. They seemed to have taken harsh measures against them as well. Burckhardt mentions that in 1817 Arnaut soldiers, who were the masters of Egypt at that time, robbed several *ghawâzî* and killed others "in fits of jealousy." Many *ghawâzî* fled from the garrison towns into the open country (1972: 178).

19. There was a considerable reserve army of unemployed women at the time, because indigenous factory production in the period of Muḥammad ʿAli and the import of European articles displaced many female workers, particularly in the textile crafts (Tucker 1986: 101).

20. The large number of common *ʿawâlim* is also indicated in the accounts of Lane and Clot Bey. Lane mentions four classes of female entertainers in 1833: the higher class *ʿawâlim*, a large class of common *ʿawâlim* who sang and danced, the *ghawâzî*, and an inferior class of *ghawâzî* (1978: 354–355; 372–377). Clot Bey at around the same time distinguishes the *ʿawâlim* from the *ghawâzî* and cautions

against mixing the two. Next, he divides the *ghawâzî* into two groups: the *ghawâzî* and the "*ᶜalma's*"! Probably this group of "*ᶜalma's*" (which is just the singular of *ᶜawâlim*) indicates the group of common singers and dancers, which had increased at that time (1840 vol. 2: 86). The ambivalent status of the *ᶜawâlim* is also indicated in the travel account of the Egyptian scholar Ṭahṭâwî, who studied in Paris between 1826 and 1829. His comparison of French actresses and the Egyptian *ᶜawâlim* reveals that they were equally educated and eloquent, but that the Egyptian singers were far more lacking in virtue than their French counterparts (1988: 117–119).

21. Mengin mentions that in the budget of the Egyptian government (1821), dancers, magicians, and itinerant entertainers for the lower and lower-middle classes paid 300 pounds (the total budget amounted to 240,040 pounds and 381 piasters) (1828 vol. 2: 380). According to Clot Bey, female dancers, musicians, and conjurers paid 60,000 francs in 1833 (total budget was 62,778,750 francs) (1840: 208). These amounts do not include revenues from prostitution, and Mengin explicitly refers to entertainers working at weddings and saint's day celebrations only, excluding the higher-class *ᶜawâlim*.

22. Measures against domestic servants in European households also demonstrate the sensitivity of this issue at the time. Opposition to the foreign presence, "often cloaked in religious sentiments," prompted Muḥammad ᶜAlî to issue an ordinance forbidding any Muslim woman or girl from entering the service of any foreign family under pain of being thrown into the Nile in a sack and drowned (Tucker 1986: 92).

23. According to Clot Bey, the government voluntarily renounced the tax revenues (1840 vol. 1: 336). Nerval states that the "devouts of Cairo" offered to pay the taxes of public women if their demands were met (1980: 246).

24. When Combes visited Minyâ, the governor invited him for an oriental dinner with male singers. There were no dancers (*ᶜawâlim*, as he called them) because Minyâ was still too close to the capital (1846 vol. 1: 162). According to him, they were also chased from Alexandria (1846 vol. 1: 129–130). St. John, however, states that they were forbidden to dance in the houses of Europeans, but allowed to perform in the many coffeehouses of Alexandria (1845: 20).

25. Several stories are told about the famous Ṣafia. Brehm mentions that she was the lover of ᶜAbbâs Basha. When ᶜAbbâs Basha found her in the arms of another lover, he had her whipped and deported to Esna. According to Brehm, she was paralyzed as a result of the beating and could no longer perform (1975: 68). Others, however, attended her singing and dancing in Esna (Combes 1846 vol. 1: 216–223). In 1851, after twenty years of public life, she is said to have retired (St. John 1852 vol. 1: 26).

26. *Khawal* means an effeminate man. Nowadays it commonly denotes a homosexual man.

27. According to Buonaventura, the *ginks* originally came from Constantinople. They were so popular that they often caused riots. In 1837, Sultan Maḥmûd outlawed them. They fled to Cairo and replaced the female dancers (1983: 48, 51).

28. According to Pückler, they were fed for half a year (1844 vol. 2: 236).

Romer mentions that they received rent-free housing, three loaves of bread, and one piaster and ten paras a day (1846 vol. 1: 272).

29. At least in the travelers' accounts. I am not sure about the Egyptian use of the word, since at the beginning of the twentieth century *ʿawâlim* meant singers and dancers for the lower and lower-middle classes, not prostitutes (see Chapter 3).

30. The disobedience of the Arnauts, usually caused by little or irregular payment, often resulted in riots.

31. The exact date is not clear. Pückler mentions 1843 (1844 vol. 2: 237), but according to Curtis the ban was lifted under ʿAbbâs Basha (1849–1854) (1860: 86). Buonaventura states (without reference) that they were allowed to return in 1866 (1989: 69). Under ʿAbbâs, Saʿîd (1854–1863), and Ismâʿîl (1863–1879), heavy taxes were levied in order to finance irrigation and infrastructural projects such as the Suez Canal.

32. Arabic sources refer to the female entertainers working at weddings and saint's day celebrations as the *ʿawâlim* who were to blossom in the first decades of the twentieth century (Buṭrus 1976: 123–126).

33. Probably they also performed in the street in front of the house if the house had no court, as happens at present-day weddings of the lower-middle class.

34. See Mitchell's *Colonising Egypt* (1988) for an analysis, based on Foucault, of the growing state control in the spheres of the army, education, housing, and health.

3. FEMALE ENTERTAINMENT IN THE TWENTIETH CENTURY

1. In my research I used the newspaper *al-Ahrâm* [*A*] (1876–1920) and the magazines *Alf Ṣanf* [*AṢ*] (1926–1929), *Magalla al-Funûn* [*MF*] (1926–1928, 1933–1935), *al-Malâhî al-Musawwara* [*MM*] (1931–1935), *al-Kawâkib* [*K*] (1933–1934), *Rûz al-Yûsif* [*RY*] (1933–1945), and *Dunyâ al-Fann* [*DF*] (1946–1948). Bracketed letters indicate the abbreviations used in text cites. *Rûz al-Yûsif* was launched by the actress Fatma al-Yûsif. It was started in 1925 as a general weekly with a strong emphasis on art and entertainment; later on it developed into a magazine of political satire.

2. The journalists sometimes radically changed from criticism to approval in their evaluation of certain nightclubs. Occasionally nightclub owners seem to have bribed them effectively.

3. Egyptian visitors to the exposition were embarrassed and disgusted by the Egyptian street. Fifty donkeys were imported from Egypt, a facade of a mosque gave entrance to a coffeeshop with dancing girls and whirling dervishes, and Old Cairo was imitated so carefully that even the paint on the buildings was made dirty (Mitchell 1988: 1).

4. The feminist Julia Ward wrote: "The Cairo dancing was simply horrid, no touch of grace about it, only the most deforming movements of the whole

abdominal and lumbar region. We thought it indecent" (cited in Allwood 1977: 90). On account of its indecent movements, *Danse du ventre* (1896) was one of the first films to be censored in the history of the cinema (Buonaventura 1989: 105).

5. At the San Francisco Exposition in 1911, complaints against the "lewd acts" performed at the Mysterious Orient Dance Hall prompted the authorities to close it down (Graham-Brown 1988: 179). It is not clear which "Oriental" dance was performed in that period.

6. It is not precisely known how the costume changed. According to Graham-Brown, it may have been influenced by the costume of the Indian nautch dancers, which was introduced by the British into Egypt and from there into the world of Western entertainment (1988: 180). Buonaventura holds that the costume was first introduced into the West and later brought back to the Middle East (1983: 108; 1989: 152). Although this point needs more detailed study, pictures of the Hollywood cabaret costume indicate that the two-piece costume already existed before the 1920s in the West, whereas it did not appear until the late 1920s in Egypt. That it was exported to Egypt from the West is substantiated by the fact that in the Egyptian wedding circuit, which was less influenced by Western fantasies than the nightclubs, the two-piece costume was adopted later (see this chapter, section 3).

7. Law 24, amending Law no. 1 from 1904 and the 1938 amendments under Farûq, emphasized that scandalous acts (*'af'âl fâḍiḥa*) were forbidden in public places and regulated when places of entertainment could remain open.

8. I describe these decades in some detail because this period has strongly influenced the present image of nightclubs. The nightclubs of the early period can be seen in films, which are often shown on television. Although important changes have occurred, the old films have a stronger impact than reality on people's ideas of nightclubs, since most people do not visit them.

9. In 1934, a journalist estimated that dancers earned 16 to 20 pounds a month from performing and 24 to 48 pounds from drinking. A drink, which normally cost about 4 piasters, was 15 piasters in the nightclubs. Of the 15 piasters, the cost of the drink was 2 piasters, 5 went to the *fâtiḥa*, and 8 to the owner. Champagne was raised from 50 to 150 piasters (*RY* 19-3-1934: 30). In 1938, a competition among *fâtiḥât* in Alexandria was won by Fardûs il-Shallabî, who drank thirty-five glasses. Mimi was second with twenty-five glasses and snacks. They received 3 piasters per glass (*RY* 20-6-1938: 51).

10. Several tourists describe the prostitution area as the Fishmarket (Guerville 1905: 79; Sladen 1911: 60–61; Bethge 1926: 54).

11. The Anglo-Egyptian Treaty of 1936 placed the responsibility for protection of foreigners with the Egyptian authorities, and it promised to assist Egypt in abolishing the Capitulations, which finally came to an end in 1948 (Sayyid Marsot 1985: 96).

12. This white-slave traffic was a subject of major concern for British officials. The Société pour la Suppression de la Traite des Blanches, founded in 1905, tried to intercept young women in the Alexandrian port and to lodge them in "honest" hotels (Tucker 1986: 154).

13. It is not clear whether the government was effective and "restored the

district's respectability," as Russell (1949) maintains. Bethge described the Fishmarket in 1926 in much the same way as Russell did ten years before. He saw heavily painted fat women smoking cigarettes while trying to attract customers (1926: 54). Yet statistics for Alexandria do indicate an increased government control on brothels after 1924. In 1919, the number of licensed prostitutes was 1,325 and the number of discovered clandestine brothels 62. In 1924, it was 1,356 and 162, respectively, and in 1925, 1,260 and 207 (Question 1930: 8).

14. It is not clear whether the *ṣâlas*, each of which bore the name of its leading female performer, were all actually owned by these performers. It seems that some owned at least a share of the property, although others held a long-term lease. They probably had financial support from male admirers (Graham-Brown 1988: 184).

15. Egyptian attitudes during the Second World War were largely inspired by anti-British feelings rather than pro-German sentiments, but generally the Egyptians did not hinder the Allied cause. For instance, Badîʿa Masabni, according to a journalist for *Rûz al-Yûsif*, was sentenced to death in absentia by Hitler on account of her critical sketches (25-5-1940: 18).

16. Ḥikmat Fahmî had contact with many officers. Her relation to two German spies proved to be her undoing. She was imprisoned for 2½ years by Egyptian intelligence forces (Bindârî 1958: 40–50). Amîna Muḥammad said she danced for Goering but refused to perform naked (*RY* 23-9-1939: 35).

17. According to Rayyis Bîra, it was the parliamentarian Sayyid Galâl, responsible for the area and campaigning for his election, who agitated against the presence of prostitution in an Islamic society. He took a minister with him to show him the "vice" in the area. One of the habits of prostitutes was to snatch the fez of passersby, and since it was shameful to walk around bare-headed, they had to follow the women. After the minister went through this experience, he was convinced that the area should be cleaned up. The law of 1949 was followed by Law no. 68 in 1951 and Law no. 10 in 1961.

18. Scandals surrounded his private life. He could be seen any evening in one of the nightclubs or at the gambling table (Sayyid Marsot 1985: 103).

19. I did not find an official regulation prohibiting the naked midriff. At any rate, films of the period no longer show the more revealing costume. The prohibition of dancing while sitting on the floor dates probably from the same period. The *shamʿidân* dance was attacked several times for its "vulgar prostrate and sitting positions." Doing the splits in a costume with side slits was considered too revealing (*MM* May 1932: 7; 5-12-1933: 6).

20. I do not know whether tip giving was a usual practice in the early period. I only once came across a note that it was habitual for the dancers to collect tips for the musicians (*RY* 11-7-1938: 51). It thus seems that tips were not an important source of income for the performers. This probably changed when the profits were drastically cut by the abolition of *fatḥ*.

21. In old films he is usually depicted as an effeminate person with a high-pitched voice who also dances to make the guests laugh. Although the *ṣabî il-ʿalma* resembles the *khawal* dancer of the past, he is not a professional dancer but merely an assistant to the female dancers.

22. The older generation of Muḥammad ʿAlî Street related with relish that if a harem ran out of females or blind musicians, sometimes they accepted a sighted male musician wearing opaque glasses.

23. The word *artiste* was also introduced into Arabic, initially to denote performers in the nightclubs. Because of its bad connotations, the word is currently avoided and has been replaced by *fannâna*.

24. As stated in the previous chapter, I am not sure whether the *ghawâzî* were Gypsies or belonged to a separate tribe during the nineteenth century. MacPherson doubts that the women working at saint's day celebrations in the first decades of this century were tribal *ghawâzî* (1941: 220). Presently, all dancers working in the countryside and at *mawâlid* are often called *ghawâzî* whether they belong to a tribe or not. It seems to be a loose catchall term to describe people whose lifestyle involves extensive travel, usually related to working in different locations.

25. MacPherson witnessed a male belly dancer dressed as a woman who also performed at weddings (1941: 83–84). I did not see any male belly dancers at weddings or saint's day celebrations. The male dancers I saw were either folk dancers or performers at religious or wedding processions. The latter spin around for a long period during which they untie a colored skirt (*tannûra*), which is pancake-shaped because of the whirling, and lift it above their heads, draw figures with it, and tie it on again while still spinning.

26. The word *usṭâ* became obsolete. The male and female employers are called "owners of the band," *ṣâḥib il-firʾa* and *ṣaḥbit il-firʾa*, respectively.

27. They are called *impresario* in Arabic as well. Licensed agencies are also named *muta ʿâhid ḥafalât* and unlicensed agencies, *nabatshî*.

28. Sometimes a person writes down exactly the name of the tipper and the amount he contributes.

29. Taking tips existed in the past as well, but presently this practice exists on a broader scale. It resembles the structure of savings clubs (*gamaʿiyya*), which are very popular in Egypt. Every member of the club pays a stipulated sum every week or month, and everyone gets the savings by turns. Entertainers also have their savings clubs. They give a *ʿuzûma*, that is, a party for entertainers at which the entertainers are colleagues who perform gratis and the host takes the tips. This enables them to raise a considerable amount at once. Entertainers usually do this in the slack winter season.

30. It is difficult to know the exact development of the costume. Some were probably ashamed and therefore claimed that they never wore a revealing costume. Besides, "revealing costume" is polyinterpretable, since the tulle and *shabaka* can be highly revealing. When I asked whether the costume of the past exposed the belly, some said yes, meaning that it was covered, but with a light material. Moreover, government dress prescriptions of the 1960s were less influential in the popular circuit, since checking is difficult in this irregular form of entertainment. So it might be that they wore revealing costumes for a longer period than the nightclub performers.

31. One of my informants has been blind since she was sixteen because of a gunshot wound she suffered when one of the guests fired at a wedding to show

his happiness. A dancer from the south related that one of her aunts was killed under similar circumstances. I visited two wedding parties with guests mostly from the south and found that shooting is still a way of celebrating at weddings.

32. The cassette industry is a somewhat exceptional case. This branch is relatively democratic but does not have very high prestige. The low costs of cassettes have made it possible for lesser-known people from the circuit of weddings and saint's day celebrations to make cassettes. Yet currently the prices asked by composers and songwriters have risen to the extent that many complain it has become a matter of money and not art. So, in this branch commercialization seems to be more important than professionalization.

4. LIFE STORIES OF FEMALE ENTERTAINERS

1. I spoke with 18 former female performers (6 extensively or repeatedly) and 20 working female entertainers (12 extensively) from the circuit of weddings and saint's day celebrations. I talked with 14 female performers working in nightclubs (6 extensively).

2. They thus earned more money because there were more people in the *ṣâla* and the atmosphere for giving tips was better after several drinks. Usually the "good" *nimar*—often interpreted as the ones that bring in good money—are presented later in the program.

3. The early piano was the same size as the present accordion.

4. A brother and two sisters were not in the trade and one of them married a butcher. Some of their children became government employees and refused to have any contact with the Madbaḥ branch.

5. Later on it appeared that she meant a costume with tulle over the belly, not one that left that area bare, as in nightclubs. She said that at weddings they had to protect themselves because they collected tips from the guests and were thus close to men.

6. The word *baladî* has several meanings. It refers to *balad*, the place one comes from and belongs to; depending on the context, it means country, nation, town, or village. In a more narrow sense, it refers to the "conservative" lower class as opposed to the "modern" Westernized middle class. See also Chapter 5 on *awlâd il-balad*.

7. This popular song sung by il-ʿAdawiyya, composed by Rayyis Bîra, is often used as an example of how common meaningless songs are today. As I learned from Rayyis Bîra, though, the words are ones mothers use in talking to small children.

8. Those whose relatives were strongly opposed often used similar expressions, such as being almost slaughtered, or being burned and shaved. It seems like a pattern of initial resistance. The expressions they used, though not necessarily literally true, indicate strong resistance from relatives.

9. He is called *nabatshî* or *shawîsh*. He has to "answer" the *nuʾṭa*—that is, to repeat the congratulations and greetings.

10. The tips amounted to 900 pounds. ʿAida received 120 pounds and Zizi

100 pounds. The *nimra* Khadra got 60 pounds, and Magda got 50. The musicians are usually paid less—depending on the instrument, between 20 and 40 pounds. After subtracting the cost of transportation and the rent for the instruments and sound system, Sayyid's net was 300 pounds.

11. Sayyid used the word *amraza*, a term belonging to the secret vocabulary of entertainers (see Chapter 5).

12. Entertainers give appropriate nicknames to the months January and February. *Janâyir* is called *Janâyim* (from the verb "to sleep") and *Fabrâyir* is called *Fa'râyir* (from "poverty").

13. *Bêt* is a house, and *wa'f* is a property placed in religious trust or a charitable endowment.

14. Celebration of the Prophet's birthday is not restricted to one location. Towns, villages, and neighborhoods throughout Egypt have their own festivals.

15. He is called *nabatshî*. Entertainers gain prestige if they do not carry their own bags.

16. The word *sha'wâza*, bewitchment, is often used to describe the effect a dancing woman in a revealing costume has on men.

17. I have the impression that new recruits to the circuit of weddings and saint's day celebrations often have a rural background, particularly since most families from Muḥammad 'Alî Street kept their daughters out of the trade. The step to nightclubs is probably too big, whereas weddings of the lower-middle class are familiar to them. The girls from Cairene lower-income neighborhoods are more attracted to the higher earnings of nightclubs.

5. MARGINALITY

1. There are communities of Gypsies, the *ghagar* of Sett Guiranha, who, among other things, engage in entertainment (Sobhi Hanna 1982).

2. The profession is not confined to Muslims, though. The famous Shafî'a il-'Ibṭiyya, mentioned in Chapter 3, was Coptic. However, Danielson states that most female singers and dancers between 1850 and 1930, contrary to popular wisdom that they were foreign or non-Muslim, were native Egyptians and that most were Muslim (Danielson 1991: 301).

3. Littman's list of Gypsy Arabic shows a small overlap of, to my knowledge, ten words (1920: 9–18).

4. It is an old word that was used by beggars in the Middle Ages for "outsider," "nonbeggar" (Bosworth 1976: xi). Also the *ghagar* of Sett Guiranha call the non-Gypsies *khashânâ* (Sobhi Hanna 1982: 46).

5. I spoke to two sisters who, although very hospitable and keen on selling their costumes, were not interested in talking about their profession, since they were about to stop. They said they were not *ghawâzî* because, as they explained, this is synonymous with prostitutes. They called themselves folk dancers of *bêt Ma'zin*.

6. I conducted interviews with 50 Egyptians: 23 lower-class and lower-middle-class people, including workers, artisans, and independent traders; 14

members of the lower-middle class and middle class, including lower government employees; and 13 upper-middle-class and upper-class people.

7. See also the discussion on the "significant others" in the next chapter.

8. *Awlâd* (singular: *ibn*) literally means sons and *banât* (singular: *bint*) means daughters. *Balad* means the place one lives, and can refer to a neighborhood, a village, or the country of birth.

9. I added this question in the second period of my fieldwork and interviewed twenty people on the topic.

10. *Miᶜallim* (feminine: *miᶜallima*) is a title of address referring to a chief, usually the owner of a small business or someone holding a similar position of authority.

11. This means the quality of being *gadaᶜ* (feminine: *gadᶜa*; plural: *gidᶜân*), said of a person with the following characteristics: nobility of character and integrity; intelligence and application; manly toughness and courage (Badawi 1986).

12. Here I only give a general outline of the *bint il-balad*. In Chapter 8, I discuss some other aspects of her attributes and behavior, since she provides a powerful model for working women.

6. HONOR AND SHAME

1. See also Chapter 1 for a similar argument and a plea to try to see things from "the native's point of view."

2. The word *ᶜawra*, a shameful thing, has religious connotations and is associated with the parts of the body that should be covered during prayer. It thus differs from the more commonly used word *ᶜêb*, which also means shame but is applied to a wide range of shameful behavior in social life.

3. During the first period, I handed the cards to 30 people of the different strata of the Egyptian society. Some cards appeared to be ambiguous or were missing. I thus changed a few cards in the second fieldwork period and played the game with 20 other persons. I also played the game with 12 female entertainers in the first fieldwork period and with 8 during my second stay. Examples of the card game played in the second period and some methodological details are included in the Appendix.

4. Dancers added that besides a customary way of creating a merry atmosphere, it is a way of earning tips, since the groom has to put a tip in their costume. They are slightly ambivalent about this practice and said that they first put the hand of the bride on their body and then that of the groom on her hand, so they are not touched by him. Yet observation reveals that this is not necessarily the case. I noticed that dancers are indeed explicitly asked to do this at weddings and that it is a hilarious occasion for taking pictures. I do not want to suggest that it has no connotations of shamefulness at all, but I was surprised that it hardly arose in conversation as the main reason for discrediting dancers at weddings, and when I asked why, it was explained away as *farfasha*. The same behavior outside the context of wedding happiness could result in a serious warning from the vice squad.

5. Acting was not part of my research. In general, it was somewhat negatively evaluated for women because it is a very visible profession and the actress sometimes has to play roles that bring her into intimate situations with unrelated men.

6. Leila Ahmed argues that the word *ʿawra* is highly suggestive of the connection which is made between women, sex, and shameful or defective things. *ʿAwra* has several meanings, including the genital area, women's bodies, women's voices, and women (Ahmed 1992: 116).

7. See also W. Jansen for the relation between movement and morality. Algerian men are considered to be "heavy" (*ṭaqîla*) in the control of their movements, whereas women have to overcome their natural tendency to be "light" (*ḳafîfa*). Lightness of movement stands for lightness in morals (1987: 183).

8. Only a few very famous female singers, such as Umm Kalthûm, are evaluated for their voice.

9. These two images—being a "responsible mother" on the one hand and being as "tough as men" on the other—will be elaborated upon in Chapter 8.

10. The fact that they have several secret words related to food indicates that they are generally interested in it. Yet it is viewed as diminishing their dignity.

7. GENDER

1. In the next two sections, I describe symbolic and structural constraints. In the next chapter, I deal with female entertainers as agents who actively change and negotiate meaning.

2. The term *berdache* is derived from the French word for male prostitute (Whitehead 1981: 86). They were recorded at the beginning of this century but seem to be disappearing (Aalten 1991: 178–179).

3. *Xanith* means effeminate, impotent, or soft.

4. A man who enters into a homosexual relationship and assumes the active role does not endanger his male identity, whereas the receiving homosexual cannot be conceptualized as a man.

5. Delaney criticizes Mernissi with this observation, which I think is unwarranted. The view of active female sexuality is present as well, as will become clear when I discuss the implicit theory of female sexuality. Contradictory views on female sexuality exist side by side, and the fact that women are seen as vulnerable does not mean that they cannot be perceived as powerful.

6. Sexual and other services are wifely duties, but not necessarily having children. There is thus no special emphasis on women's generative capacity, in contradistinction to past and present oral culture. It should be borne in mind, though, that the orthodox perspective which is discussed was influential but not the only voice (Ahmed 1992: 92–93).

7. In *Khul-Khaal, Five Egyptian Women Tell Their Stories*, by Nayra Atiya, one of the women relates that her mother went to religious lessons. Her daughter asked her what Sheikh Ahmad taught her that day. Her mother replied: "He said that a woman must care for her husband, that she must wear clean clothes before

going to bed, that she should smell good. A woman before she drifts off to sleep should ask her husband three times, 'Is there anything you desire?' And if not, then she can sleep" (1982: 59).

8. *Fitna* also means a beautiful women or a femme fatale whose attraction makes men lose their self-control (Mernissi 1975: 4).

9. See also Musallam (1983) for the theory of the equality of the sexual nature and the equal contribution to conception.

10. I do not intend to suggest that this view is exclusive to Islam or the Middle East. It is a familiar concept in the West as well.

11. The models for women are not exhausted by these two dominant images. In the next chapter, I return to the image of the *bint il-balad*, as a more experience-near model for working women.

12. Veiling was a recurrent theme in the research I conducted for graduation among female students of Cairo University (1983). They explained the need for veiling as a double protection—that is, against harassment by men and against seduction by men.

13. In terms of the previous section, my argument could be summarized as follows. The explicit theory on women (weak women) and the implicit theory (femmes fatales) coexist in daily life and converge in the definition of women as sexual beings. The total reversal emanating from the erotic discourse, centering on the disruptive and insatiable sexual needs of women, however, seems experience-distant.

14. I restrict myself to the relation with the husband because affairs with other men are hazardous for women. They risk not only loss of reputation, but more important, divorce. Even the slightest suspicion, justified or not, can result in repudiation.

15. I am not sure whether this image of the "omnisexual woman" from the erotic discourse is also experience-distant in daily life male discourse. Yet, as I shall shortly argue, most informants, male and female, do not regard a dancer as an insatiable femme fatale in search of sex, but rather as a woman in search of money.

16. Actresses are also feared for the bad example they set, which can be imitated by other women.

17. *Waqf* is a religious foundation that makes endowments for religious or charitable purposes.

8. FEMALE ENTERTAINERS: FEMININE AND MASCULINE

1. For the self-presentation of female nightclub performers, see Chapter 6, section 3.

2. See also Wikan (1980) about the lack of friendship among the poor of Cairo. Male entertainers do fraternize in coffeehouses, which cannot be visited by women. The agencies in Mansûra, however, provide a better opportunity for socializing for female and male performers.

3. I do not have the impression that smoking on the part of women is solely a "strong symbol of prostitution," as W. Jansen suggests for Algeria. Market women, who occasionally smoke cigarettes or a water pipe in public, are, unlike female entertainers, not associated with prostitution. I think that it indicates male behavior, which is improper for women, but not necessarily prostitution. It is interesting that Algerian prostitutes assume male behavior as well. Besides smoking, they use the male spatial idiom. In body posture and in their movements, they appropriate a larger space, usually a symbol of masculinity (W. Jansen 1987: 175–190).

4. A *fitiwwa* is usually the strong *man* of a neighborhood. See also Chapter 5 on *awlâd il-balad* and the next section.

5. She thus had to go alone, without the protection of a group of musicians.

6. A nightclub dancer who was murdered by a bodyguard; see Chapter 3.

7. This literally means place, but it also connotes a community. It has physical and social boundaries that may extend from an alley to a whole quarter (Messiri 1978b: 525).

8. *Muᶜallima* is standard Arabic. I generally use the colloquial Egyptian pronunciation. Hence I use the transcription *miᶜallima.*

9. I now refer to this combination of femininity and masculinity. As discussed in Chapter 5, a *bint il-balad* is perceived as respectable and could thus not earn such a "shameful" living.

APPENDIX. METHODOLOGICAL NOTES

1. The mourner and money lender are *ḥarâm*; for that reason, they are usually put very low.

2. The *zâr* is considered *bidᶜa*, an innovation, and therefore frowned upon in Islam. A number of lower-class people, the group mostly involved in the *zâr*, however, regarded it as a therapeutic session.

3. The assistant to the dancer is despised for his effeminate manners; he is not "a real man." According to some, he is a pimp.

4. This class includes the middle class and civil servants, who are lower-middle class.

5. This group comprises the lower-class and the lower-middle-class independent tradespeople and artisans.

GLOSSARY

ʿalma/ʿawâlim (pl.): a "learned woman," a trained female singer or dancer, performing for a female audience
ʿawâlim: women's wedding party
awlâd il-balad: country people
awlâd il-kâr: tradespeople
ʿawra: a shameful thing
badrona: madam
baladî: local (lit.); usually translated as traditional or lower-middle class
barrâda: to collect money or attract an audience (secret language)
bint il-balad/banât il-balad (pl.): daughter of the country
dôsa: Sûfî ceremony
ʿêb: shame
fannâna: female artist
fatḥ: system of sitting and drinking with customers
fâtiḥa/fâtiḥât (pl.): performers or other women who sit and drink with customers
fitiwwa/fitiwwât (futûwa) (pl.): strongman of a neighborhood who protects the quarter
fitna: chaos; sexual disorder initiated by women; femme fatale
gadaʿ (m.)/gadʿa (f.)/gidʿân (pl.): noble, tough, and manly
gallabiyya: long, flowing gown
ghagar: Gypsy
ghazîya/ghawâzî (pl.): group of dancers (in the countryside and at saint's day celebrations)
ghurza/ghuraz (pl.): small coffeehouse with entertainment (at saint's day celebrations)

ḥarâm: forbidden thing in Islam
ibn il-balad/awlâd il-balad (pl.): son of the country
kabarêh: negative term for nightclub
khawal: effeminate man (lit.); in the nineteenth century it was applied to male dancers; presently, it denotes homosexuals
khushnî/khashânâ (pl.): nonentertainers, "intruders"
lêla: night
lêla il-dukhla: the night on which the consummation of the marriage takes place
lêla il-galwâ: the night at which the bride shows her finery to female visitors
lêla il-ḥenna: the night that the hands and feet of the bride are dyed with henna
makrûh: rejected, blameworthy
milâya-laff: square black overwrap for women
*mi*ᶜ*allim (m.)/mi*ᶜ*allima (f.) (mu*ᶜ*allim):* title of address referring to the head person (man or woman)
mûlid/mawâlid (pl.): saint's day celebration
munulogist: singer of the *munulôg*
munulôg: type of popular song consisting of a solo on varied themes followed by a refrain of one or two lines which is repeated after each section
muṣannafât (il-fanniyya): censorship and licensing department for the arts and entertainment
muṭayibâtî: "the good-time maker," arranges parties and pays the entertainers advance money
nabatshî: (unlicensed) impresario
nimra/nimar: entertainment act; also used as shorthand for entertainers
*nu*ʾ*ṭa/nu*ʾ*ûṭ (pl.):* tips
*ra*ʾ*âṣa:* dancer
*ṣabî il-*ᶜ*alma:* servant of a ᶜ*alma*
sahra: men's wedding party
ṣâla: neutral term for nightclub
*sham*ᶜ*idân:* candelabra (lit.), dance act with a candelabra
shamla: a "complete" performer, one who combines singing and dancing
*sha*ᶜ*wâza:* bewitchment
sheikh: an honorary title of address usually applied to religious scholars
sîm: secret language
*subû*ᶜ*:* celebration for a seven-day-old baby

tashnîb: "begging" money (secret language)
teatro/teatrât (pl.): variety theater
ʿulamâʾ: religious authorities
usṭâ/usṭâwât (pl.): head of a group of performers
zaffa: wedding procession
zaffit il-ʿarûsa: procession of the bride
zaffit il-gihâz: procession of the bride's furniture and trousseau
zaffit il-ḥammâm: procession to the bathhouse
zikr: Sûfî ritual

BIBLIOGRAPHY

Aalten, A. (1991) *Zakenvrouwen: Over de grenzen van vrouwelijkheid in Nederland sinds 1945*. Amsterdam: Sara/Van Gennep.

Abou Zeid, A. M. (1965) "Honour and Shame among the Bedouins of Egypt." In *Honour and Shame*, J. G. Perestiany (ed.), pp. 243–260. London: Weidenfeld and Nicolson.

Abu Lughod, L. (1987) *Veiled Sentiments*. Cairo: American University in Cairo Press.

Aegypten, wie man es am besten bereist. (1908) Leipzig and Hanover: A. Sponholtz Verlag.

Ahmed, L. (1992) *Women and Gender in Islam: Historical Roots of a Modern Debate*. New Haven and London: Yale University Press.

Alloula, M. (1986) *The Colonial Harem*. Theory and History of Literature, vol. 21. Minneapolis: University of Minnesota Press.

Allwood, J. (1977) *The Great Exhibitions*. London: Studio Vista.

ʿArafa, A. (1947) *Târîkh âʿlâm al-mûsîqâ al-sharqiyya*. Miṣr, Egypt: Matbâʿa anâni.

Atiya, N. (1982) *Khul-Khaal, Five Egyptian Women Tell Their Stories*. Syracuse, N.Y.: Syracuse University.

Auriant [pseud.] (1948) *Koutchouk-Hanem, l'almée de Flaubert*. Paris: Mercure de France.

Badawi, el Said, and Martin Hinds (1986) *A Dictionary of Egyptian Arabic*. Beirut: Librairie du Liban.

Badger, R. (1979) *The Great American Fair: The World's Columbian Exposition and American Culture*. Chicago: Nelson Hall.

Baedeker, K. (1885) *Ägypten: Handbuch für Reisende*. Leipzig: Karl Baedeker.

Baer, G. (1964) *Egyptian Guilds in Modern Times*. Jerusalem: Israel Oriental Society.

——— (1969) *Studies in the Social History of Modern Egypt*. Chicago and London: University of Chicago Press.

Balen, J. H. van (1884) *De Dadels van Khartoem: Reizen en avonturen in het land van den Mahdi*. The Hague: Mouton.

Berland, J. C. (1982) *No Five Fingers Are Alike: Cognitive Amplifiers in Social Context*. Cambridge, Mass., and London: Harvard University Press.

Berland, J. C., and M. T. Salo (1986a) "Introduction." In J. C. Berland and M. T. Salo (issue eds.), "Peripatetic Peoples" (special issue). *Nomadic Peoples* 21/22: 3–6.

——— (issue eds.) (1986b) "Peripatetic Peoples" (special issue). *Nomadic Peoples* 21/22.

Bethge, H. (1926) *Ägyptische Reise*. Berlin: Euphorion Verlag.

Biegman, N. (1990) *Egypte: Derwisjen, Heiligen, Kermissen*. The Hague: SDU.

Bindârî, J. (1958) *Raqiṣât Miṣr*. Cairo: Akhbâr al-Yawm.

——— (1962) *Shafî ʾa il-Ibṭiyya*. Cairo: Akhbâr al-Yawm.

Blok, A. (1980) "Eer en de fysieke persoon." *Tijdschrift voor Sociale Geschiedenis*: 211–231.

——— (1981a) "Infame beroepen." *Symposion* 3 no. 1/2: 104–128.

——— (1981b) "Rams and Billy-Goats: A Key to the Mediterranean Code of Honour." *Man* 16: 427–440.

——— (1984) "Over het begrip van eer." *De Gids* 147(8–10): 667–671.

——— (1985) "Infamous Occupations." In *Essays on Structural Change: The L. H. Morgan Symposium*, T. Vuyk (ed.), pp. 29–42. Leiden: ICA Publication.

Bosworth, C. E. (1976) *The Mediaeval Islamic Underworld: The Banû Sâsân in Arabic Society and Literature*. Leiden: Brill.

Bourdieu, P. (1965) "The Sentiment of Honour in Kabyle Society." In *Honour and Shame*, J. G. Perestiany (ed.), pp. 191–242. London: Weidenfeld and Nicolson.

Brandes, S. (1987) "Reflections on Honor and Shame in the Mediterranean." In *Honor and Shame and the Unity of the Mediterranean*, D. D. Gilmore (ed.), pp. 121–135. American Anthropological Association Special Publication no. 22.

Brehm, A. E. [1863] (1975) *Reisen im Sudan 1847 bis 1852*. Tübingen and Basel: H. Erdmann Verlag.

Brown, P., and L. J. Jordanova (1981) "Oppressive Dichotomies: The Nature/Culture Debate." In *Women in Society*, Cambridge Women's Studies Group (eds.), pp. 224–241. London: Virago Press.

Browne, W. G. (1800) *Nieuwe reize naar de binnenste gedeelten van Afrika, door Egypte, Syrië en le Dar-Four waar nimmer te voren eenig europeaan heeft gereisd,– gedaan in den jaare 1792–1798*. Amsterdam: Johannes Allart.

Brunschvig, R. (1962) "Métiers Vils en Islam." *Studia Islamica* 16: 4–61.

Budge, E. A. Th. Wallis (1925) *Cook's Handbook for Egypt and the Egyptian Sûdân*. London: Thos. Cook and Son.

Buonaventura, W. (1983) *Belly Dancing*. London: Virago Press.

——— (1989) *Serpent of the Nile: Women and Dance in the Arab World*. London: Saqi Books.

Burckhardt, J. L. [1875] (1972) *Arabic Proverbs; or, The manners and customs of the modern Egyptians, illustrated from their proverbial sayings current at Cairo*. Reprint. London: Curzon Press.

Burke, P. (1978) *Popular Culture in Early Modern Europe.* New York: Harper and Row.

Burton, R. F. (1857) *Personal Narrative of a Pilgrimage to el-Medinah and Meccah.* London: Longman, Brown, Green, Longmans, and Roberts.

——— (1898) *The Jew, the Gypsy and el-Islam.* London: Hutchinson.

Buṭrus, F. (1976) *a'lâm al-mûsîqâ wal-ghinâ' al-'arabî.* Cairo: Al-hay'a al-miṣriyya al-'âma lilkitâb.

Caplan, P. (ed) (1987) *The Cultural Construction of Sexuality.* London: Tavistock.

Carré, J. M. (1956) *Voyageurs et Écrivains Français en Égypte.* 2 vols. Le Caire: Institut Français d'Archéologie Orientale.

Casagrande, C., and S. Vecchio (1979) "Clercs et jongleurs dans la société médiévale." *Annales Economies Sociétés Civilisations* (34) no. 5: 913–930.

Chabrol, M. de (1822) "Essai sur les moeurs des habitants modernes de l'Égypte." In *Description de l'Égypte,* vol. 18(1). Paris: Panckoucke.

Charmes, G. (1883) *Five Months in Egypt.* London: R. Bentley and Son.

Chelebi, K. (1957) *The Balance of Truth.* London: G. Allen and Unwin.

Clot Bey, A. B. (1840) *Aperçu général sur l'Égypte.* 2 vols. Paris: Fortin, Masson.

Combes, E. (1846) *Voyage en Égypte, en Nubie.* 2 vols. Paris: Desessart.

Corbin, A. (1978) *Les Filles de Noce: Misère sexuelle et prostitution (19e et 20e siècles).* Paris: Aubier Montaigne.

Cromer, Earl of (1908) *Modern Egypt.* 2 vols. London: Macmillan.

Curtis, G. W. (1860) *Nile Notes of a "Howadji"; or, The American in Egypt.* Leipzig: Alphons Dürr.

Dalby, L. C. (1985) *Geisha.* New York: Vintage Books.

Danckert, W. (1963) *Unehrliche Leute. De verfemten Berufe.* Bern and Munich: Francke Verlag.

Danielson, V. (1991) "Artists and Entrepreneurs: Female Singers in Cairo during the 1920s." In *Women in Middle Eastern History,* Nikki R. Keddie and Beth Baron (eds.), pp. 292–310. New Haven and London: Yale University Press.

Davenport Adams, W. H. (1894) *Egypt Past and Present.* London: Nelson and Sons.

Davis, S. Schaefer (1978) "Working Women in a Moroccan Village." In *Women in the Muslim World,* L. Beck and N. Keddie (eds.), pp. 416–434. Cambridge, Mass. and London: Harvard University Press.

Delaney, C. (1987) "Seeds of Honor, Fields of Shame." In *Honor and Shame and the Unity of the Mediterranean,* D. D. Gilmore (ed.), pp. 35–49. American Anthropological Association Special Publication no. 22.

Denon, V. (1803) *Reize in Opper—en Neder Egipte Gedurende den Veldtocht van Bonaparte.* 3 vols. Amsterdam: Johannes Allart.

DuBois-Aymé, M. M., and Jollois (1822) Voyage dans l'intérieur du Delta. In *Description de l'Égypte,* vol. 15. Paris: Panckoucke.

Duff Gordon, Lady (1902) *Letters from Egypt.* London: R. Brimley Johnson.

Ebers, G. (1879) *Aegypten in Bild und Wort.* 2 vols. Stuttgart and Leipzig: Eduard Hallberger.

Encyclopaedia of Islam (1965) Rev. ed. Leiden: E. J. Brill.

Farmer, H. G. [1929] (1973) *A History of Arabian Music to the XIIIth Century*. London: Luzac.

Faruqi, Lois Ibsen al- (1985) "Music, Musicians and Muslim Law." *Asian Music* 17 (1): 3–37.

——— (1979) "The Status of Music in Muslim Nations: Evidence from the Arab World." *Asian Music* 12 (1): 56–85.

Flaubert, G. (1979) *Flaubert in Egypt*. Ed. F. Steegmuller. Chicago: Academy Chicago Limited.

Fromentin, E. (1881) *Notes d'un voyage en Égypte*. Ed. M. L. Gonse. Paris: A. Quantin.

Gabârtî, al ʿAbdarraḥman (1983) *Bonaparte in Ägypten*. Zürich and Munich: Artemis Verlag.

Geertz, C. (1983) *Local Knowledge*. New York: Basic Books.

Ghazâlî, Imâm al- (1901–1902) "Ihyâ ʿUlûm ad-Dîn of al-Ghazâlî" (Emotional religion in Islam as affected by music and singing). Trans. D. B. MacDonald. *Journal of the Royal Asiatic Society* April 1901: 195–253; October 1901: 705–749; 1902: 1–29.

Gilmore, D. D. (ed.) (1987) *Honor and Shame and the Unity of the Mediterranean*. American Anthropological Association Special Publication no. 22.

——— (1987) "Honor, Honesty, Shame: Male Status in Contemporary Andalusia." In *Honor and Shame and the Unity of the Mediterranean*, D. D. Gilmore (ed.), pp. 90–104. American Anthropological Association Special Publication no. 22.

Gilsenan, M. (1973) *Saint and Sufi in Modern Egypt*. Oxford: Clarendon Press.

Ginzburg, C. (1980) *The Cheese and the Worms: The Cosmos of a Sixteenth-Century Miller*. Baltimore and London: John Hopkins University Press.

Graham-Brown, S. (1988) *Images of Women*. London: Quartet Books.

Guerville, A. B. de (1905) *New Egypt*. London: William Heinemann.

Hackländer, S. W. (1842) *Daguerreotypen aufgenommen während einer Reise in den Orient in den Jahren 1840 und 1841*. 2 vols. Stuttgart: A. Krabbe.

Hamilton, W. (1809) *Remarks on Several Parts of Turkey*. Part 1: *Aegyptica, or some account of the ancient and modern state of Egypt, as obtained in the years 1801, 1802*. London: Richard Taylor.

Harding, S. (1986) *The Science Question in Feminism*. New York: Cornell University Press.

Henniker, Sir (1824) *Notes during a Visit to Egypt, Nubia, the Oasis Boeris, Mount Sinai and Jerusalem*. London: J. Murray.

Herzfeld, M. (1980) "Honour and Shame: Problems in the Comparative Analysis of Moral Systems." In *Man* 15: 339–351.

——— (1987) "'As in Your Own House': Hospitality, Ethnography, and the Stereotype of Mediterranean society." In *Honor and Shame and the Unity of the Mediterranean*, D. D. Gilmore (ed.), pp. 75–90. American Anthropological Association Special Publication no. 22.

Hopkins, D. (1982) *Egypt: Politics and Society 1945–1981*. London: George Allen and Unwin.

Jansen, G. W. (1987) *Een roes van vrijheid, kermis in Nederland*. Meppel and Amsterdam: Boom.

Jansen, W. (1987) *Women without Men: Gender and Marginality in an Algerian Town*. Leiden: E. J. Brill.

Jomard, M. (1822) Description de la ville du Kaire. In *Description de l'Égypte*, vol. 18 (1). Paris: Panckoucke.

Jong, F. de (1978) *Ṭuruq and Ṭuruq-Linked Institutions in Nineteenth Century Egypt*. Leiden: E. J. Brill.

——— (1980) "Islamitische Mystiek." *De Gids* 143 (9–10): 743–756.

Kabbani, R. (1986) *Europe's Myths of Orient*. London: Pandora Press.

Kahle, P. (1926–1927) "Eine Zunftsprache der Ägyptischen Schattenspieler." *Islamica II*: 313–323.

Kasson, J. F. (1978) *Amusing the Millions: Coney Island at the Turn of the Century*. New York: Hill and Wang.

Keer, P., Jr. (1870) *Naar en uit Egypte*. Maatschappij: Tot nut van 't algemeen.

Kemeid, H. (1898–1899) *Cairo and Egypt and Life in the Land of the Pharaohs*. London: Simpkin, Marshall.

Koskoff, E. (ed.) (1989) *Women and Music in Cross-Cultural Perspective*. Urbana and Chicago: University of Illinois Press.

Kramer, K. S. (1971) "Ehrliche/unehrliche Gewerbe." In *Handwörterbuch zur deutschen Rechtsgeschichte*, A. Erler and E. Kaufmann (eds.), pp. 855–858. Berlin.

Landau, J. M. (1958) *Studies in the Arab Theater and Cinema*. Philadelphia: University of Pennsylvania Press.

Lane, E. W. [1836] (1978) *Manners and Customs of the Modern Egyptians*. The Hague and London: East-West Publications.

Lapidus, I. M. (1967) *Muslim Cities in the Later Middle Ages*. Cambridge, Mass.: Harvard University Press.

Larrey, M. le baron (1822) "Mémoires et observations sur plusieurs maladies." In *Description de l'Égypte*, vol. 13. Paris: Panckoucke.

Leland, C. G. (1873) *The Egyptian Sketch-Book*. London: Strahan.

Lever, A. (1986) "Honour as a Red Herring." *Critique of Anthropology* 6 (3): 83–106.

Linant de Bellefonds (1872–1873) *Mémoires sur les principaux travaux d'utilité publique exécutés en Égypte*. Paris: Artus Bertrand Éditeur.

Littman, E. (1920) *Zigeuner Arabisch*. Bonn and Leipzig: Kurt Schroeder Verlag.

MacCormack, C. P. (1980) "Nature, Culture and Gender: A Critique." In *Nature, Culture and Gender*, C. MacCormack and M. Strathern (eds.), pp. 1–23. Cambridge: Cambridge University Press.

MacPherson, J. W. (1941) *The Moulids of Egypt*. Cairo: Ptd N. M. Press.

Mengin, F. (1828) *Geschiedenis van Egypte onder de regering van Mohammed-Ali, of verhaal der staatkundige en militaire gebeurtenissen, die plaats gehad hebben sedert het vertrek der franschen tot in 1823*. 2 vols. Amsterdam: J. C. van Kesteren.

Mernissi, F. (1975) *Beyond the Veil: Male-Female Dynamics in a Modern Muslim Society*. New York: Schenkman.

Messiri, S. el- (1978a) *Ibn al-Balad: A Concept of Egyptian Identity*. Leiden: E. J. Brill.

——— (1978b) "Traditional Urban Women in Cairo." In *Women in the Muslim World,* L. Beck and N. Keddie (eds.), pp. 522–541. Cambridge, Mass.: Harvard University Press.

Mitchell, T. (1988) *Colonising Egypt.* Cairo: American University in Cairo Press.

Montagu, Lady Mary Wortley (1965) *The Complete Letters of Lady Mary Wortley Montagu.* Vol 1. Ed. R. Halsband. Oxford: Clarendon Press.

Moore, H. L. (1988) *Feminism and Anthropology.* Cambridge: Polity Press.

Mostyn, T. (1989) *Egypt's Belle Epoque: Cairo 1869–1952.* London and New York: Quartet Books.

Musallam, B. F. (1983) *Sex and Society in Islam.* Cambridge: Cambridge University Press.

Naamane-Guessous, S. (1990) *Achter de schermen van de schaamte, de vrouwelijke seksualiteit in Marokko.* Amsterdam: Dekker.

Nanda, S. (1990) *Neither Man nor Woman: The Hijras of India.* Belmont, Calif.: Wadsworth.

Nefzawi, Shaykh Umar ibn M. (1963) *The Perfumed Garden.* Trans. Sir R. Burton. London: Granada.

Nerval, G. de (1980) *Le Voyage en Orient (I).* Paris: Garnier-Flammarion.

Niebuhr, C. (1776) *Reize naar Arabië en andere omliggende landen.* 2 vols. Amsterdam: S. J. Baalde.

Nieuwkerk, K. van (1990) *Female Entertainment in Nineteenth and Twentieth-Century Egypt.* MERA Occasional Paper no. 6.

——— (1992) "Female Entertainers in Egypt: Drinking and Gender Roles." In *Alcohol, Gender and Culture,* D. Gefou-Madianou (ed.), pp. 35–48. London and New York: Routledge.

Ortner, S. B. (1974) "Is Female to Male as Nature Is to Culture?" In *Woman, Culture and Society,* M. Z. Rosaldo and L. Lamphere (eds), pp. 67–87. Stanford, Calif.: Stanford University Press.

Ortner, S. B., and H. Whitehead (eds.) (1981) *Sexual Meanings: The Cultural Construction of Gender and Sexuality.* Cambridge: Cambridge University Press.

——— (1981) "Introduction: Accounting for Sexual Meanings." In *Sexual Meanings: The Cultural Construction of Gender and Sexuality,* S. B. Ortner and H. Whitehead (eds.), pp. 3–27. Cambridge: Cambridge University Press.

Otis, L. L. (1985) *Prostitution in Medieval Society: The History of an Urban Institution in Languedoc.* Chicago and London: University of Chicago Press.

Perestiany, J. G. (ed.) (1965) *The Values of Mediterranean Society.* London: Weidenfeld and Nicolson.

Peters, R. (1982) "The Mysteries of the Oriental Mind: Some Remarks on the Development of Western Stereotypes of Arabs." In *The Challenge of the Middle East,* I. A. El-Sheikh, C. Aart van de Koppel, and R. Peters (eds.), pp. 73–91. Amsterdam: University of Amsterdam.

Pina-Cabral, J. de (1989) "The Mediterranean as a Category of Regional Comparison: A Critical View." *Current Anthropology* 3: 399–407.

Pitt-Rivers, J. (1965) "Honour and Social Status." In *The Values of Mediterranean Society,* J. G. Perestiany (ed.), pp. 19–78. London: Weidenfeld and Nicolson.

Pückler Muskau, H. L. H. Fürst (1844) *Aus Mehemed Ali's Reich.* 3 vols. Stuttgart: Hallberger'sche Verlagshandlung.

Qaraḍâwî al- Y. (1985) *al-Ḥalâl wal-Ḥarâm fî al-Islâm.* Cairo: Maktabit wahba.

La question de l'abolition de la règlementation officielle de la prostitution. (1930). Publié sous les auspices du comité central pour l'Égypte du bureau international pour la suppression de la traite des femmes et des enfants. Alexandrie.

Quran (n.d.) *The Meaning of the Glorious Koran.* M. M. Pickthall (trans.). New York: New American Library, Mentor Religious Books.

Racy, A. J. (1981) "Music in Contemporary Cairo: A Comparative Overview." *Asian Music* 13(1): 4–26.

——— (Sept. 1982) "Musical Aesthetics in Present-day Cairo." *Ethnomusicology* 26(3): 391–407.

Raymond, A. (1957) "Une liste des corporations de métiers au Caire en 1801." *Arabica* 4: 150–164.

Robson, J. (ed.) (1938) *Tracts on Listening to Music.* London: Royal Asiatic Society.

Rodinson, M. (1974) "The Western Images and Western Studies of Islam." In *The Legacy of Islam,* J. Schacht and C. E. Bosworth (eds.), pp. 9–63. Oxford: Clarendon Press.

Romer (1846) *Temples and Tombs of Egypt.* 2 vols. London: R. Bentley.

Rosaldo, M. Z. (1974) "Woman, Culture and Society: A Theoretical Overview." In *Women, Culture and Society,* M. Z. Rosaldo and L. Lamphere (eds.), pp. 17–42. Stanford, Calif.: Stanford University Press.

——— (1980) "The Use and Abuse of Anthropology: Reflections on Feminism and Cross-cultural Understanding." *Signs* 5: 389–418.

Rowson, E. K. (1983) "Cant and Argot in Cairo Colloquial Arabic." *American Research Center in Egypt Newsletter* 122: 13–25.

Rubin, G. (1975) "The Traffic in Women: Notes on the 'Political Economy' of Sex." In *Toward an Anthropology of Women,* R. R. Reiter (ed.), pp. 157–211. New York. Monthly Review Press.

Russell, T. (1949) *Egyptian Service, 1902–1946.* London: John Murray.

Rydell, R. W. (1984) *All the World's a Fair. Visions of Empire at American International Expositions, 1876–1916.* Chicago: University of Chicago Press.

Sabbah, F. A. (1984) *Woman in the Muslim Unconscious.* New York: Pergamon Press.

Said, E. W. (1979) *Orientalism.* New York: Vintage Books.

St. John, B. (1852) *Village Life in Egypt.* 2 vols. London: Chapman and Hall.

St. John, J. A. (1845) *Egypt and Nubia.* London: Chapman and Hall.

Savary, M. (1787) *Lettres sur l'Égypte.* 3 vols. Amsterdam and Leiden: Les Libraires Associés.

Sawa, G. D. (1985) "The Status and Roles of the Secular Musicians in the 'Kitab al Aghani' (Book of Songs), of Abu al-Faraj al-Isbahani (D. 356 A.H./967 A.D.)." *Asian Music* 17(1): 69–82.

Sayyid Marsot, A. L. al- (1985) *A Short History of Modern Egypt.* Cambridge: Cambridge University Press.

Scherer, D. J. (1848) *Dagboek eener Reize in Egypte.* Amsterdam: G. J. A. Beijerinck.

Seetzen, U. J. (1854) *Reisen durch Syrien, Palästina, Phönicien, die Transjordan-Länder, Arabia Petraea und Unter-Aegypten*. 3 vols. Berlin: G. Reimer.

Shawan el- S. (1980) "The Socio-Political Context of al-Musika al-ʿArabiyyah in Cairo, Egypt: Policies, Patronage, Institutions, and Musical Change (1927–1977)." *Asian Music* 12(1): 86–129.

Silverman, C. (1986) "Bulgarian Gypsies: Adaptation in a Socialist Context." In J. C. Berland and M. T. Salo (issue eds.), Peripatetic Peoples, *Nomadic Peoples* 21/22: 51–63.

Sladen, D. (1911) *Oriental Cairo, the City of the Arabian Nights*. London: Hurst and Blackett.

Sobhi Hanna, N. (1982) *Ghagar of Sett Guiranha: A Study of a Gypsy Community in Egypt*. Cairo Papers in Social Science no. 5. American University in Cairo Press.

Sonnini, C. S. (1798) *Voyage dans la haute et basse Egypte*. 3 vols. Paris.

Spruit, J. E. (1969) *Van vedelaars, trommers en pijpers*. Utrecht: A. Oosthoek's Uitgeversmaatschappij.

Stigelbauer, M. (1975) *Die Sängerinnen am Abbasidenhof um die Zeit des Kalifen Al-Mutawakkil*. Ph.D. dissertation, University of Vienna.

Sugarman, J. (1989) "The Nightingale and the Partridge: Singing and Gender among Prespa Albanians." *Ethnomusicology* 33(2): 191–215.

Ṭahṭâwî, R. (1988) *Ein Muslim entdeckt Europa*. Leipzig and Weimar: Gustav Kiepenheuer.

Thevenot, J. de (1681) *Gedenkwaardige en zeer naauwkeurige reizen van den Heere de Thevenot*. Amsterdam.

Tucker, J. E. (1986) *Women in Nineteenth-Century Egypt*. Cairo: American University in Cairo Press.

Villiers Stuart, H. (1883) *Egypt after the War*. London: John Murray.

Villoteau, M. (1822) De l'état actuel de l'art musical en Égypte. In *Description de l'Égypte*, vol. 14. Paris: Panckoucke.

Warburton, E. (1864) *The Crescent and the Cross; or Romance and Realities of Eastern Travel*. London: Henry Colburn Publisher.

Whitehead, H. (1981) "The Bow and the Burden Strap: A New Look at Institutionalized Homosexuality in Native North America." In *Sexual Meanings: The Cultural Construction of Gender and Sexuality*, S. B. Ortner and H. Whitehead (eds.), pp. 80–116. Cambridge: Cambridge University Press.

Wikan, U. (1977) "Man Becomes Woman: Transsexualism in Oman as a Key to Gender Roles." *Man* 12: 304–320.

——— (1978) "The Omani Xanith: a Third Gender Role?" *Man* 13: 473–476.

——— (1980) *Life among the Poor in Cairo*. London: Tavistock.

——— (1984) "Shame and Honour: A Contestable Pair." *Man* 19: 635–652.

ARABIC NEWSPAPERS AND MAGAZINES

al-Ahrâm (1876–1920), Dâr al-kutub, Cairo.

Alf Ṣanf (1926–1929), Dâr al-kutub, Cairo.

Dunyâ al-Fann (1946–1948), Dâr al-kutub, Cairo.
al-Kawâkib (1933–1934), Dâr al-kutub, Cairo.
Magalla al-Funûn (1926–1928, 1933–1935), Dâr al-kutub, Cairo.
al-Malâhî al-Musawwara (1931–1935), Dâr al-kutub, Cairo.
Rûz al-Yûsif (1933–1945), Dâr al-kutub, Cairo.
al-Wafd (1989), Cairo.